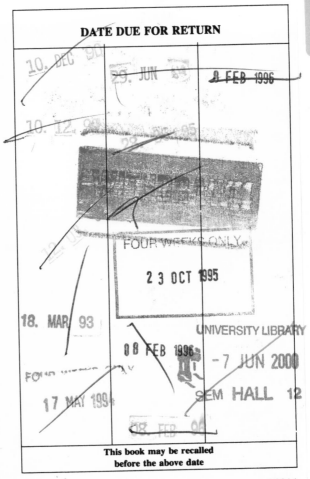

DATE DUE FOR RETURN

10. DEC '90

29. JUN

8 FEB 1996

10. 12.

FOUR WEEKS ONLY

2 3 OCT 1995

18. MAR 93

UNIVERSITY LIBRARY

0 8 FEB 1996

-7 JUN 2000

FOUR

17 MAY 1994

SEM HALL 12

08 FEB 06

This book may be recalled
before the above date

90014

Vision Critical Studies

General Editor: Anne Smith

Günter Grass

Currently available: *Vision Critical Studies*

GÜNTER GRASS

Keith Miles

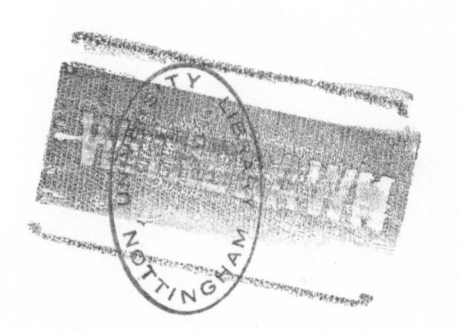

VISION

Vision Press Limited
11–14 Stanhope Mews West
London SW7 5RD

ISBN 0 85478 353 9

For Rosalind, Helena and Conrad

Printed in Great Britain
by Clarke, Doble & Brendon Ltd., Plymouth
MCMLXXV

Contents

Editorial Note

The authors of the *Vision Critical Studies* apply the critical theory and techniques of the seventies to the literature most relevant to our own age, but with the aim of the best critics of every age: to stimulate in the reader what T. S. Eliot called 'a development of sensibility'; to enlarge, and challenge, his own perceptions of the original work, and to make him want to go back to it, with a deepened sense of engagement.

A.S.

Acknowledgements

For permission to quote from the works of Günter Grass acknow-
ledgements are due to Günter Grass and Luchterhand Verlag, and
to the publishers of English translations as follows: to Martin
Secker and Warburg Ltd., and Pantheon Books, a Division of
Random House Inc., for permission to quote from *The Tin Drum*
translated by Ralph Manheim (translation copyright (c) Pantheon
Books, 1961, 1962); to Martin Secker and Warburg Ltd., for the
British Commonwealth, excluding Canada, and to Harcourt Brace
Jovanovich Inc. for the U.S.A. and Canada for quotations from
*Cat and Mouse, Dog Years, The Plebeians Rehearse the Uprising,
Local Anaesthetic, Speak Out, From the Diary of a Snail* and
Four Plays (all, with the exception of the speech from A. Leslie
Willson's translation of *The Wicked Cooks* in *Four Plays*, trans-
lated by Ralph Manheim); to Martin Secker and Warburg Ltd.,
and to Harcourt Brace Jovanovich Inc. for 'Stadium at Night'
(translated by Michael Hamburger), 'Open Air Concert' (trans-
lated by Michael Hamburger), and an extract from 'Diana—or
the Objects' (translated by Christopher Middleton) from *Selected
Poems*; to Martin Secker and Warburg Ltd., for 'Prevention of
Cruelty to Animals' (translated by Michael Hamburger) from
Selected Poems; to Harcourt Brace Jovanovich and Penguin Books
for extracts from 'Sale', 'Marriage' and 'Kleckerburg' (all translated by Michael Hamburger) from *New Poems*; to Frederick
Ungar Publishing Co., for the extract from 'The Stork' (translated
by John Conway), quoted in *Günter Grass* by Kurt Lothar Tank.
Other translations are by me.

Acknowledgements are also due to the following for their kind
permission to quote from copyright material: to Eyre Methuen,
Brecht on Theatre, and *The Messingkauf Dialogues* (both trans-

9

lated by John Willett); to Edward Bond and Eyre Methuen, *Lear*; to Jupiter Books, Calder and Boyars Ltd., *The Man Outside* (translated by David Porter); to *Encounter* and Hans Magnus Enzensberger, *In Search of a Lost Language*; to C. M. Bowra and the Cambridge University Press, *Poetry and Politics* (1900–60); to David Caute and Audre Deutsch Ltd., *The Demonstration* copyright © 1970 by David Caute; to Arthur Miller and Martin Secker and Warburg Ltd., *Incident at Vichy* copyright © 1965 by Arthur Miller; to Penguin Books and to the estate of Philip Wayne, translator, *Faust I*; to the estate of C. Day Lewis and The Hogarth Press, *The Aeneid*.

I should like to thank many German friends for discussing Grass tirelessly with me and, in particular, I wish to record my debt to Karl-Jürgen Voigt of Kiel for tracking down some evasive material for me in Germany. I must also thank Jane Barton for typing the manuscript, the staffs of libraries in Coventry, Birmingham, Oxford and London for unlimited help, David Jones of the Royal Shakespeare Company for discussing his production of *The Plebeians Rehearse The Uprising* with me, and Dr. Anne Smith for her constructive criticism and enthusiasm at every stage. Above all, I must thank my wife, Rosalind, whose support and understanding have been remarkable at all times.

10

Introduction

And I grew up, was reared between
the Holy Ghost and Hitler's photograph.
'Kleckerburg', *Poems of Günter Grass*, 1969, p. 80

Günter Grass is the most consistently interesting and disturbing writer at work in Europe today. With his prodigious talents, unmistakable voice, alarming energy, wayward genius and sheer physical presence, he has made himself a tremendous force in modern European literature. He has faults, naturally: as befits a great writer, he sometimes has great faults. But—as he himself might say—this much is certain: for the German novel he has once more gained an international audience. At a time when the economic miracle dominates the German scene, he has focused attention on the country's artistic achievements. He has even given a hope, an ideal, of a cultural future in West Germany which accepts the painful facts of the nation's military past.

To the student of paradox, Günter Grass is a gift. Profoundly serious in aim, he is often cynical or flippant in approach; monstrously eclectic, he has a devastatingly original style; operating firmly within the traditions of the German novel, he mocks, even subverts, those traditions; having helped to make German literature respectable again, he remains, legally, a pornographer;[1] having satirised the German language itself, he has emerged as one of its saviours; having repudiated Roman Catholicism, he is

[1] *Kunst oder Pornographie: Der Prozess Grass gegen Ziesel*, 1969. Herr Ziesel described Grass as "an author of the worst pornographic obscenities and defamations against the Catholic Church". Grass sued him for libel, but lost the case. Ziesel thus had the legal right to call Grass a pornographer—in a specifically literary context.

11

still fascinated by its forms; supremely convinced of the importance of the artist's role in society, he has grave doubts about his effectiveness—"Ladies and Gentlemen, I have no other weapon than the word, my possibilities are limited" (*Speak Out!*, 1969, p. 123); and, finally, though a true lover of democracy in the Whitmanesque vein, he has become, unwillingly but strictly on merit, a literary aristocrat. For in dedicating his rich abilities to the German people, Günter Grass has set himself impossibly apart from them—"My Fame, children, is someone I ask indulgence for. . . ." (*From the Diary of a Snail*, 1972, p. 75).

The facts of Grass's life have been repeatedly recorded in his fiction. In the Danzig Trilogy—*The Tin Drum, Cat and Mouse* and *Dog Years*—the suburb of Langfuhr is presented to us with such ferocious devotion and in such meticulous detail that we almost feel we could find our way around the area like residents. We should have no difficulty locating Winterplatz or Schwarzer Weg or Osterzeile, and we could with confidence direct strangers to the Horst-Wessel School, explaining that before the last war it was known as the Crown Prince Wilhelm School. Regardless of our religious views, we could check our watches against the Christ Church clock, which "provided the whole of the neighbourhood, from Max-Halbe-Platz to the Catholic and clockless St. Mary's Chapel, from Magdeburger Strasse to Posadowski Weg near Schellmühl with the time of day, enabling Protestants as well as Catholic factory workers and office workers, salesgirls and schoolboys to reach their schools and places of work with interdenominational punctuality" (*Cat and Mouse*, 1961, p. 27).

Yet Grass is not an autobiographical writer in the sense that O'Neill is in *Long Day's Journey into Night* or Joyce is in *A Portrait of the Artist as a Young Man*. Grass begins with familiar events and places, but then transforms his own experience into highly artistic fiction. What may start out in the realm of fact can quickly and deftly be developed in terms of allegory or fantasy or legend or fairy-tale. Grass's emphasis on his personal history is not merely a case of providing a firm, recognisable basis from which his novels can take flight. It has two other functions. In the first place, that personal history is offered as a set of credentials—"I, too, born almost late enough, am held to be free from guilt. Only if I wanted to forget, if you were unwilling to

12

learn how it slowly happened, only then might words of one syllable catch up with us: words like guilt and shame; they, too, resolute snails, impossible to stop" (*From the Diary of a Snail*, p. 13). Grass wants to hide nothing. As he told an Israeli audience in 1967:

> I was born in Danzig in 1927. At fourteen I was a Hitler Youth; at sixteen, a soldier, and at seventeen an American prisoner of war. These dates mean a great deal in an era that purposefully slaughtered one year's crop of young men, branded the next year's crop with guilt and spared another. You can tell by my date of birth that I was too young to have been a Nazi, but old enough to have been moulded by a system that, from 1933 to 1945, at first surprised, then horrified the world. . . . Innocent through no merit of my own, I became part of a post-war period that was never to be a period of real peace.
>
> (*Speak Out!*, 1969, pp. 89–90).

Grass's claim to speak on behalf of his generation has by no means been acknowledged by all of his contemporaries. Many of them are not seeking a spokesman, least of all a man of such abrasive honesty who dwells on certain recent events. This brings us to the second reason why Grass uses his own biographical details as a starting-point for much of his fiction: he is obsessed with the historical process itself. The present is an extension of the past and quite inseparable from it. Furthermore past and present can co-exist. At one and the same time, Eberhard Starusch in *Local Anaesthetic* can be a patient in a dentist's chair, leader of a gang of wartime delinquents, a teacher of German and history, an indifferent lover, a dilettante philosopher. He is a prisoner of his past actions in the most demonstrable way, as is his colleague Irmgard Seifert, former squad leader in the League of German Girls. Grass's preoccupation with the importance of history and antecedent informs his whole creative approach. In the Grass universe, everybody has a pedigree.

Oskar Matzerath, for instance, begins his bizarre memoirs in *The Tin Drum* with an exhaustive account of his maternal grandmother, Anna Bronski of the Wide Skirt. In *Dog Years*, Walter Matern is also equipped with an eccentric grandmother and the ancestry of Eddi Amsel and Tulla Pokriefke is hardly disguised from us. Hermann Ott and Anton Stomma are likewise studied in terms of their backgrounds in *From The Diary of a Snail*, the symbiosis between past and present being indicated by clever juxtaposition of paragraphs dealing with Ott's wartime privations and Grass's own post-war activities. Even in a work as lean and economical as *Cat and Mouse*, where there is little formal delineation of character, Grass finds it necessary to tell us early on that "Mahlke was an only child. Mahlke was half an orphan. Mahlke's father was dead". In *Local Anaesthetic*, which is set in the present day, the insidious influence of the past is vividly described and then summed up succinctly—"Afterwards begins beforehand". And in the title of the dramatic version of the same story, Grass obligingly reduces his obsession to one word, *Davor* —before.

It is not only human beings who are provided with a tell-tale genealogy. Animals, insects, buildings, ideas, geographical areas, inanimate objects such as penknives, even names themselves are accorded the same treatment. When we learn that ". . . . Perkun sired Senta; and Senta whelped Harras; and Harras sired Prinz; and Prinz made history. . . ." (*Dog Years*, p. 15), we are not merely being offered a biblical parody. Grass is giving us serious proof of the dog's impeccable pedigree, and this achieves its full effect when placed beside the Führer's own more suspect origins. Again, in the same novel, the name of Osterwick, home of the Pokriefkes, comes under scrutiny. Grass takes time off to list the various spellings of Osterwick in use between the middle of the fourteenth century and the date of Tulla's birth, 1927. In *The Tin Drum* the story of the city of Danzig is traced back to the Rugii, the Goths and the Gepidae. And there are countless other examples.

This concentration upon the past as the Janus-face of the present has a number of effects on Grass's work. Most obviously, it enlarges the physical dimensions of his novels. *The Tin Drum* and *Dog Years*, in particular, are filled out generously with historical digression. The attention to background detail also gives the works their density, their extraordinary texture, their quality of documentary accuracy which has led some critics to invoke the name of Dos Passos and *U.S.A.* Again, the cumulative effect of this aspect of Grass's technique is to convey not just the individual stories of the protagonists involved—Oskar Matzerath, Eddie

Amsel, Walter Matern, Mahlke, Starusch—but a multi-dimensional picture of a nation's history over a period of forty years. His novels are at once particular and general, minutely parochial and grandiosely national. In this sense, Grass approaches Carlyle's definition of history as "The essence of innumerable biographies"; though Grass adds the rider that the biography of a dog, a scarecrow, a church, a suburb, a toothache can be equally revealing and pertinent.

To understand the impact which Grass has made upon German language and literature, it is necessary to follow his own example and establish historical context. While he himself would probably go as far back as Gutenberg, we must limit ourselves to little more than a hundred years. In 1871 under the leadership of Bismarck and at the expense of France, Germany achieved unification. The nation was given a new status and a greater stability. Its priorities included the build-up of military and material strength. At a time when one might expect a great literary outpouring to celebrate the success of national aspirations, one finds German culture at its lowest point for a century. The very forms in which German writers had hitherto excelled—the lyric, the poetic drama, the *Bildungsroman*—now seemed lifeless. All the creative energy appeared to have been squandered on political objectives. Less than a decade later Nietzsche could observe that the Franco-Prussian War had destroyed German culture, and a more independent witness, Strindberg, could lament in the Preface to *Miss Julie* (1888) that "in those cultural strongholds which have nurtured the greatest thinkers of our age, namely England and Germany, the art of writing plays is, like most of the fine arts, dead". It was a sad obituary on a country which had produced Lessing, Goethe, Schiller, Kleist, Büchner, Grillparzer, Hoffmann and Hebbel. To those concerned about the moribund state of German culture it must have rankled that France, the defeated nation, had in the period since the war produced a Zola, a Verlaine and a Rimbaud, that Russia still boasted the active talents of Tolstoy, Dostoevsky and Turgenev, that America had discovered Melville and Mark Twain and that even Norway and Sweden had made their mark in world drama through the respective works of Ibsen and Strindberg. England, too, had its Hardy, its Meredith, its

15

Gissing, and, on loan from Scotland, its young Robert Louis Stevenson.

The situation in Germany altered abruptly. In 1889 Gerhart Hauptmann's first play, *Before Sunrise* was performed before an astonished audience in Berlin—an audience which could have been even more astonished if Hauptmann had not deleted the scene in which a woman is shown in labour. *Before Sunrise*, which deals with the effects of industrialisation on the Silesian peasantry, was more than a social documentary and a powerful drama. It signalled the belated arrival of Naturalism in Germany. For this reason—though far from being Hauptmann's best play—it made an enormous impact, quite out of proportion to its intrinsic merits. Seldom has an unknown author transformed the literary scene so radically with a first work and one might compare Hauptmann's play with John Osborne's *Look Back In Anger* (1956) in England, and with Grass's *The Tin Drum* (1959) in Germany, in this respect. In each case the unpreparedness of the existing scene is crucial. One might also note that all three works were written by embarrassingly young men.

Given Hauptmann's lead, the tide of Naturalism was able to flow freely in Germany in the drama and in the novel. By 1901 it had produced its greatest masterpiece in Mann's *Buddenbrooks* and he himself commented that "realism is the backbone of all literature". Many other writers emerged to enliven German literature, several of them reacting against the Naturalist Movement —Stefan George and his Aestheticism, Rilke and his Symbolism, Schnitzler and Hofmannsthal with their neo-Romanticism, and that strange original, Wedekind, with his Expressionism. The German lyric had been reborn, the German drama had been refashioned, the German novel had been rediscovered.

The outbreak of the First World War checked these developments. Ironically, in its early stages, the war stimulated the form it was to maim most severely later on—the realistic drama. For in contrast to the Franco-Prussian War this new encounter provoked a number of patriotic plays in the historical-realistic tradition. Great figures from the Prussian past were exhumed to remind Germans of their noble heritage. Playwrights like Emil Ludwig, Hermann Burte and Paul Ernst delivered dramas about Frederick the Great when the war was barely a few months old,

16

and even Wedekind responded to the need for heroic prototypes by writing *Bismarck* in 1916. An appeal to history at times of national self-assertion has always been strongly characteristic of the Germans and the Nazis were later to adopt the same technique. One could therefore argue that an additional feature of Grass's retrospective approach is that he is attacking his enemies with their own weapons—searching the past for success but finding only failure. In 1916, too, success suddenly began to look like failure for the Germans. It was the turning-point of the War. Military resistance from outside the country was strengthened, finding its counterpart in a growing opposition to the war from within. By 1917, Frederick the Great and Bismarck were hanging up their uniforms in the dressing room. It was the anti-war plays of Stefan Zweig, Fritz von Unruh and Reinhard Goering which, in their published form, were collecting sympathisers. The war ended in 1918 with Prussianism defeated and discredited. The Weimar Republic was created. What the Allies intended as the gift of democracy could not help looking like a punishment.

If the Franco-Prussian War, which they won, had dampened the culture of the Germans, the First World War, which they lost, gave it an unprecedented boost. For in the period 1918–33 there took place what can only be described as a creative explosion, a sustained outburst of artistic experiment and attainment. The record is awesome—Kaiser's *Gas* trilogy (1917–20); Toller's *Transformation* (1919); Rilke's *Duino Elegies* and *Sonnets to Orpheus* (1922); Thomas Mann's *The Magic Mountain* (1924); Feuchtwanger's *Jew Süss* (1925); Kafka's *The Trial* (1925) and *The Castle* (1926); Hesse's *Steppenwolf* (1927); Brecht's *The Threepenny Opera* (1928); and the first volume of Musil's *A Man Without Qualities* (1930). Although Hofmannsthal could complain in 1929 that "We have no German literature. We have Goethe and a few beginnings . . .", the facts belied his jaundiced view. Moreover, the above list is even more impressive when Hofmannsthal's own superb comedy, *The Difficult Man* (1922) is added. Another work which must be mentioned is Alfred Döblin's *Berlin Alexanderplatz* (1929), a novel which has a special relevance in any study of Günter Grass.

As will be seen from the violently disparate nature of the talents of the writers named here, the mainstream of German literature in the 1920's did not develop in an ordered, homogeneous way towards a common goal. On the contrary, the literary scene became a battleground as disputed as Verdun or Passchendaele, with entrenched attitudes coming under fire from exciting if unpredictable new weapons, with heavy casualties among the infantry, and with the same mood of uncertainty and disillusion creeping in. There were riots during performances of Toller's *Hinkemann* (1923) which portrays a soldier who returns from the war rendered impotent through injury, and who makes a living in a fairground, biting the heads off rats. Zuckmayer's *The Merry Vineyard* (1925), a totally different work, a realistic, rustic comedy, also offended the patriotic sections of its audiences. Hasenclever's play *Marriages are Made in Heaven* (1928), another comedy, was involved in legal action for "undermining Christian values". Brecht's *Rise and Fall of the City of Mahagonny* (1929), an operatic attack on the evils of capitalism, aroused bitter protest from many quarters. George Grosz, the artist, was convicted of blasphemy for depicting Jesus wearing a gas mask. German culture in the 1920's had a startling immediacy to the life around it.

Grass has been more influenced by the Early Expressionists like Toller and Kaiser than by the later ones like the young Brecht. Not surprisingly, many of the charges levelled against those Early Expressionists—obscenity, corruption, blasphemy—have been reproduced to meet the publication of Grass's own fiction. In his fine study, *The German Tradition in Literature (1871–1945)*, Ronald Gray remarks that a feature common to the Early Expressionist dramas is "a ghastliness, an emotional excess" and this has clearly rubbed off on Grass in the two major novels of the Danzig Trilogy. There is a frantic eloquence in *The Tin Drum* and in *Dog Years*, a linguistic energy which at times is in danger of being its own justification and which recalls some of the more intoxicated passages in the works of Early Expressionism. Unlike his predecessors, Grass is alive to these dangers of verbal and emotional extravagance and can, in work such as *Cat and Mouse* and *Local Anaesthetic*, produce fiction which is distinguished by the austerity and artistry of its form.

This brief history of German literature must continue at the point where it was forcibly discontinued—in 1933, when the Nazis assumed power with frightening ease. Almost at a stroke,

18

the creative upsurge of the last fifteen years was cut dead within Germany itself. Books were burned, authors were blacklisted, any association that could be found between Jews and German culture was ruthlessly obliterated. Some writers died in concentration camps. Others, like Toller and Walter Benjamin, sickened by what they saw, eventually committed suicide. But many of the greatest writers survived in exile—Brecht, Zuckmayer, Thomas Mann, Heinrich Mann, Franz Werfel, Stefan Zweig, Lion Feuchtwanger, Alfred Döblin, Hermann Broch. The National Socialists attempted to woo Thomas Mann back to lend tone and dignity to their cultural life, but the novelist remained abroad. He was never forgiven for this, and, as Grass himself pointed out in a political speech, was never welcomed back to his homeland. What Grass says of Willy Brandt could equally well apply to Mann's reception in his homeland—"Once again the word 'emigrant', pronounced in German, demonstrated its value as a word of vilification" (Speak Out!, pp. 33–34). Of the writers who stayed in Nazi Germany, none were allowed free expression and, notwithstanding the labours of Ernst Jünger, Werner Bergengruen, Ernst Weichert and others, no worthwhile contribution was made to German literature in this period from within the nation itself. Suffice it to say that the most popular book of the time was Mein Kampf by Adolph Hitler, who had exposed his literary shortcomings in his original title for the work—Four and a Half Years of Struggle Against Lies, Stupidity and Cowardice. By a cruel twist of fate, sales of this work reached in 1940 the figure of six million.

When living authors deserted the Third Reich, Hitler turned to those who were beyond escape—the dead, the hallowed. the unprotesting. Under National Socialism, the popularity of Heinrich von Kleist knew no bounds. As the first major literary figure to concern himself directly with politics, Kleist was a convenient court of appeal for the Nazis. Had he not urged the use of any lie, deception or atrocity in order to save the Fatherland from foreign domination? For similar reasons, Nietzsche, too, was pressed into service. Wagner, Hegel and Hebbel joined him. These illustrious names added a spurious glamour to the Nazi philosophy and helped to conceal from the German people what was happening to their literature and, more significantly, to their language. As Hans Enzensburger, the poet, has argued:

19

The mental state of a people is nowhere mirrored more exactly and mercilessly than in its language, and during those twelve years the German language was debauched in an unheard of manner. Long before the first bombs fell it lay in ruins. In the mouths of the holders of power and their helpers even apparently simple and innocuous words—like Raum, Heimat, Boden, Blut, Ehen, Schulung, Pflicht, Vorsehung, Opfer, Zucht—were so corrupted that they still bear the stigma, and have become unusable. . . . After the entry of the Allies, Germany was mute, in the most precise meaning of the word, a speechless country.

('In Search of a Lost Language', *Encounter*, Sept. 1963, pp. 44–5)

Many other commentators have examined the disastrous effects of totalitarianism upon the German language. In a famous and hotly-debated essay. *The Hollow Miracle*, George Steiner decided that the Nazis found in the German language itself exactly what they needed—"Hitler recognised in his native tongue the latent hysteria, the confusion, the quality of hypnotic trance" (*Language and Silence*. Essays 1956–66). Steiner also emphasises the weakness of the German people for slogans and long words and loud voices and categorical imperatives. Language under Nazism had an appalling unity of tone. It was used to convey commands, not to describe nuances of feeling. It was ransacked by philistines.

A German writer returning to his homeland in 1945, therefore, was confronted not only by a cultural desert. The basic tools of his craft—German words—had been disgraced and perverted. An official "rehabilitation of the language" was undertaken but could hardly flourish in the context of Allied Occupation, with its censorship, its impulse to democratise, and its hyper-sensitivity to the vestiges of Nazism. Wolfgang Borchert, one of the first writers to emerge after the war, was understandably sceptical about foreign pronouncements on how his native language should be reclaimed. In *Generation Without Farewell*, Borchert summed up the mood of nihilism, despair and self-pity which prevailed among his contemporaries immediately after the war:

We are the generation without ties and without depth. Our depth is the abyss. We are the generation without happiness. Our sun is narrow, our love cruel, and our youth is without youth. And we are the generation without limit, without restraint and without

20

protection—thrown out of the playpen of childhood into a world made for us by those who now despise us because of it.

(*The Man Outside*, 1966 edition, p. 39)

Borchert, who died in 1947 at the age of twenty-six, was to be the first post-war casualty of this dislocated generation. In the year of his death the *Kahlschlag* or Clean Sweep Movement began, committed to honesty of language and straightforwardness of theme. It was no formal or statutory endeavour but a concerted attempt on the part of a number of individuals to return to the language of popular usage and to the literature of personal experience. At the heart of this movement was *Gruppe 47*, a remarkable organisation which owed its existence to the reflex action of the American Occupying Forces, who closed a periodical because it criticised the attempts by the Allies at 're-education'.

Gruppe 47 was not a literary movement where the members subscribe to common beliefs and have a mutually-accepted policy. Nor was it an exclusive society for the intellectual elite. Its meetings were informal, its membership by invitation. Yet in the first twenty years of its existence, the poets, dramatists, novelists and critics who attended its readings were between them responsible for most of the finest literature and criticism produced in Germany. What *Gruppe 47* did was to reverse the trend set by National Socialism—it began to restore the language to its proper use, to win back faith in the written word, and to make the craft of a writer an honourable one again. Even by the end of the 1950's it's achievements were considerable. Then, in 1958, it invited a young author by the name of Günter Grass to read sections of his work *The Tin Drum* to its members. Grass did so and as a result won the annual literary prize offered by *Gruppe 47*. It was the best recommendation possible for his work. When *The Tin Drum* was published in 1959 it was given a tremendous reception in Germany and, later, abroad. Grass had once more connected the German novel with the world market. He had created that sophisticated handicap—a novel, a first novel, that is also a masterpiece.

A fuller discussion of *The Tin Drum*'s claim to this title must be left to a later chapter. Here we must simply appreciate some of the features of the novel, and the time in which it was published, in order to explain some of the reverberations it set up. To begin with, there is the bold arrogance of the theme: an investigation of a whole, sensitive period of German history, a forbidden area as far as many of Grass's countrymen were concerned. Grass is not the only author to reconstruct the story of the nation from the last days of the Weimar Republic through the horrors of National Socialism and on to the war. Heinrich Böll in *Billiards at Half-Past Nine* (1959) deals with the same subject-matter. Böll, the realist, the committed moralist, the radically Christian observer of the human condition, gives us a work of subtlety, irony and compelling craftsmanship. It appeals to the mind, and occasionally to the heart. *The Tin Drum*, on the other hand, assaults the intellect, the soul and the emotions, makes impossible demands on the reader, leaves him exhausted. *Billiards at Half-Past Nine* confirms our prejudices against Nazi Germany with skill and humour and is oddly reassuring: *The Tin Drum* explores the darkness beyond our worst suspicions and is constantly unnerving. Böll contrives something approaching a happy ending. Grass's ending spreads unease.

For Böll and Grass alike the main target is the middle-classes, that traditional scapegoat for the artist with blame to allot. Ibsen had attacked the middle-classes for mediocrity and compromise: Brecht had exposed their hypocrisy: Thomas Mann, following Checkhov, had flinched from their materialism and lack of culture —"All my work is an attempt to free myself from the middle-classes". In *Billiards at Half-Past Nine*, Böll pours scorn on their complacency, their knowing complicity in certain Nazi crimes: his method is controlled, astringent understatement. Grass, on the other hand, is more strident and all-embracing in his accusations. He does not only indicate the vast share of guilt attaching to the middle-classes for their role in twentieth-century German history. He mounts a scathing attack on the whole fabric of their lives, on their religious convictions, their sexual habits, their political views, their preoccupation with business, their concept of morality. What is staggering is that Grass does all this and more within the limits of what is, at one level, a comic novel. *The Tin Drum* is the artistic reply to—and indictment of—that self-made tribute to the German middle-classes, the *Wirtschaftswunder*.

Another feature of Grass's first novel which places it apart

22

from, and above, any competitors is the quality of its language. The vitality, thrust and range of Grass's language is stunning. He writes freely and convincingly in a bewildering variety of modes— a dialect, schoolboy slang, biblical parody, officialese, idiom, literary allusion, fairy-tale, dramatic dialogue, prose-poetry— and yet manages to blend them into a single, coherent mode. Here is no Thomas Mann, writing graceful, detached prose, which is marked by its linguistic refinement. Grass has an immense gusto for words themselves and uses every device in the language, sometimes out of sheer enjoyment. Yet he never permits himself to be completely overwhelmed by his love of language. Beneath all the profusion one senses that he is—to borrow a phrase with which Dylan Thomas described himself—"a conscientious, involved and devious craftsman in words".

Throughout Grass's work, no matter how grim the subject-matter, there remains this feeling of joy in the language itself, of delight in its richnesses, its sounds, its multiple shades of meaning. *The Tin Drum*, as a result, communicates an immense enthusiasm for the medium of the novel itself and this, in post-war Germany, in a country with a blighted language, is a striking achievement.

1

Beginnings

Man is what he eats.
Ludwig Feuerbach

The writer must put a name to the house which everyone is helping to build. To the different rooms as well. He must call the sick-room 'The Sad Room', the attic 'The Windy Room' and the cellar, 'The Gloomy Room'. He may not call the cellar 'The Beautiful Room'.

Wolfgang Borchert: *The Writer*

In his novel, *From the Diary of a Snail*, Grass describes how Hermann Ott, confined to a cellar for the duration of the war, entertains his hosts by solo performances of classic dramas of the German theatre. To differentiate between characters, he employs a series of old hats, making discarded headgear the basis of his art. Grass's poetry anticipates Ott's cellar presentations. Like Ott the snail-collector, Grass the poet wears a variety of hats; he takes on the roles of lyric poet, educationist, jester, moralist, realist, surrealist, traditionalist, experimentalist. His poems can evoke the light-heartedness and delicacy of a Paul Klee or the nightmarishness and abrasiveness of a Georg Heym. They can be playful celebrations of innocence or grim reflections of experience. They can reproduce the exterior world or exist in a realm of their own. Where Grass's art is more subtle than that of Ott is in his ability to wear all the hats at the same time, to fuse the disparate personalities into one. The artist does not vanish when the political activist speaks: the jester does not disappear in the presence of the moralist. It is the characteristic feature of Grass's poetry that it finds a way to make each cap, separately and simultaneously, fit.

For a man who is such a dynamic figure on the European literary scene, Günter Grass emerged relatively without trace. After the war, he worked as a farm labourer, a potash miner and a stone mason before becoming a student of sculpture and painting at the Düsseldorf Academy of Art. In the evenings he earned some money as a jazz drummer. After travelling in Italy and France, he settled in 1953 in West Berlin where he has lived with his wife and family ever since. Until the mid-fifties he was sculptor, graphic artist and writer, increasingly drawn to express his vision in poetic and dramatic form. Literary recognition came in 1955 when he was awarded third prize in a poetry competition organised by the Süddeutscher Rundfunk (the South German Radio Network). With the publication in the following year of a slender volume called *The Merits of Windfowl*, Grass took a first, modest and inconspicuous step forward into print. He illustrated this collection of poems with weird, fantasticated drawings of fabled beasts, birds, objects, images, expressionistic motifs. These drawings at once strengthen the impact of the poems and are themselves given substance and movement by the works to which they correspond. *The Merits of Windfowl* is the earliest example of that productive interplay between the visual and the written which has become a hallmark of Grass's work.

While Günter Grass was still struggling with the problem of how to begin his literary career, the two most prominent poets of the older generation were approaching the end of theirs. Gottfried Benn and Bertolt Brecht represented the twin poles of artistic practice. They were aestheticism and didacticism personified. Benn saw poetry as the articulation of the individual soul, while Brecht measured it by its social and political usefulness. Each man had had his poetic credo tested by the pressure of real events. Benn, the advocate of poetry that was "pure and absolute", had refused to believe that his work could in any way be influenced or compromised by the rise of National Socialism. He remained in Germany but was disenchanted when his work was banned. Brecht, by contrast, had fled before Hitler and worked in exile. True to his belief in the social, moral and political function of art, he returned to live in East Germany, subjugating his immense talent to the Communist regime. Benn was shaken by what he saw under the Third Reich: Brecht was disturbed by his part in the events of 17 June 1953, a situation which Grass himself has explored in his best play, *The Plebeians Rehearse the Uprising*. But when Benn and Brecht both died in 1956, in their respective sectors of Berlin, they were unrepentant believers in their opposing concepts of poetry. It seemed that whoever tried to step into the enormous gap left by their passing was bound, in a sense, to choose between them. They were self-appointed captains of rival teams wearing very different colours. Even posthumously they would continue to lead those teams on to the field of play.

Critics who sought to assign Grass to the relevant changing-room on the evidence of *The Merits of Windfowl* were in grave difficulties. The poems appeared to qualify their author for both teams and for neither at one and the same time. Moreover, Grass even used a footballing metaphor to justify his equivocation:

> Slowly the football rose in the sky.
> Now one could see that the stands were packed.
> Alone the poet stood at the goal
> but the referee whistled: Off-side.
>
> ('Stadium at Night', p. 26)

By lifting two things—football and poetry—completely away from their normal context, Grass lets them associate and interact to form new, unexpected and arresting relationships. His language is simple and precise, the poem has epigrammatic force, and yet it is impossible to paraphrase. It is not devoid of meaning. A whole range of ideas is opened up—the poet as goalkeeper, as the last line of defence, as the one player restricted to a definite area of the field, as the solitary man who works under the harsh flood-lights of public gaze, the source of entertainment, the individual subject to a higher authority, the victim of rules, the artist whose work is always seen in artificial light and whose poems, the football, is destined to be kicked about by others, the confused figure who is always permanently and innocuously off-side. What 'Stadium at Night' lacks, and deliberately so, is any single, exclusive meaning. Freedom of imagination is paramount here as in all of Grass's poetry. By connecting the artistic and sporting worlds in his playful fantasy, he revalues them both and compels

27

further revaluations on the part of the reader. The poetry consists in the setting up of these new potentialities.

Grass, then, is a disciple neither of Benn nor of Brecht. He strives neither for the poetry of pure self-expression nor for that of public purpose. And yet he does not reject these categories. Grass seeks to balance them, to confront imagination with reality, to exploit the tension between them. In his essay, 'Content as Resistance',[1] which was written shortly after the publication of *The Merits of Windfowl*, Grass discusses the nature of the creative process. He does not see form and content as natural allies but as inevitable enemies. Content is inimical to form. It prizes its freedom and resists any organisation. Grass announces his intention to sow mistrust between form and content; indeed, mistrust is the ruling providence in his theory of aesthetics. It ensures that form and content are kept on full alert against each other, so that neither dominates. When form is imposed upon content, it does not subdue it: when content is structured by form, it does not atomise that structure. Art is produced from the tension between form and content, a tension which the artist must maintain at all times. In a work of art, therefore, fantasy and observation can coexist. Opposites are not synthesized: they are preserved in opposition.

In the middle section of his essay, Grass illustrates his argument in terms of a dialogue between two poets. Pemplefort and Krudewil represent antithetical viewpoints. Pemplefort is a romantic, esoteric poet who is obsessed with the validity of his private vision. Paradoxically, his art has a most unromantic basis in indigestible food. He confesses that he gormandises before going to bed in order to provoke nightmares. Jolted awake by the force of his dreams, he then reaches for the waiting pencil and pad to record his 'inspiration'. Krudewil is a much more realistic, commonsensical, down-to-earth person. As they stroll along, he nudges away at molehills with his walking-stick, a pragmatist who is interested in the observable world and not in inducing fantasies. Grass takes care to side with neither of his poets. If Pemplefort's method of writing poetry is patently absurd, then Krudewil's

---

[1] "Der Inhalt als Widerstand", in *Über Mein Lehrer Döblin und andere Vorträge* (Berlin: Literarisches Colloquium, 1968).

is equally ridiculous. The latter's art rests on crude superstition. He switches the light on and off three times before sitting down to compose a poem so that he can ward off the very fantasties which Pemplefort believes to be the essence of poetry. Krudewil persuades his companion to "knit a new Muse", who is practical and sceptical and who takes the shape of a "meticulous house-wife". The worlds of Benn and Brecht are subsumed in the char-acters of Pemplefort and Krudewil respectively, but it is a mis-take to identify the fact that Krudewil takes the initiative as proof of Grass's preference for the Brechtian values. He remains ironically impartial throughout, accepting neither standpoint, re-jecting neither credo. The moderation which he shows in the dialogue is fundamental to his work as a poet. The new muse will be created by the two knitting needles of form and content. In the clash and stab of this metaphor, Grass gives us an insight into his own method of writing.

'Content as resistance' is a valuable warning against too literal an approach to Grass's poetry. Many of the poems in *The Merits of Windfowl* defy interpretation. They are explorations rather than statements, purveyors of mood rather than of meaning. The follow-ing poem, for example, makes no attempt at formal coherence. Its effect lies in the way it conjoins the human, animal and in-animate in a startling, concentrated image:

> The piano into the zoo.
> Quick, get the zebra into the best room.
> Be kind to it.
> It comes from Bechstein.
> Scores are its fodder.
> and our sweet ears.
> 'Prevention of Cruelty to Animals', p. 26)

Colour links the animal with the musical. The black and white markings of the zebra become interchangeable with the notes on a piano. Whole new chains of associations are opened up, especi-ally when one considers the title of the poem. This technique of placing the familiar object in the strikingly unfamiliar environment is central to Grass's work. Its effect is sometimes grotesque, some-times humorous; but it always makes possible new, original re-lationships and calls in question old, conventional assumptions.

29

The indentification between the zebra and the piano is taken a stage further in Grass's early play, *Rocking Back and Forth* (1954). Here the animal becomes pianist rather than piano. Conelli notes at one point that "Even at birth zebras know how to play four hands".

The first volume of poems contains many of the ideas and motifs which Grass later develops in novel and play form. 'Gassing', 'Polish Standard', 'Three Our Father' and 'The Eleventh Finger' all prefigure elements in *The Tin Drum*; and Osker's inhabitation of Nurse Dorothea's wardrobe in the same novel is anticipated in 'Open Wardrobe', a poem which shows its author's incredible eye for detail. Poems like 'Bird Flight' and 'The Bird' foreshadow *Dog Years*, which also is adumbrated in 'Open Air Concert', another poem in which the animal and the musical worlds are related:

> When the yellow dog ran over the meadow
> the concert expired.
> Later the bone could not be found.
> The scores lay under the chairs,
> the conductor seized his airgun
> and shot all the blackbirds.

('Open Air Concert', p. 23)

Much of the subject matter of Grass's early poems is grim and oppressive. He concerns himself with death, murder, violence, betrayal and terror. He searches for the sinister implication in the mundane happening. He points up the ambiguous relationship between past and present in his country. And yet his poems remain exuberant, buoyant, even genial at times. Treatment redeems content. Grass maintains a resolute innocence which enables him to see the world through the uncomplicated eyes of a child, and in doing so he makes that world at once more accessible and more unnerving. In spurning the solemn and the sombre, he does not become flippant. His simplicity and total lack of self-consciousness heighten the power of his poems. Casual, naive, matter-of-factness conceals the darker elements: when they are realised, their impact is all the more shattering. Fear and unexplained violence can be contained in an over-turned garden seat in 'Furniture Out of Doors'. The straightforward

30

account given in 'The Midge Plague' can encapsulate a nation's desperate unease. A single line from 'Music for Brass'—"Those days we slept in a trumpet"—can sum up absurdly but accurately the plight of those who live on the edge of a political and social volcano.

The themes, motifs and object-mania of *The Merits of Wind-fowl* were carried over into Grass's second volume of poems which appeared in 1960. By this time *The Tin Drum* had transformed Grass from an unknown sculptor into a novelist of world-wide fame. *Railroad-Track Triangle*, the second volume of poetry, suggests no major changes in its author's method or perception. There are, however, shades falling across the childhood innocence in some cases and a more serious, adult note is sounded at times. The moralist's hat is worn along with the jester's coxcomb. Object-mania not only holds its former sway, it even defines itself in 'Diana—or the Objects'. Here, promoting the goddess of the chase to the position of patroness of poets, Grass welcomes the pain of her arrows:

> When she hit me,
> her object hit my soul
> which is to her like an object.
> ('Diana—or the Object', p. 38)

The artist's soul is no abstract concept. It is a tangible object, as capable of being wrested from its context as any of the other objects which exert such an influence in and upon Grass's poetry. If the goddess can objectify him, he in turn can objectify her:

> But you, Diana,
> With your bow,
> are to me objective and answerable.
> ('Diana—or the Object', p. 38)

What is being established here is the autonomy of the object, the supremacy of the thing. It is a concept which is fundamental to all of Grass's work and which accounts, in his poetry, for the proliferation of such objects as beds, doorbells, hats, mirrors, chairs, tables, cigarettes, scissors, spoons, forks, musical instruments and so on. Grass objectivises everything, even language itself:

31

> While I was selling it all
> five or six streets from here they expropriated
> all the possessive pronouns
> and sawed off the private shadows
> of little innocuous men.
>
> ('Sale', p. 39)

This stanza is an interesting example of a political interpolation in a relatively personal poem. It is difficult to miss the reference by a West Berliner to the other sector of his city. Under Communism nothing is private. A man's most intimate thoughts are sawn up like logs. The title poem, too, has a marked political tone. *Railroad-Track Triangle* refers to the railway junction in Berlin at a time when traffic to and from the Eastern Sector was relatively free. But the poem conveys the restlessness and the fear and the impermanence generated by the political situation, and is oddly prophetic of the attitudes which led to the building of the Berlin Wall. 'Fireproof Walls' and 'The Big Rubble Woman Speaks' are also compassionate comments on the city of Berlin. But it is in a poem about Poland that Grass was to achieve his most moving and alarming effect. 'The Stork' does not take refuge in fantasy or innocence. Its tone is measured, insistent, accusatory:

> Time was when in Treblinka on Sundays
> There was much smoking flesh, stork-blessed,
> Heated air by which the gliders cleared the ground.

We have left the world of *The Merits of Windfowl* in this poem and are given a glimpse into the Danzig Trilogy and, further ahead, into *From the Diary of a Snail*. With a poem like 'The Stork' Grass answered those who had tried to dismiss him as an irresponsible joker, as a poet incapable of any deeply felt experience. 'The Stork' may not be a purely subjective reflection, but it is charged with disgust, human sympathy, controlled rage and a very real pain. In its balancing of form and content, in its setting of the lyrical against the factual, it anticipates some of the finest passages in the novels.

When Grass's third volume of poetry was published in 1967, many critics judged it by criteria which had little to do with literary excellence. For reasons which are discussed later in this book, Grass had become directly involved in party politics in the mid-sixties.[2] His poems thus became fair game for political commentators who interpreted any treatment of topical themes as outright propaganda. Even some established literary critics decided that Grass had forsaken the freedom of the court jester for the questionable glamour of the public platform. Such attitudes are as unjust to Grass as they are damaging to his poetry. His third volume of poetry, *Questioned*, is no essay in didacticism. The illustrations may have taken on a more savagely realistic shape, the number of poems which relate to political issues may be considerably higher than in the two previous collections, and the title-poem itself may be unequivocally about the modern German; but the volume is still pre-eminently the work of a remarkable lyric talent.

Questioned marks a development in the direction of realism and adult observation, but this development does not take place at the expense of the qualities which enlivened the earlier volumes. The zest remains, the innocence is not lost, the amoralist can be called upon when needed. 'The Steam Boiler Effect' ("Hisso-maniac. Hissoplex. Hissophile.") is a polemical poem in which the jester is as energetic as ever. 'Placed Amid Old Men' is a highly topical poem with the stark simplicity and effect of some of the earlier work. 'Don't Turn Around' combines laughter and unease in the old proportions. Even when Grass sets out to produce political satire, as in 'The Jellied Pig's Head', the artist takes over from the political activist and asserts his love of cooking. The poem reads less like polemicising than it does an advance extract from a work which, in *From the Diary of a Snail*, the author promises one day to write—"a narrative cookbook . . . about man as an animal who can cook". With the smell of the kitchen in his nostrils, Grass turns his back completely on his didactic intentions.

The force and nature of Grass's commitment were bound to arouse the familiar complaint that the artist had no place or function in the political arena. To support such an argument is to ignore the long and distinguished partnership which politics and poetry have enjoyed since the time of the Greeks. From the days of Simonides and Aeschylus onwards, public events have been

[2] See the chapter on *The Plebeians Rehearse the Uprising*.

not only a proper subject for the creative artist, but an essential one. Poets as diverse as Aristophanes, Chaucer, Dante, Milton, Marvell, Heine, Byron, Wordsworth and Tennyson have put their artistic abilities at the disposal of political ends. In our own century the names of Blok, Auden, Neruda, Trakl, Mayakovsky, Brecht, Quasimodo, and Pasternak have kept the tradition alive and honourable. As C. M. Bowra reminds us in his incisive lectures on *Poetry and Politics (1900–1960)*:

> Poetry on public events has as much right to exist as poetry on any other subject, since it helps us to grasp them from unexpected angles and to treat them seriously without yielding to the numbing effects of lower methods of communication. Nor is there any reason why it should not be as good as poetry in other fields. . . .[3]

Grass's political poems are no less artistically viable for being concerned with public events. A poem like 'Do Something' is as delicate in its structure and as memorable in its phrasing ("Lovely is rage in the paddock, /before it is fed") as most of the poems in the volume. Yet along with 'Powerless, with a Guitar' it was seen by many as a direct attack on the radical left. Two objections must be registered against this interpretation; one, political, the other, artistic. In the first place, none of Grass's political poems is in any way the product of blinkered partisanship. They have general application, disturb the attitudes of colleagues as well as of opponents. Secondly, in conceiving these two poems against protest, Grass is himself making a protest and hence, by the laws which he is himself laying down, courting impotence. 'Do Something', in particular, is a personal as well as a public poem, an act of self-examination which leaves its author uncertain about the most effective mode of protest. That the poem is no assault on one element in the political world is shown by the way its themes are amplified in the novel, *Local Anaesthetic*. In the poem as in the prose, Grass asks pertinent questions about the nature of protest and the role of the artist in presenting it.

The shift from realism to surrealism is seen most clearly in the autobiographical poems. 'Marriage' is at once highly intimate and universal. It offers an honest, dispassionate, ironic picture of

C. M. Bowra, *Poetry and Politics (1900–1960)* 1966, p. 137.

Grass's own marriage ("We deduct each other from income tax"), which accords with the fuller insights into his family life given in *From the Diary of a Snail*; and it makes general comments on the marital state and the mechanics of its survival ("Exhaustion simulates harmony"). Greater realism does not compel Grass to forfeit the child's imaginative freedom and exuberance. In his most uncompromisingly autobiographical poem, 'Kleckerburg', he exploits the tension between the childhood world and the sardonic adult view of that world. Innocence and experience coexist and produce a poem which at all times refrains from overt moral judgement:

> Baptised and vaccinated, schooled, confirmed,
> Bomb splinters, meanwhile, were my toys.
>
> ('Kleckerburg', p. 80)

The disarming simplicity is intact: the perspective of naïveté still has the power to arrest and unsettle. The poet has not been obliterated by the politician. The partnership between them has been provocative and fruitful, and has contributed to the maturing of Grass's poetic talent which is revealed in his third volume of poems.

Grass the poet is indistinguishable from Grass the dramatist. The same principles inform his approach, the same bewildering variety of hats is worn. In a much-quoted discussion in 1961, Grass explained that poetry, plays and prose were, for him, all built upon dialogue. The transition from the lyric to the stage play was thus smooth and natural: Grass wrote poems in dialogue form and elaborated upon them. This process is at its clearest in the plays *Flood* and *The Wicked Cooks*, which have their origin in poems from the first and second collections respectively. It accounts for the strengths and the weaknesses of Grass's earliest dramas.

Rocking Back and Forth was Grass's first play, a one-act curtain-raiser which wonders if the curtain should be raised at all. For this slight piece is both drama and debate on the theory of drama. Its subtitle 'A Prelude on the Stage', identifies it as a parody of the 'Prelude' to Goethe's *Faust I*. Goethe draws together Director, Poet and Comedian to discuss the nature of theatrical presentation. The Director, a witty, down-to-earth man, begins by stating the eternal problem facing those who live under the tyranny of the paying audience:

You two, Sirs, have been my stay
In many a time of storm and stress,
What does our theatre want today,
What are the chances of success?

The Director wonders how best to combine the talents of writer and performer, in order to produce a work which will edify and entertain, instruct and amuse. In the ensuing discussion, it is the Comedian, the practical man of the theatre, who makes the most perceptive comments. The calm, ordered debate in verse is terminated by the Director. It is time to replace words with action.

Rocking Back and Forth replaces action with words. In its convoluted theorising about dramatic action, it effectively negates it. A Clown sits on a rocking-horse in the middle of an empty stage. Time has made his art anachronistic. The circus wishes to dismiss him. He is no longer funny because the world around him is more comic than he is. A Director, Playwright and Actor enter and rule out the Clown as a legitimate member of the theatre. They try all manner of ways to incorporate him in another guise, but he remains true to his art and stays in the saddle. After speculating on ideas from the intellectual theatre (Cocteau, Beckett), the three practitioners fall back on the more conventional dramatic devices. To introduce sexual conflict, a bed is literally dragged onto the stage and the Actor obligingly leaps into it, even inventing a wife to keep him company beneath the sheets. The Clown is not to be tempted off his rocking-horse, however. Another ploy is used—a piano is rolled on to the scene, bringing a whole new element into the drama. When this fails to hold the Clown's attention, the Actor falls back on one of the oldest methods of dramatic surprise and points a gun at him. This, too, fails to gain the Clown's participation. The Director's comment that "The conflict is long overdue" is an exact summary of the whole play. The Clown refuses to dismount from his undramatic rocking-horse. He will only consider joining the Actor in bed if the horse can join them, too. He takes up the ultimate position of the non-dramatic by pretending to be dead.

In his first play, Grass is not contending that the writing of drama is an obsolete mode of expression. He is questioning the assumptions which underlie theatre, separating form and content, theory and practice. As his play rocks to and fro between ideas and dramatic realisation of those ideas, he scatters mistrust liberally into the void. The Clown is not only a symbol of the contracting world of the circus; he has associations with the older traditions of theatre as well. His name, Conelli, links him with the *commedia dell'arte* and he shares its delight in the unmotivated, the unscripted, the mimed, and in the sheer freedom of play. Again, he is the artist as court jester, professionally irreverent. He holds fast to the childhood perspective which is represented by the rocking-horse, unconvinced that any of the adult experiences on offer are worth the loss of his innocence. Like a child, he has named his horse, and treats it as a live animal with needs and feelings of its own. Grass throws the notion of the Clown as child into relief by making him in turn a father. His daughter, Dorothy, arrives to accuse him of hindering her love affair with a film-splicer. What she and Karl-Heinz hope will blossom into marriage, the Clown insists on opposing. In life, as on the stage, the Clown bars the development of conventional drama. Instead of letting the real-life plot which involves Dorothy and Karl-Heinz develop into marriage, he turns the love-lorn film-splicer into a buffoon and makes him part of his act. In every situation, the Clown insists on seeing only comic possibilities, and the comedy must be low and broad and unserious enough to appeal to children. The world of the child is paramount. The Director concedes this in the last line of the play—"children don't like to be kept waiting, you know". Left alone once more, the Clown rocks vigorously. Neither his vision nor his freedom have been influenced.

Rocking Back and Forth is an ingenious, inventive play, propelled by a simple idea. It has wit, satire and surrealistic values which recall the poems. Its shortcomings are equally obvious. It is too theoretical, too discursive, too pointlessly obscure. That Grass is able to make a first-rate play out of a discussion of theatre in a theatre is shown later in *The Plebeians Rehearse the Uprising*. As we shall see, in that drama it is the Boss who mounts the rocking-horse of his dialectical method and rejects the various roles offered to him. Grass's first play, however, is more than just an interesting experiment. It is an engaging and stimulating work that is of a piece with his poetry, commending innocence, respecting imagination and reality as separate entities which must be balanced carefully against each other. In its parallels with Goethe's 'Prelude', *Rocking Back and Forth* uses a device which its author employs with more assurance in some of his novels—that of selecting an established artistic talent as a reference point. It is worth remembering that the last words spoken by Goethe's comedian have a direct bearing on Grass's play:

> It's not age that brings childhood back again,
> Age merely shows what children we remain.

The themes and images of Grass's next play, *Flood* (1955), are largely contained in his poem, 'The Flood'. The two-act play has the same cool acceptance of disaster, the same air of fatalism, the same dominating objects. In contrast to the bare stage of his first play, Grass supplies a setting which is redolent of a definite dramatic situation—a house threatened by the rising flood. In times of catastrophe people try to save what is dearest to them. As the play opens, Noah, the owner of the house, is struggling up the cellar steps with a box. He is anxious to preserve his collection of historic inkwells and candelabras: he learns that water can dissolve the written word as easily as it can extinguish the flame of truth. His sister-in-law, Betty, is more concerned to save photograph albums, those reminders of a time when the children were at their happiest in the child's world, those symbols of a drowned past. In the room above them, Yetta, Noah's daughter, and her fiancé, Henry, have more practical tendencies: they have saved their magazines, phonograph records, the last crate of beer and, ironically, preserving-jars. On the roof itself are two rats, Pearl and Point, whose only thought is to save themselves.

The flood waters rise with an insistence which recalls the growth of the corpse in Ionesco's *Amédée* (1953). But whereas the swelling body is a visual image which externalises the neuroses of the protagonists, the flood is an unseen thing which is only measured by the watermark it leaves on the individuals, human and animal, in the play. Again, while the cadaver provides a focal point and stimulus to the drama, the flood has no power to alarm or to provoke any dramatic action. The love-triangle which was suggested as a possible situation in *Rocking Back and Forth* is adopted in *Flood* but it, too, fails to lead to any real conflict or drama. The sensual Congo steps in between the engaged couple without ceremony. Henry submits with only meek protest to being put out on the roof while Yetta jumps into bed with Congo. Overheard by the rats, who mistake him for a philosopher, Henry muses about the sudden, unhappy turn of events. But the thwarted lover promises no dramatic confrontation or recrimination. He decides that he has already forgiven his fiancée and will say nothing to her—"Silence comes easy to me".

Henry's calm resignation pervades the whole play. Aunt Betty sews parasols against the sunny times that are sure to come. While she busies herself with symbols of readiness and hope, Leo and Congo tell stories, Yetta sings, Noah sorts out his inkwells, the rats chat amiably. When the flood subsides at the end of the play, there is no enthusiastic response. The flood disappears quietly and unobtrusively. Yetta sums up the mood of anticlimax. She wants the rain to start again in earnest. After the excitement of the flood, and the physical and emotional changes forced upon them, normality seems dull and prosaic. Life at ground level is its own kind of catastrophe. Yetta leaves slowly and reluctantly as the curtain falls, to be re-united with Henry on the mud in the garden.

Like some of the poems discussed earlier, *Flood* liberates humans, animals and objects from their recognised settings and juxtaposes them in new relationships. The whole house is, in effect, turned upside down. Cellar rats occupy the roof. Their nibbling rodent-conversations counterpoint the human reactions to the crisis. Down below them, people are so conditioned by the disaster to accept anything that they are not surprised when Leo and Congo arrive in a box from the cellar, or when an Inspector of Flood Damage steps briskly out of a grandfather clock. The clock is only one of the many objects which feature in abundance, ejected from their usual context, given comic and symbolic value in the process. In a characteristic speech, Yetta watches some beds float by:

> I wish I could be a bed like that, empty, tossing about. Not standing on four legs under an idiotic oil painting, tied to a chamber pot and the bedside table, false teeth in glass of water, detective

story with bookmark, dreaming the murder to the bitter end and putting up with the seventy years that some people spend on earth from sheer habit. . . .

(*Flood*, Act One)

The real and surreal join hands here. Detailed observation is matched with wild fantasy to produce a touching, wistful moment—until Grass reminds us that Yetta's lyrical response has been set off by a scene of utter devastation. There is violence and loss and futility in the sight of a bed drifting along on flood water, but Yetta interprets the picture in terms of freedom. A bed liberated from its function makes her yearn for a life which is liberated from conventional expectations. This is why she bemoans the return to reality. Yetta would rather consort with aggressive and corrupt fantasy figures like Congo and Leo than settle down with the pedestrian Henry in the boredom of the real world.

The autonomy of objects is stressed even more forcefully in Grass's next play, *Onkel, Onkel* (1956). Like its predecessor, this four-act play reveals genuine anarchic talent which specialises in the grotesque. The putative hero of *Onkel, Onkel* is Bollin, a 'systematizer', a man who is in theory that most dramatic of stage characters—a professional murderer. In practice, however, Bollin repudiates all the guarantees he seems to give of action and surprise. He resembles the three men of the theatre in *Rocking Back and Forth*, trapped hopelessly in the lift that rises from thought to action. Dedicated to murder in a most single-minded way, he is yet unable to carry through any of his carefully planned killings. For Bollin is a pedantic criminal, a man who needs his pencil and pad as much as his revolver if he is to instil order and harmony into the world. Because events do not proceed in a logical, ordered way, he is frustrated in his ambitions. Each of his victims refuses to behave in the accepted way by showing fear. His first assignment is a teenager, Sophie, confined to bed with influenza. Vulnerable and immobilised, Sophie is not in the least upset when Bollin emerges from beneath her bed. She calmly warns him that he must not come close for fear of infection—a subtle parody on Bollin's plans for her physical well-being—then asks him to help her finish her crossword. Deprived of a successful murder, he takes his revenge on her doll, Pinky, plunging a knife into its stomach.

The forester, Greensward, is the next intended murder victim, and Bollin devises a suitable death for the man, first catching him in a pit like a wild animal. But the forester will not play the role of the frightened victim either. He continues with a botanical lecture, remaining steadfastly in character as a forester. This time Bollin axes a Christmas tree to release his pent-up violence. Bollin finds his third victim, a famous Prima Donna, relaxing in a bath, an ideal venue for a classic sexual murder. But the assassin fails once again to instil any fear. The Prima Donna's endless prattle deflects him from his mission, and when she makes advances he throws her aside and flees. In the last act, Bollin waits in the middle of an abandoned building site, a visual comment on the failure of his own plans to mature. He is joined by the children who pestered him in the prologue at the beginning of the play. They taunt him with their songs and with their repeated chant of the play's title—'Mister, Mister'. Gradually, they confiscate his watch, pen and revolver. As she plays with the revolver, Sprat, the girl, accidently pulls the trigger and shoots Bollin dead ("Look. His eyes are all white"). Planned assassination has failed. Casual death ensues. Bollin has found a role which he can play properly at last: he has succeeded as an innocent victim where he failed as a calculating murderer.

Onkel, Onkel has considerable lightness of touch and several fine comic moments. Notwithstanding his profession, Bollin emerges as a kindly, sympathetic character whose problems engage an audience. His death is as shocking as it is ironic, and gives the play its deeply disconcerting conclusion. Objects can become the controlling agents in life. The revolver, which has refused to react to Bollin's bidding, has more claim to being called the protagonist than he has. It asserts its independence from the start. Placed in the unknowing hands of a child, it wreaks its revenge on Bollin for the damage he did to the other objects—the doll, the tree. Beneath the humour and the black farce, Grass makes an unnerving case for the supremacy of the inanimate. The final song, appropriately, concentrates on objects:

> Mister, mister, aintcha, aintcha,
> aintcha, aintcha, aintcha got
> any little dingus

41

Hidden in your pocket.
(*softly*) Mister, mister. . . .

(*Onkel, Onkel*, Act Four)

Only Ten Minutes to Buffalo (1957) re-introduces the characters
of Pemplefort and Krudewil from the essay, 'Content as Resistance', In this lively one-actor, Grass transforms Pemplefort into a
fireman and the other poet into an engineer. They are discovered
on a rusty engine in the middle of a Bavarian meadow. Cows
surround them, moss tells of the engine's long disuse, pastoral
serenity dominates. But in their fantasy, Pemplefort and Krudewil have endowed the machine with locomotion, speed and destination. They must reach Buffalo at all costs. When they have
anxieties over the coal supply, they shovel cow pats into the fire-
box. Bowel-movement leads to engine-movement. For Pemplefort
and Krudewil, then, there is fierce progress in their stasis.

Working in the foreground is the painter, Kotschenreuther.
Though he takes the bucolic scene around him for his subject,
what appears on his canvas is a seascape. Axel, the bovine cow-
herd, is baffled. His perception of reality is simple and limited:
he sees cows, not ships. The painter introduces him to the potentialities of the imagination. His words have a bearing on the
message of this play and on the principles which underlie Grass's
approach to poetry:

> You've got to attune yourself to the new spirit.
> You've got to dive down under the old values. . . .
> Then you'll discover new aspects, sensitive instruments,
> prophetic mechanisms, a virgin continent . . . and first
> of all you've got to throw all these stupid titles
> overboard. Cow, ship, painter, buttercup. They're all
> delusions, hallucinations, complexes. Do you think a
> cow minds if I call it a sailboat . . . or even a steamer?

Axel proves to be a ready pupil. With his intuitions awakened,
he shows a firmer grasp on artistic truth than either Pemplefort,
Krudewil or Kotschenreuther. At the end of the play, the men on
the engine are rejoined by Frigate, a domineering female. She
forces them to abandon their own play situation, and enter into
hers again. Caught up in a nautical fantasy, which has been anticipated by the painter, they pretend to row off across the ocean

42

in search of whales. References to Moby Dick and quotations from Melville's novel established the scale of their joint fantasy. Axel reappears to take charge of the engine. His dog, Jonah, is far too realistic to be swallowed up by the invention of a whale. Axel determines that the engine will reach Buffalo. It replies to his command and moves slowly offstage.

The argument of 'Content as Resistance' is given visual expression here. Axel, crude, untutored, rustic, has found a way to combine form with content so that art is generated. He does not resort to the sophisticated fantasies of Pemplefort and Krudewil, for their whimsies are self-defeating. In the end their antics become a case of amusement for amusement's sake, play without a purpose. Again, Axel rejects the conceptualising of Kotschenreuther, who is revealed in his true light when he tries to render the flight between the two men on the engine in terms of a symbolic religious picture. Axel is unhindered by any traditional theories about art and unaware of experimentalist notions as well. He approaches the engine in the true spirit of intellectual adventures, and finds the means to fuse imagination and reality. His liberated fantasies are the form which harmonises with the content as represented by the engine. When form and content achieve the right balance, art moves forward.

As in Grass's previous plays, objects enforce despotic rule. The engine resists Pemplefort and Krudewil metaphorically and literally. Kotschenreuther is the prisoner of his artist's materials. Frigate is controlled by her spyglass and her boatswain's whistle. And even when the engine does consent to roll, it is another object —a pistol—which has the last word. It explodes in the smokestack, a starter's gun signalling that someone at least and at last has set off on the right track. Fittingly, when dramatic action begins to take place, the curtain falls. Grass has already mocked the conventional devices of film melodrama—the fight on the train, the body across the line—and he persistently checks any real development or confrontation. Action is internalised in the fantasies of the characters. The play's title thus becomes ironic. *Only Ten Minutes to Buffalo*, refers to the ballad of 'John Maynard', a steersman on Lake Erie who gallantly remained at his job when fire broke out aboard his steamer. Heroism and self-sacrifice become, in Grass's drama, anti-heroism and self-indulgence.

43

Dramatic potential is stifled. Grass breaks all the rules of play-writing in order to argue, through the example of Axel, that the rules must be broken and scrapped and ignored if art is to make any meaningful progress. In its precision, invention, concentrated imagery, sureness of control and uninhibited fun, *Only Ten Minutes to Buffalo* is the most effective and appealing of Grass's early plays.

The Wicked Cooks (1957) is an altogether more ambitious play, and one which is prefigured in the poem, 'Chefs and Spoons'. Grass's obsession with cooks and with cooking is proverbial. Metaphors from the kitchen have eaten hungrily into his poetry, prose and drama. *The Wicked Cooks* is a scarifying but irrepressible allegory in five acts. Its plot centres around a mysterious recipe for cabbage soup, greatly sought after despite its unappetising taste of ashes. Two rival factions of cooks compete for the recipe which is in the sole possession of the man they call the Count. To secure their ends, the cooks will go to any lengths and they merrily discuss trickery, intimidation, bribery and worse. The Count, whose real name of Herbert Schymanski has anything but the ring of nobility about it, resists all blandishments and threats. Then the cooks realise their bargaining strength. The Count is in love with Martha, a nurse who is engaged to Vasco, one of the cooks. Vasco agrees to put his professional needs before his emotional ones. He lets Martha marry the Count on condition that the latter parts with the secret. The Count is given the recipe for his happiness: he must give the cooks the recipe for theirs.

When it is time to divulge the secret, however, the Count cannot remember the recipe. Paradoxically, it is Martha, offered in exchange for the recipe, who has put the secret ingredients beyond recall:

> THE COUNT: I've told you all often enough, it is not a recipe, it's an experience, a living knowledge, continuous change—you ought to be aware that no cook has ever succeeded in cooking the same soup twice. . . . This last few months, this life with Martha, with my wife. . . . It has made the experience superfluous. I have forgotten it.
>
> (*The Wicked Cooks*, Act Five)

Unable to keep up their end of the bargain, the Count and Martha commit suicide. The cooks make running exits. Petri, the trumpet-playing cook, is the last to leave. Deprived of a specific aim (the recipe) Petri feels that perhaps seeking is more important than finding—"But in my legs, too, something is getting ready to strike out for a hypothetical goal". Martin Esslin has pointed out the religious parallels, discerning, in the washing of the Count's feet shortly before his death and in the association of the soup with the Eucharist, a strong analogy with the Passion.[4] To support this view one could cite the setting of Act Five in a garden, a suitably Biblical venue, and the identification of Martha with her New Testament namesake as a practical, domesticated, highly industrious woman. With blasphemy and reverence, Grass sets up clear affiliations between the Count of the cooks and the King of the Jews.

The problem with this interpretation is that it does not contain all of the values and elements in *The Wicked Cooks*. No single reading can do justice to the multiple ambiguities of the play. It moves between its levels of meaning and suggestion with mercurial speed. Drama, ballet, music, fairytale, song, tragedy, comedy, the tyranny of objects, satire, lyric poetry, echo effects, and outright absurdity all make their contribution. As in earlier plays, dramatic potential is first located then nullified: the suicide is kept in the wings. Again, like *Onkel, Onkel*, the play explores the dark side of innocence, finding in childish repetitions a sinister kind of persecution. Bollin, the potential murderer, is killed by the unwearying persistence of the two children, Sprat and Slick. The Count, a potential saviour, is sent to his death by the child-like single-mindedness of the cooks who keep asking "And the recipe?"

Another reading of the play is to see it, along with *Rocking Back and Forth*, as a parable on the dilemma of the artist. The Count desperately tries to preserve his artistic integrity and his individuality in the face of a menacing conformism. To surrender his secret is to become at one with the cooks, corrupt, dehumanised, consigned to the uniformity of whiteness. It is better to die than to lose one's artistic identity. In its spirited defence of individuality, the play has affinities with *The Tin Drum*, another work with ample supplies of food, nurses, recipes, objects,

[4] Martin Esslin: *Theatre of the Absurd*, Pelican edition, 1968, p. 261.

45

trumpets, betrayals, persecution, suicides and powerful religious overtones. It is interesting that in the Berlin premiere of *The Wicked Cooks* in 1962 (a ballet version, *Five Cooks*, was performed in 1959), the Count wore a mask which resembled Grass's own face. Such an explicit identification of the protagonist as artist confuses as much as it clarifies. To emphasise any one element in the drama is to subdue others, and to disguise the fundamental ambiguity of the play.

The political analogies must not be neglected—the recipe as the blue-print for a perfect society, the white of the cooks as the black evil of National Socialism, the Count and Martha as victims of a system which ruthlessly imposes rigid standards. Again, the commercial parallels must not be lost sight of—the cooks as business tycoons, the recipe as the ultimate source of monopoly, the marriage of the Count and Martha as pure financial transaction. Arnold Wesker's ebullient naturalistic play, *The Kitchen* (1959), finds in the work situation of its cooks a microcosm of the world. Grass's effervescent fantasy finds in the clownish villainy of its cooks, a perturbing microcosm of Germany.

Whether any production of *The Wicked Cooks* can realise all of its latent values remains a matter for grave doubt. The author himself must take some blame for this. The play is unnecessarily handicapped by obscurity and impetuosity. Grass has been at once too niggardly and too prodigal. *The Wicked Cooks* lacks the substance to sustain interest over five acts. It needs more development, more co-ordination, more sense of direction. At the same time, it needs to tighten, to limit, to condense some of its metaphors. The play is too diffuse, too wasteful of its considerable resources. The poems from which it grew is exemplary in its construction, unerring in its images, and subtle in its shifts of meaning and in its repetitions. The play is unable to translate these qualities into stage terms. While the poem is able to distil its essence into a single line—"No death is here but leads back to the spoon"—the play, for all its boisterousness, becomes sluggish in the statement of its themes.

None of Grass's early plays achieved any lasting success in the theatre. *Flood* was first performed in Frankfurt in 1957, *Onkel, Onkel* was first performed in Cologne in 1958, and *Only Ten Minutes to Buffalo* had its première in Berlin in 1959. (Another short play, *Thirty-Two Teeth*, written in 1958, was an absurdist fantasy about a schoolteacher obsessed with dental hygiene. Grass withdrew the play, but took up its themes at a more realistic level in *Local Anaesthetic* and its stage counterpart). The relative failure of Grass's first ventures into drama must not lead to their being considered as no more than apprentice works. They deserve a far better fate than to be consigned to a preserving jar marked 'Theatre of the Absurd'. The plays are clever, original, coruscating creations, full of poetry, zest and a refreshing innocence. Grass the dramatist has great mental agility, immense theatrical flair and an uncanny ability to fuse the comic and the serious. Like his poems, his plays provide no categorical answers, no neat solutions. They glorify uncertainties, anxieties, unpalatable truths. They institute a search.

Rejection bestows its own blessings. Bernard Shaw tried to begin his literary career as a novelist in nineteenth-century style. When his books found little favour, he turned to drama. The fumbling novelist became the most assured theatrical talent of his day. Günter Grass made a similar journey from disappointment to acclaim. The unenthusiastic reception of his early plays made him concentrate on the writing of a novel. It was a long, painstaking process which called for nerve, stamina and faith. It transformed an unsung poet and daunted playwright into an impossibly accomplished novelist. Grass's first novel drew heavily on his earlier work, collecting themes, motifs and perspectives from his poetry and plays. It lost none of their qualities. It kept their innocence and extended their exuberance. It maintained their blending of imagination with reality. It sharpened their satire. Finally, it preserved their wonderful sense of freedom, notwithstanding the fact that the novel was under the sovereignty of that most autocratic of Grassian objects—the tin drum.[5]

[5] This book was at the proof stage before the publication of John Reddick's excellent *The 'Danzig Trilogy' of Günter Grass*. I am able only to record my admiration for Dr. Reddick's scholarly and exhaustive work.

2

The Tin Drum

It was not out of modesty that I wanted to become a drummer.
That is the highest thing, the rest is a trifle.

Adolph Hitler, Munich People's Court, 1924

When I go down to the cellar
There to draw some wine
The little hunchback who's in there
Grabs that jug of mine.

Des Knaben Wunderhorn, ed.
Arnim and Brentano (1805–8)

Literary criticism is born of suspicion. When a new author makes
such a thunderous impact as Günter Grass did with *The Tin
Drum*, the literary critic uses doubt and distrust as his book-
marks. He seeks to explain and absorb that impact by catalogu-
ing the many writers who have so clearly "influenced" the novel.
Now the search for source and affinity is a valuable activity, which
enriches our apprehensions of a work. Moreover, it is impossible
to gauge a writer's full significance until he is set alongside his
literary forbears and contemporaries. But all too often the task
of doing this is approached with a hearty scepticism. Many
modern critics seem to equate the detection of an influence with
catching an author out in the very act of plagiarism. To be moved
sufficiently by another's work to want to borrow from it is somehow seen as a grave weakness, as proof of glaring unoriginality.
As if literature should arise spontaneously, or as if the business of
an author should at the very least be to disguise his borrowings
instead of openly acknowledging them, or, as is sometimes the
case with Grass, of actually celebrating them. It was T. S. Eliot
who warned against the pursuit of a spurious originality in writers,

48

and his words have a special relevance here—"we shall often find that not only the best, but the most individual parts of his work may be those in which the dead poets, his ancestors, assert their immortality most vigorously" (*Tradition and the Individual Talent: Selected Prose*, Penguin Edition, 1953, p. 22). In *The Tin Drum* we shall hear many of the voices of Grass's literary ancestors, some loud, some soft, some mere whispers, some returning echoes. And these voices, far from diminishing the power of the novel, enhance it and confirm its impression of towering individuality.

Grass's first novel not only invites comparisons with the work of other writers, it compels them. An author immediately summoned to mind is Herman Melville, and Grass has readily admitted his debt to the American—"But the decisive influence for me was Herman Melville and his object mania, his *Moby Dick*."[1] And in another interview Grass singled out two other qualities of the novel—its realistic precision and its pursuit of fantasy as *part* of reality—"That's what Melville gave me".[2] One can see many other features of *Moby Dick* reflected in *The Tin Drum*: the epic structure, the delight in fable, the true ambiguity of symbols, the Biblical affiliations, the exploration of uncertainty and terror (as the ship leaves the security of the land or as the country sails into the great black unknown of the Third Reich), the love of the big dramatic scene, and, most of all, the fine lyricism. For, as Grass emphasised in that same *Encounter* interview, "Everything I have written has its origin and impulses in the lyrical." Finally, there is a bond between Ishmael, who has "Doubts of all things earthly, and intuitions of some things heavenly," and who ends up as "neither believer nor infidel"; and the Oskar who declares the basic paradox of his existence—". . . though today I am at home neither in the sacred nor the profane but dwell on the fringes, in a mental hospital" (*The Tin Drum*, p. 146).

In his play, *Only Ten Minutes to Buffalo* (1959), Grass expresses his affection for Melville by quoting directly from *Moby Dick* at the climax of the drama. For another of the key influences upon his work, Grass has expressed more than affection. His lecture, *On My Master Döblin* (1967) draws attention to the

---

[1] Interview published in *Frankfurter Neue Presse*, 14 November 1959.
[2] Interview published in *Encounter*, September 1970.

neglected talents of Alfred Döblin (1878–1957), whose master-piece, *Berlin Alexanderplatz*,[3] remains the archetypal metropolitan novel. Technically, this work foreshadows many of the devices used in *The Tin Drum*, but Grass does not concentrate on the finer details of Döblin's prose composition. He dwells on the latter's role as a writer-politician, a role which he himself has attempted to fill with fluctuating success. To illustrate his theme, Grass does not use Döblin's masterpiece, but selects his *Wallen-stein*, a choice which is not as perverse as it may at first appear.

Apart from the fact that *Wallenstein* satisfies Grass's pre-dilection for the historical, it is a work about an aggressively political animal, whereas Franz Biberkopf in *Berlin Alexanderplatz* is fundamentally apolitical. Again, the character of Wallenstein connects directly with the German imagination. He is a national hero who has inspired many novels and plays—including Schiller's drama—and who has proved equally irresistible to biographers. The Thirty Years War, in which he operated, was the last of the wars of religion and its intrigues, futility and farcical aspects have been immortalised in a number of works, from Grimmelshausen's *Simplicius Simplissimus* (1669) down to Brecht's *Mother Courage and her Children* (1939). In other words, Grass—through Döblin —is dealing with a period which is very familiar to his audience and which he makes even more familiar by relating it to Germany of the twentieth century. For Döblin does not present his readers with a great military hero. His Wallenstein is a cold-blooded master of finance, an opportunist, who, like Krupp, invested his money in armaments. "Krupp and Wallenstein each bought a Kaiser" (*Über Mein Lehrer Döblin*, p. 17). Grass points up other parallels, then concludes by insisting that literature can and should have an educational impulse. And yet it is not from the idea of the novel as manifesto that Grass has learned most from his master. It is surely from Döblin's approach to the historical process that he has gained one of his main intellectual character-istics—his belief in the possibility of simultaneous existences. Döblin thought that the present contained both the past and the future, and decided that "This simultaneity in the present is a single truth, a meaningful event" (*Unser Dasein/Our Existence*,

---

[3] For a comparison between *The Tin Drum* and *Berlin Alexanderplatz*, see W. Gordon Cunliffe, *Günter Grass* (New York: Twayne, 1969, p. 57).

1953, p. 217). We shall find that his belief underlies much of Grass's writing.

Great writers are great readers. *The Tin Drum* is a monument to its author's profound love of literature and abounds in parody, quotation, allusion, burlesque. Exemplifying Synge's dictum that "All art is collaboration", it is a work of such range and copiousness that it is possible to attach an endless list of comparisons to it.

Two writers who must be mentioned in any discussion of Grassian parallels are Lawrence Sterne and Thomas Mann. Sterne has always exercised a strong appeal to the German mind and when the first volume of *Tristram Shandy* was published in Germany in 1769, in a translation by Johann Friedrich Zückert, it caused a sensation. Writers as diverse as Goethe ("Yorick-Sterne was the most beautiful spirit who ever lived"), Novalis, Jean Paul, Hegel, Heine and Herder have paid tribute to its effect upon them. Many novelists have tried to thumb a lift from *Tristram Shandy* but there are times in *The Tin Drum* when Grass actually seems to be behind its driving wheel. There is the same idiosyncratic autobiographical approach, with the narrator constantly reminding us that he is undertaking a literary work. In both novels the tone is firmly established in the opening paragraph, with Tristram speculating cheerfully about his conception or with Oskar playing with the notions of the observer and the observed, friend and enemy, abnormality and normality, as a child plays with its bricks. Grass, too, shares Sterne's delight in documentation, his capricious attitude to the novel's structure, and his merciless mockery of folly, pretension and authority. We are told that in the library of the Reverend Sterne, vicar of Coxwold, there were five editions of Rabelais. Grass joins Sterne in borrowing from Rabelais his zest for language, for learned wit, and for the obscene. Another work of literature which we can safely assume was on Sterne's shelves was the Bible, and both he and Grass introduce a great deal of Biblical language and reference into their works. This, set against the more Rabelaisian qualities, makes for a glorious interpenetration of the sacred and the profane. Another writer whose presence links the worlds of *Tristram Shandy* and *The Tin Drum* is Shakespeare, whose *Hamlet* preoccupies both Sterne and Grass.

51

What separates the two novelists is their narrative skill. Sterne, like Rabelais, deliberately loses his narrative thread, meandering off into all manner of digressions. Grass never loses sight of his story and, more important, never breaks faith with it. Another apparent difference between the two works is in their tone, with Sterne's sentimentality having little in common with Grass's cynicism. Yet are these qualities so unrelated? Oscar Wilde was at his most perceptive when he discerned, in *De Profundis*, that "A sentimentalist is a cynic at heart. Indeed, sentimentality is the bank-holiday of cynicism". To complete this list of affinities between Sterne and Grass we must return to Melville who, having finished *Moby Dick*, confessed to Nathaniel Hawthorne that "I have written a wicked book". No such authorial confirmation is needed in the cases of *Tristram Shandy* and *The Tin Drum*: they gleefully proclaim their own wickedness.

Wickedness is not a quality which one easily associates with Thomas Mann, that urbane master of German prose. To many critics Mann and Grass are poles apart, coming, as they do, from totally different backgrounds, adopting contrasting life-styles, and viewing their work in very different ways. There is a patrician air about Mann which sorts ill with the air of a well-rehearsed plebeian which Grass often conveys. Mann appeals primarily to the intellect while Grass, in *The Tin Drum* certainly, appeals chiefly to the visual imagination. Mann prizes economy: Grass, in his first novel, exalts abundance. And one could go on. Let us extend the comparison to other terms, and let us bear in mind *The Magic Mountain* and *The Tin Drum* as we do so.

Consider two fully-realised works of architecture: a Greek temple and a Gothic cathedral. The former is stately and restrained, the latter is ornate and urgent. There is simplicity, unity and a harmony of proportion in the temple: in the cathedral there is elaboration, disunity and a wilful disproportion. The calmness of the former's horizontal line is in sharp contrast to the striving of the latter's vertical line. In the marble walks of the temple, one sees things which would have excited a Wincklemann—a power, an imagination, a creative thrust that is at once heightened and kept in check by the exquisitely symmetrical form. In the cavernous interior of the cathedral, one notices the shattered windows, the proliferation of grotesque stone-carvings and of dog-tooth ornaments, the sudden unexplained cries from the crypt, and the overwhelming feeling that the whole edifice is in the process of de-consecration.

Yet the more closely one examines the two constructions the more one realises the extent to which they are both clever optical illusions. The temple may indeed seem to be a triumph of light and of linear perfection, but it has dark, sinister corners where a jagged irregularity of line breaks out. It may appear serene and pure and dedicated to the worship of Apollo, and then one senses the passions and the impurities and the violent presence of Dionysus. Even that antiseptic atmosphere, which was so all-pervading at first, is now no longer so: the aroma of death and decay keeps drifting into one's nostrils.

As in the temple, so it is in the cathedral—first impressions are misleading. It is not the gigantic, rambling, unplanned, perverse creation that one had assumed. In the repeated intricacies of the tracery, in the crazy geometry of the sculpture, and in the abrupt surges of the central arches into higher space, there is order and pattern. The windows, though bereft of most of their stained glass, still possess a variegated poetry. The gargoyles, which at first unsettle, can also reassure. And the strange three-year old Quasimodo who squats in the topmost part of the bell-tower, may have come to mock God but he has not forgotten how to praise him.

The work of Mann and Grass, then, is not as totally opposed in conception or execution as some have argued. It may be that in Grass—to borrow once more from *Tristram Shandy*—we have an example of the judgement surprised by the imagination, whereas in Mann we see an instance of the imagination, even at its most mettlesome, reined in by the judgement. But beyond this there are similarities worth noting, and they occur especially when we compare Mann's *The Confessions of Felix Krull* (1954) with *The Tin Drum*. In a penetrating essay, Arrigo Subiotto has suggested that the similarities between Felix and Oskar are "so striking as to be suspect" (*German Men of Letters*, vol. 4, 1966, p. 230). Both are self-absorbed heroes who relate their tales with disarming innocence. Oskar, like Felix, is an imprisoned criminal, though he has chosen the asylum instead of the jail. Like Felix again, he is a beautiful boy who is irresistible to both sexes. Each hero has a succession of names and guises, and each claims Mercury as his protector.

These similarities need to be qualified. Both heroes may be totally self-involved as they narrate, and act as protagonists in, their respective stories. But their starting-point is hardly identical. Felix Krull is able to take up his pen "at leisure and in complete retirement" in order to give us the confessions of a confidence trickster, a special insight into the trade secrets of a professional criminal. Oskar, on the other hand, writes out of a compulsion and is grateful to Bruno, his keeper, for making the paper available to "this mind of mine which persists in excreting syllables". Again, Felix does not change as a result of the retelling of his life history, whereas Oskar hints at a very definite change in his life at the end of the novel. In his final chapter, *Thirty*, Oskar tries to pull all his images and memories about him in one frantic movement, like Grandmother gathering in her wide skirts. For the Black Witch is at hand and she provokes the dramatic change which is distilled into the sentence "Words fail me". After the verbal plentitude of the rest of the novel, this announcement brings the reader to a sharp halt. At the end of *Felix Krull*, Mann gives us a moment of ecstatic ascent rather than a sudden and disturbing descent. Seized by "a whirlwind of primordial forces", Felix embraces with Zouzou's mother—"And high and stormy, under my ardent caresses, stormier than at the Iberian game of blood, I saw the surging of that queenly bosom" (*Felix Krull*, Penguin edition, p. 347).

The comparison of Oskar and Felix as beautiful boys must also be modified. Oskar exploits his abnormality in order to pass among his victims: Felix exploits his normality. Oskar chooses his path through life at the age of three, deciding that he has reached the stature which suits him, and resolving to stay at that height by an act of will-power. For anxious parents, he considerately supplies a medical explanation of his condition by pretending to fall down the cellar steps. Felix, however, only gradually becomes aware of his powers, and those powers rely strongly on the classical perfection of his body and the natural dignity of his bearing. Oskar is throughout the complete outsider, and, notwithstanding the detail into which Grass goes about his parentage, it is the freakish aspect of Oskar which is stressed. Grass

54

supports this with his drawing of the drum-beating dwarf on the book-jacket.

Oskar does indeed follow Felix in undergoing a change of names but he has a far greater variety of identities. Also, his adventures take him much further afield than is the case with Mann's hero, whose operations are limited to a few locations. After the failure of the Krull family business—a sparkling wine of inferior quality —Felix moves to Paris and takes a job as a lift boy. Realising his talent for ingratiation, Felix rises from this lowly station, via the willing arms of the cultured wife of a manufacturer of lavatory fittings, past the widening eyes of the impressionable Miss Eleanor Twentyman from Birmingham, to full aristocratic status. Impersonating Louis Marquis de Venosta, he consorts with members of the Portuguese Royal Family and writes home long and graciously obsequious letters to his "parents". In the tradition of confidence tricksters, Felix cannot only establish a relationship immediately, he can pursue it with care and intensity. Oskar, however, has no such facility. He tends to eliminate, rather than develop, serious friendships.

There are many other smiles of recognition between the two novels. One could compare them as wonderfully playful novels, as works which help to destroy the myth that the German genius is too high-minded to produce comic literature of this order. One could compare them as travesties of the *Bildungsroman*, the great novel of development and education. Felix is hardly an example of the "growth to wholeness", and he underlines this when he speaks of education as "the fruit of freedom and apparent idleness; one does not achieve it by exertion, one breathes it in" (*Felix Krull*, p. 65). Oskar, too, resolutely blocks any possibilities of development or growth in himself, and like, Felix, sees "education" as the learning of new ways to exploit his power over others. Another point of comparison between the two novels is the subtle use of homosexuality. It is lightly introduced into *The Tin Drum*, and in *Felix Krull*, the queer peer, Lord Nectan Strathbogie, is used as a means of affirming Felix's fascination for either sex, as well as his adroitness in avoiding the consequences of becoming valet at Aberdeen and Nectan Castle.

Notwithstanding all these affinities, Grass's novel is anything but a slavish copy of Mann's. Confronted with *The Tin Drum*, one can imagine Mann borrowing the words from one of his own characters in *Tristan*: "You write a villainous hand, sir, you would not get a position in my office, let me tell you." The truth is that Thomas Mann and *Felix Krull*, Herman Melville and *Moby Dick*, Alfred Döblin and *Berlin Alexanderplatz*, and Lawrence Sterne and *Tristram Shandy*, are only four of the countless literary partnerships which can be identified in Grass's work. This does not mean that *The Tin Drum* is simply a second-hand bookshop specialising in classic novels. On the contrary, the book has an astonishing freshness, because everything which Grass touches he makes irredeemably his own. His novel transcends its sources and achieves a depth, resonance and originality which is quite remarkable.

There is no surer guide through the undergrowth of Grass's first novel than that which he himself provides in his title. For *The Tin Drum* is primarily about just that. It is not a study of Oskar Matzerath and his problems: it is a novel about the tin drum and its relationship to Oskar. Throughout, the drum stands central. It is the key symbol, the mainspring of the narrative, and the controlling influence on the imagery and style of the work. In designing the book-jacket, Grass emphasised the centrality of the drum by enlarging it out of proportion, and by framing it in Oskar's stippled garb so that it stands out in sharp relief. This drawing is not merely a visual aid for *The Tin Drum*: it is a highly skilful précis of it. In the drawing, as in the book, the drum is at once an organic part of Oskar, and something quite separate which has to be strapped on to him; a gaping red wound, and a proudly-held weapon: a source of vulnerability and a perfect protection. The drumsticks, too, are both organic and separate: monstrous growths or bone-like sticks held by the embryo hands. The duality is even more pronounced in the figure of Oskar. He is at once simple and complex, child and adult. The pointed hat and the apparel suggest a dwarf, but the face is that of a baby. Malevolence competes with innocence, protest with pathos, freakishness with normality. The novel starts here, with this striking demonstration of realism at one with surrealism. Imagine the drawing without the drum, and one realises how much it contributes.

Whether one prefers to see more of the dwarf than the baby,

or vice versa, one factor remains constant. The tin drummer is giving a peformance, and is strongly aware of his audience. This awareness of spectators is stressed in the opening paragraph:

> Granted: I am an inmate of a mental hospital; my keeper is watching me, he never lets me out of his sight; there's a peephole in the door, and the keeper's eye is a shade of brown that can never see through a blue-eyed type like me. (*The Tin Drum*, p. 15).

The casual, conversational tone conceals the amount of information that is packed into this paragraph. Oskar is a patient in an asylum and his condition is serious enough to warrant constant observation by his own keeper—who seems to be a combination of a male nurse, a prison warder and an attendant at a zoo. The scrutiny of Oskar is as total and continuous as it is possible to be. Words like "watching", "sight", "peephole", "eye", "see through", and "blue-eyed" not only reinforce this point, they establish the primacy of the visual element in the novel. Oskar is not alarmed by his incarceration or by the fact that he is under surveillance. What is vital to him is an audience, even if that audience is only represented by the brown eye of his keeper. Oskar can perform. He can do what he has always done: assume an appropriate role and play it to the hilt.

It is essential to grasp this theatrical aspect of Oskar because it dictates so many of his activities throughout the book. When Oskar is born, Alfred Matzerath first speaks as a man of business —"He will take over the store when he grows up. At last we know why we've been working our fingers to the bone" (*The Tin Drum*, p. 47). His next words are more prophetic: "When little Oskar is three, he will have a toy drum" (p. 47), and the moth which is drumming on the two sixty-watt light bulbs helps to fix this promise firmly in Oskar's mind. At the age of three, Oskar sees in a drum what all children do. It is a toy, a brightly-coloured, lacquered instrument, simple to play, and gifted with noise. With noise the child can get attention, and with attention he has the opportunity to indulge in role-playing. Oskar soon comes to understand that when the drum is around his neck, and only then, he is the leading actor in any situation. This is why, later, he has an immediate kinship with Bebra, the musical clown. It is not just lack of height which unites them, but the instinct to exploit that lack of height in front of an audience. As Bebra insists, Oskar's place is on the rostrum; and his pupil soon demonstrates that, even from beneath it, he can command an audience magisterially. At a Nazi Party Meeting, renowned for its order, seriousness, and martial music, Oskar's drum takes control and leads the musicians in The Blue Danube Waltz.

The audience begins to sing and dance and Löbsack, one of the Nazi speakers for the night, "stood there fuming and surprisingly disgruntled by my three-quarter time. He was used to being escorted to the rostrum by rectilinear march music" (*The Tin Drum*, p. 124). Oskar here is both performer and spectator, leading the music with his drum and peering through the knothole to judge the audience reaction just as Bruno later peers through the peephole at him. Oskar is moved by Löbsack's plight, noting with fine irony of the Nazi that "These frivolous sounds shook his faith in the people" (p. 126). Feeling sorry for Löbsack, he switches the music to a Charleston, "Jimmy the Tiger", taking up the rhythm of Bebra the clown who had played in the circus on empty seltzer siphons. Even when Oskar rests his instrument, his influence lasts and the drummer boys continue to play on. Later, having wrecked the meeting completely, he tucks his "very unbiblical drum" under his sweater and makes good his retreat. It should be remembered that once again a visual element, colour, has dominated the scene. The brown of the Nazi uniforms has been defeated by the blue of Strauss's waltz, a colour relationship which recalls the opening paragraph's statement that the brown eye of Bruno can never see through a blue-eyed type like Oskar.

The performance under the rostrum is not solely anticipated by the meeting with Bebra. Even earlier, Oskar is taken to see the play, *Tom Thumb*, and this makes a deep impression on him. What strikes him most is that Tom Thumb, though controlling the action, is not visible on the stage. At the Party Meeting, he, too, is invisible but undeniably central. Tom Thumb enjoys the comforts of a cow's, and then a wolf's, stomach. Oskar is enclosed in the "bowels" of the rostrum. And just as Tom's adventures end with domestic reunion, so does Oskar return from his fantastic feats to the more mundane, but reassuring, world of dinner with the family.

Oskar's theatricality is not only limited to public performance, such as his appearance in Bebra's Theatre at the Front or in the trio at the Onion Cellar. The urge to adopt roles informs his whole psyche. Sometimes it is a defensive action, as in the many instances where he pretends to be an innocent child caught up in a guilty situation, exonerated by his age. On other occasions, he enters into certain roles in order to manipulate or assess relationships with his family or friends. A cemetery in Fortuna North prompts thoughts of the Gravedigger Scene in *Hamlet*, and Oskar, in the true tradition of Sterne, imagines himself to be a Yorick. In this role, he can usurp Hamlet and use his musings about the nature of existence to confront a more practical problem—"To marry or not to marry, that is the question". Maria, no yearning Ophelia, turns him down. An even greater role beckons Oskar when he encounters Sister Dorothea in the darkness of the Ziedler toilet. "Oh heavens, it's the Devil!" whispers Sister Dorothea as she feels the fibre rug in which Oskar has wrapped up his naked body. "Slowly I felt my way into the role, and Satan was my prompter", comments Oskar, delighted that the fibre rug seems to have the same aphrodisiac qualities for Sister Dorothea which the Fizz Powder held for Maria. As the nurse falls forward, Oskar catches her and holds her up long enough to "arrive at a decision in keeping with my Satanic role" (*The Tin Drum*, p. 515). But the moment lacks the celebration it requires. Oskar finds that he is impotent—"I aimed an unloaded pistol at the bull's eye" (p. 516). Sister Dorothea awakens to the realities of the situation and flees.

It is significant that in the roles of Yorick and Satan he is required to play opposite women who exert a tremendous power over him. In both cases—a rejected proposal, impotence—he fails because his drum has not been an essential part of the performance. When the drum, or the glass-shattering voice developed to safeguard the drum, are fundamental to a particular role, it is usually crowned with success. For the tin drum is the symbol of Oskar's potency and, shocked by the thought that the supply of drums might actually cease, he develops a castration complex. He is even able to date it to the 9 November 1938, for "that was the day when I lost Sigismund Markus, who had kept me supplied with drums" (*The Tin Drum*, p. 210). Later, after a spell in hospital, he revisits his nurses and "might well have attempted a conquest in the hospital if I had still had my drum, if I had still been able to count on my reliable drummer's potency of former years" (p. 438). And when he is confined to a mental hospital the power of drum and voice is gone, so that he is "unable to shatter even a toothbrush glass with his singing" (p. 72). Ironically, it is only by using a drum "adroitly and patiently" in the asylum that he can recall the former potency of the instrument, which is rather as if Samson had been made the prison barber at Gaza, forced to discuss his past with his customers.

From an early age Oskar is aware of his utter dependence on the drum. In his first theatrical pose, before the eye of the camera at the age of eight months, he assumes an attitude most natural to him—"My little claws hover in earnest concentration on a level with my head, ready to descend, to strike. To strike what? The drum!" (*The Tin Drum*, p. 59). When he finally acquires his first drum he determines that he will never be separated from it. Only a child can logically wear and play a toy drum, so he decides to remain, physically, a child of three. An open trap door leading to the cellar gives him his opportunity. He places the drum in a safe position at the bottom of the stairs, then rehearses his fall like a born actor, experimenting with the number of steps he will have to mount before he tumbles. Every effect is gauged, even down to noise and smell. When Matzerath and Mama arrive, the tableau which Oskar has arranged speaks with dramatic suddenness. His assumed role—that of a child who has wandered unwittingly into an open trap door—has been played to perfection. The unharmed drum, as important a feature of the tableau as the injured child, can now be Oskar's permanent possession.

But the tin drum is not only a symbol of potency. Like all true symbols, it has no single inner meaning. It lends itself to a large number of interpretations, some complimentary, others contradictory. Many critics have seen the drum as a symbol of artistic creation[4] and, clearly, Oskar is, at one level, an example of that favourite character in German literature: the artist at odds with a philistine society. The medium of his art is the drum, a child's

[4] Idris Parry, *Forum for Modern Language Studies*, No. 2, 1967; John Mander, 'Variations on a Tin Drum', *Encounter*, No. 110, 1962; Alexander Gelley, *Forum for M.L. Studies*, No. 2, 1967; and *TLS*, 5 October 1962, p. 776.

tin drum, lacquered, with red and white flames on the side. Nor is it one particular tin drum which Oskar beats. He does not have the professional musician's reliance on a single, loved instrument. Such is the force and intensity of his drumming that the mortality rate among his drums is high. Indeed this mortality rate can be linked directly to his progress as a musician: "In that period, roughly between the ages of seven and ten, I went through a drum in two weeks flat. From ten to fourteen I demolished an instrument in less than a week. Later, I became more unpredictable in my ways; I could turn a new drum into a scrap in a single day" (*The Tin Drum*, p. 99). It is the tin drum's power of regeneration which holds so much attraction for Oskar and which provides him with a degree of stability—"for it did not die as a mother dies, you could always buy a new one or have it repaired. . . ." (p. 174).

To identify the presence of Oskar the Artist is far easier than to analyse the nature and purpose of his art. The crucial question must always be whether or not his drumming has a moral function. For many critics, it has not; they see the drum as a symbol of amoralism, of irresponsibility, of strongly anti-social attitudes.[5] Others can discern a moral basis and a seriousness in Oskar's art. Marcel Reich-Ranicki comes nearer to the heart of the matter when he separates the novel from the fact of its existence, arguing that while the text itself may evince a "cruel amoralism", there is a fiercely moral impulse behind the author's very decision to come to terms with Germany's Nazi past.[6] In fact, it is not necessary to isolate intention from achievement in this way. For in *The Tin Drum*, Grass has many mansions and can accommodate all critical factions, without any danger of their meeting each other in the corridors. His novel unites two apparent extremes and brings off a bizarre, morganatic marriage between the moral and the amoral.

Grass's tendency to deal with polar opposites which are yet capable of fusion is hardly an innovation in the novel. This tendency has been the dominating intellectual trend in German literature of the past century, and is especially noticeable in the

---

[5] Idris Parry, op. cit.; R. C. Andrews, *Modern Languages*, March, 1964; Theodor Weiser, *Merkur*, 13, 1959; Karl Migner, *Welt und Wort*, vol. 15, 1960.

[6] M. Reich-Ranicki, *Deutsche Literatur in Ost und West*, 1963.

work of Thomas Mann.[7] *The Tin Drum* belongs very much in this dualist tradition and it declares its aim unequivocally in the drawing on the book-jacket: to achieve a synthesis of good and evil *in artistic terms*. The drum is the means to this end. It should be remembered that the drum, too, is imprisoned in the asylum and kept under observation; and that, like Oskar, it is a vastly weakened instrument recalling its own former glories but ever-conscious of the approach of the Black Witch who brings with her the ultimate mark of impotence for drum and drummer alike—silence. No other art-form can compete with the drum at its peak. Even Lankes, the cigarette-smoking master of concrete art, admits this—"Man, Oskar, if only I could paint like you drum" (*The Tin Drum*, p. 542). And Bruno, commissioned by Oskar to render the figures of Goethe and Rasputin into a single knot construction, fails dismally to manage "a valid synthesis of the two extremes" and remains "restless and dissatisfied; for what I knot with my right hand, I undo with my left, what my left hand creates, my right fist shatters" (p. 424). It is no accident that Oskar asks that the figures should "present a striking resemblance to himself" be-cause Grass has merged the qualities of Rasputin and Goethe in Oskar. Or, to be more exact, he has invested the drummer with the qualities of the Russian faith healer and the German poet-prince *as those qualities are perceived by Oskar*. Following the "Well-known inner voice", Oskar chooses Goethe's *Elective Affinities* and *Rasputin and Women* as the two books which are going to form the basis of his education; and it is significant that the latter work is "copiously illustrated". With the aid of the childless Gretchen Scheffler he works his way through the books time and again. Oskar realises that they are of equal importance, as each provides a corrective for the other. "I didn't want to stake everything on Rasputin, for only too soon it became clear to me that in this world of ours every Rasputin has his Goethe, that every Rasputin draws a Goethe or if you prefer every Goethe draws a Rasputin in his wake, or even makes one if need be, in order to be able to condemn him later on" (*The Tin Drum*, p. 93).

When Oskar is about to depart from Paris with Bebra, he is so involved with the question of whether or not he should take

[7] Ronald Gray, *The German Tradition in Literature (1871–1945)*, 1965.

his two favourite authors with him, that he carries on "negotia-tions" with his two gods Dionysus and Apollo. At first the former advises against any reading matter being taken and the latter suggests that the trip itself is a mistake; they then make the obvious choices between the books. Oskar takes both authors—"If Apollo strove for harmony, and Dionysus for drunkenness and chaos, Oskar was a little demi-god whose business it was to harmonise chaos and intoxicate reason. In addition to his mortal-ity, he had one advantage over all the full divinities . . . Oskar could read what he pleased, whereas the gods censored them-selves" (p. 323). This determination of Oskar to unite the forces of good and evil, in a way that makes them mutually-enriching rather than self-defeating, reveals itself even more clearly during his illness after Matzerath's funeral. Matzerath's death as a result of the swallowing of the Nazi Party pin symbolises the demise of the Third Reich itself. In Oskar's life, too, it marks the end of an era. He hurls his drum and drumsticks into the grave and promptly begins to grow. Oskar's growth—his short journey in the direc-tion of normality—brings with it a crisis for his health. Fever grips him and, in one of his most febrile moments, he sees the figures of Rasputin and Goethe moving even closer together. Oskar envisages a merry-go-round, tended by God our Father, who, from an excess of benevolence, gives children more rides than they really want. Oskar notices, on each accelerating circuit, that the merry-go-round owner has a different face each time: "he was Rasputin, laughing and biting the coin for the next ride with his faith-healer's teeth; and then he was Goethe, the poet prince, holding a beautifully-embroidered purse, and the coins he took out were all stamped with his father-in-heaven profile; and then again, Rasputin, tipsy, and again Herr von Goethe, sober. A bit of madness with Rasputin and a bit of rationality with Goethe. The extremists with Rasputin, the forces of order with Goethe" (The Tin Drum, p. 412). What brings Oskar's vision to an abrupt close is the application of Mr. Fanjgold's disinfectant, and Grass signals the sudden change from the surreal to the real, disinfectantly, with the astringent information that Fanjgold once worked in Treblinka Concentration Camp as a disinfector.

The interchangeability of Rasputin and Goethe as the ruling providence in this sequence is an example of that fusion of light and darkness for which Oskar is striving. And the very fact that he places the two authors in such antithesis indicates a moral judgement of some kind on his own behalf. He is by no means as devoid of ethical awareness as some critics have claimed. He is capable of guilt, of self-examination, and of distinguishing between right and wrong. It is usually in the presence of death that these things happen. The death of his mother—the only parent of whose identity he can be absolutely certain—is a great blow to him, not least because she has been responsible for the purchasing of the drums from her admirer, Sigismund Markus. Oskar's grief finds its expression in his drumming, and he stands beside the death-bed and re-creates "the ideal image of her grey-haired beauty on my drum" (p. 162). And the drum itself responds to the tragedy, the red flames on its casing paling a little, and the white lacquer intensifying to a dazzling brightness. Oskar feels genuine guilt at his mother's death but is not above exaggerating that guilt for effect. Again, he has a profound feeling of guilt over the execution of Jan Bronski, his presumptive father—"Even when I feel most sorry for myself, I cannot deny it: It was my drum, no, it was myself Oskar the drummer, who dispatched my poor mama, then Jan Bronski, my uncle and father to their graves" (p. 247).

Oskar is not only referring to his own personal guilt here, but also to the collective guilt of a nation which sent so many of its uncles and fathers and brothers and sons needlessly to their deaths. This interplay of the personal and collective has already been seen in the defence of the Polish Post Office, an event of international significance which is seen by Oskar as a battle for his drum. The only reason that he and Jan are in the Post Office at the time of the Nazi attack is that they have gone there to have the drum repaired: they have chosen old-fashioned Polish skills, as embodied in Kobyella, over modern German technology. Here we have one of many examples of the way in which the drum is used to advance the narrative and to place important historical events in a peculiar perspective. Because of the drum's role in the action, Oskar feels guilty over Jan's execution; but he has learned to cope with his guilt in the same way as so many Germans coped with the exposure of Nazi Atrocities—by denying that they knew what was going on, by taking refuge in ignorance. It was an

"ignorance which came into style in those years and which even today quite a few of our citizens wear like a jaunty and oh, so becoming little hat" (*The Tin Drum*, p. 248). Normally, Oskar would not have learned the details of Jan's execution and burial, for, as he himself observes with mordant irony—"Out of consideration for the men's relatives, who would have been crushed by the expense of caring for so large and flower-consuming a mass-grave, the authorities assumed full responsibility for the maintenance and perhaps even the transplantation" (p. 249). The introduction of the notion of responsibility here gives the sentence a vicious edge, following as it does upon the fashionable German disclaimer: "We didn't know it was happening."

The information which throws all this collective and personal guilt into focus is brought, appropriately, by Leo Schugger, that richly symbolic figure "who like us believed in paradise". Leo, in common with many other characters in the book, is first introduced and explained by way of his occupation. But that occupation—"to turn up at funerals"—immediately sets him apart from the Bakers and the Greengrocers and the Nurses and the Doctors and the Stone-cutters and the Artists. For Leo Schugger belongs with Bruno, Bebra, Raguna, Raskolnikov, and Oskar himself among Grass's collection of grotesques. All the elements of the grotesque are contained in Leo. There is the fundamental disharmony, expressed in his madness ("meschugge", in German, is a slang word for crazy). There is the absurdity of his vision and of his appearance. There is the morbid abnormality of his occupation and the strange, telepathic powers which make that occupation possible. And there is his ability to be at once comic and terrifying, a clown with a suit several times too big, and an ever-extending obituary column in human form. This last aspect of Leo is at its clearest in the chapter, 'He Lies in Saspe'. The man from whom "no burial, however discreet, could be kept secret" (p. 249), guides Oskar to the cemetery where Jan lies, by means of an empty cartridge case. During the macabre journey, Oskar tries to turn back but Leo defeats him with his own weapon of musical allurement, turning the empty cartridge case into a whistle and himself into a Pied Piper. With orchestral support from the sirens and foghorns in the harbour, Leo finds that it is, quite literally, "child's play . . . to draw a frozen Oskar after him" (p. 254).

Leo Schugger is an angel of death, a white-gloved hand welcoming victims to the beauties of the after-life, a carrion crow feeding on the emotions of the mourners and knowing by instinct when and where a burial is taking place. He is also an artist, performing a deliberate and unvarying ritual, "moving with the lightness of a dancer, for grace had touched him" (p. 167), arriving on cue at all times. Again, he symbolises the uncertainties and contradictions of the Church under the Third Reich. Grass is careful to establish that he was a student at a seminary, for whom "the world, the sacraments, the religious, heaven and earth, life and death had been so shaken up in his mind that forever after his vision of the world, though mad, had been radiant and perfect" (p. 167). In short, Leo is an unresolved clash of opposites. His glove may hold genuine compassion but his mouth slavers compulsively. Christian duty is balanced by an enlightened necrophilia. For Leo represents the horrifying ambiguity of the situation which confronted the Church in Hitler's Germany. Deeply opposed to the more pagan manifestations of Fascism, the Church, with a few honourable exceptions, was oddly quiescent under its sway. Many historians have catalogued the paradoxes of organised religion under the Nazis, and the ambivalence, frustration and disillusion which afflicted Catholic and Protestant Churches alike.[8]

As Grass underlines again and again, the staggering truth is that Hitler viewed the Christian Church and its members as highly amenable to his purpose. Catholics were persecuted by Nazism yet found its patriotism and anti-Semitism distinctly attractive; in 1939, the Catholic clergy in Germany were even urging soldiers to fight for the Führer against France, one of the most Catholic countries in the world. Protestants were in a far more susceptible position. Their founder, Martin Luther, had been a rabid anti-Semite and an advocate of obedience to political authority. It was not difficult for the Nazis to concentrate attention upon these two aspects of Lutheranism at the expense of the others. They were helped by the divided nature of German Protestants which was such that no effective or cohesive opposition to Nazism emerged. Like Leo, many Christians must

[8] W. L. Shirer, *The Rise and Fall of the Third Reich*, 1959, pp. 234–40; R. Grunberger, *A Social History of the Third Reich*, 1971, pp. 548–70; Gunter Lewy, *The Catholic Church in Nazi Germany*, New York, 1964.

have felt that all their certainties had been shaken up wildly into a state of permanent confusion. As the power of the State grew, that of the Church declined. With their attenuated functions, the churches could simply look on in despair. In only one area of Christian duty was there a sudden boom: the burial of the dead and the comforting of the mourners. Leo Schugger is a distorted symbol of the Church, bewildered, yet seeming to have a rationale, repeating meaningless rituals, making a living out of the celebration of death.

The association between Leo Schugger and the Christian Church are fully explored in the chapter which ends Part One of the novel, 'Faith, Hope, Love'. This chapter has rightly been identified as the fulcrum of the whole book, and the place where Grass's most serious criticisms of his countrymen are located.[9] Leo Schugger expresses sympathy to all the mourners at the funeral of Herbert Truczinski, until he comes to Meyn the Trumpeter. Fear grips him and he flees across the tombstone. Leo, the harbinger of death, has recognised an even more powerful agent of death in Meyn; Leo, the artist, has acknowledged the superiority of Meyn's trumpet, an instrument which even shines besides Oskar's drum in this context; Leo, the symbol of an apprehensive Church, has bolted before the Storm Trooper. What gives this sequence even more impact is that Meyn is dressed half in civilian clothes and half in SA Uniform, thus emphasising the dichotomy of so many Germans, good citizen, and good Nazi, mourner and destroyer. Meyn has already been responsible for the expulsion of Sigismund Markus from Agnes's funeral.

There is no finer example of Grass's command of language in the novel than that offered in this chapter, nor is there a more memorable instance of his skill in weaving from his ideas a series of vivid, intricate, mobile patterns. The reader's response to the chapter is conditioned in three interacting ways. First, there is the fairy-tale beginning of "There was once . . ." and its constant repetition, postulating a world in which any horror is acceptable and in which evil has a permanent role. Then there is the liturgical quality of the chapter, and its use of Biblical words and phrases, all of which serves to sharpen the satire upon re-

[9] Ann Woods, *A Study of Die Blechtrommel,* M.A. Thesis, Liverpool, 1966.

67

ligious beliefs. Finally, there is the musical element. Oskar's drum is conspicuous by its silence, but Meyn's trumpet is very much in action; and the chapter has the improvised brilliance of jazz music, investigating themes with musical freedom, but always in touch with the melody which is restated stridently on the trumpet.

Behind this complex structure, controlling it and speaking through it, is Oskar. Not Oskar the amoral picaro, but Oskar the engaged and ethically aware individual. For while much of the chapter is delivered in a flat, matter-of-fact, objective voice, there are several moments when Oskar shows regret and compassion. At these moments—the description of Markus's suicide and its implications (pp. 202–3)—Oskar moves from third- into first-person narrative. His concern over Markus is not only concern for the security of his supply of drums. It is sympathy for a human being who has been treated without humanity. He underscores the point by keeping the saga of Meyn and his four cats before us. Meyn can win praise for burning down a synagogue and for taking part in all manner of atrocities against fellow human-beings who are Jews: but when he attempts to kill his cats with a poker, he is reported to the Party and expelled from the SA. A further refinement is included in the fact that the man who informs on Meyn is Laubschad, a Nazi: "he was a kindly man who liked to help all tired humans, sick animals and broken clocks back on their feet" (p. 199). This description is savagely ironic in the context of Crystal Night, in which many tired humans are victimised, called by names of animals, and placed on short rations of that Time, which Laubschad, as a watchmaker, has dedicated his life to measure.

What prompts Oskar to leave the burning synagogue and dash to the toy store is an intuitive recognition of the pact between himself and Markus. Oskar is the protestor against Nazism and Markus is its victim; he is the drummer who is unable to live without his drum, while Markus is "the keeper of the drums". But the SA members have reached the store before him, smashed the window and climbed in among the toys. There the ultimate act of sacrilege is committed—the drums are outraged. "Some had taken down their pants and had deposited brown sausages, in which half-digested peas were still discernible, on sailing vessels, fiddling monkeys, and on my drums" (*The Tin Drum*, p. 202). Oskar is shown that there are strict limits to his protest. "My own drum couldn't stand up to their rage; there was nothing it could do but bow down, and keep quiet" (p. 202). Markus is out of reach of the Nazi rage and his suicide is described with poetic simplicity: "Before him on the desk stood an empty water-glass; the sound of the crashing shop-window had made him thirsty no doubt" (p. 202). The poignance of this is increased when we recall Markus's earlier scene with Agnes, kneeling ridiculously before Oskar's mother and imploring her not to "do it no more with Bronski, seeing he's in the Polish Post Office. He's with the Poles, that's no good. Don't bet on the Poles; if you got to bet on somebody, bet on the Germans, they're coming up, maybe sooner, maybe later" (p. 106). Markus is the prophet of his own destruction.

Oskar leaves the dead supplier of drums and makes his way towards the Stadt-Theater and there sees a banner held up by "pious ladies and strikingly ugly young girls", proclaiming "Faith . . . hope . . . love." He begins to play with these words and to relate them to the realities of the times. The three great absolutes of the Christian religion have been perverted beyond rescue. Faith has become faith in the holy Gasman, Hitler, who has announced that "I am the Saviour of the world, without me you can't cook." Oskar has already united the use of gas for domestic and for extermination purposes at the beginning of the chapter—"And no one who sets his kettle on the bluish flames suspects that disaster is bringing his supper to the boil" (p. 197). In his fantasizing upon the concept of Faith, he supports the Christian allusion with the myth of Santa Claus, the most appeal-ing and paternal of figures in a child's imagination. Santa Claus is but another instrument of death, turning the celebration of Christmas into a complete travesty of itself. Faith in the Third Reich is faith in the powers of darkness, and the argument is hammered home relentlessly.

So corrupt have the Germans become under the Third Reich that they cannot even keep to the progression of Faith, Hope, Love, as set down by Paul the Apostle in the thirteenth chapter of his First Epistle to the Corinthians. Exemplars of order, the Germans yet betray Biblical placing. After Faith, they turn to

Love. It should be remembered that the Greek word αγαπη "Agape", is rendered in the English Authorised Version as "Charity"; in the German Bible, it is translated as "Liebe", Love, a word which has definite sexual, as well as spiritual connotations. Under the Nazi regime, Love degenerates into a self-love which knows no compromise, and which expresses itself nationally in a brutal patriotism. Love of God has become love of the Führer, but this is only an extension of self-love because the Führer is only a projection of the German's love of himself. Carnal appetite dominates the relations between the sexes—"And from sheer love they called each other radishes, they loved radishes, they bit into each other, out of sheer love one radish bit off another's radish. And they told one another stories about wonderful heavenly love, and earthy love, too, between radishes, and just before biting, they whispered to one another, whispered with all the fresh sharpness of hunger: Radish, say, do you love me? I love myself, too" (*The Tin Drum* p. 204). This debasement of Love is the worst disgrace because it is Love which forms the theme of the thirteenth chapter of Paul's Epistle, and which is set firmly above the others in the final verse: "And now abideth faith, hope, charity, these three; but the greatest of these is charity" (*English Authorised Version*).[10]

After exposing the degradation of Faith and Love, Oskar turns to the "Third white elephant of the Epistle to the Corinthians: hope" (p. 204). This, too, has been vitiated. Hope has lost all definition. There is nothing to hope for. Even the Final Solution has failed as a cradle of hope. The people are "hoping after or even during the finale that the end would soon be over. The end of what?" (p. 204). The Final Solution to what? If every end is also a beginning, what does that beginning promise? It is not known nor is it sought. Hope under Nazism is the denial of hope, it is an obsession with ending and destroying rather than beginning and building. "As long as man hopes, he will go on turning out hopeful finales" (p. 204). After one Final Solution there will come another. Hope, in fact, is the philosophy of despair.

Oskar now moves from the objective to the subjective, discarding the detachment of the third-person narrative and becoming

[10] c.f. *The New English Bible*: "In a word, there are three things that last for ever: faith, hope, and love; but the greatest of them all is love."

totally involved in the situation he is describing—"For my part,
I don't know. I don't know, for example, who it is that nowadays
hides under the beards of the Santa Clauses, nor what Santa
Claus hides in his sack; I don't know how gas cocks are throttled
and shut off" (*The Tin Drum*, p. 204). What he does know and
fear is that "Advent, the time of longing for a Redeemer" has not
been banished from the German calendar. Oskar is not certain if
it is flowing again or still flowing, but he is aware of its presence,
of the readiness within the German people to welcome, promote
and obey another political Deliverer. For the Redeemer is essentially a secular figure, and the promises which he brings must be
viewed in secular terms. Oskar stresses this by depriving Paul of
his religious conversion and his apostolic status and by regarding
him as "Saul, and a Saul he was", palming off the ideas of faith,
hope and love on a gullible public. Oskar is not indulging in blasphemy here. At no point in the novel is he more exercised by
moral concern. Men need to believe in something and their belief
is as fundamental to their lives as food, a point Oskar makes by
relating words to sausages. What he has depicted in the chapter
so far is a world in which the notions of faith, hope and love
have been so abused that the very words have lost their meaning.
The political and moral evils of the Third Reich are the result of
this perversion of the Christian absolutes. And yet, paradoxically,
there are those ready to remedy the veils with the same concepts
of faith, hope and love. Oskar is not arguing that these three are,
in the abstract, pernicious. He is insisting that they have been,
and always will be, cruelly misunderstood as guiding precepts;
and when he sees them being offered again by latter-day Sauls, he
shudders at the prostitution of language—"words communicate,
butchers won't tell, I cut off slices, you open books, I read what
tastes good to me, but what tastes good to you?" (p. 205). The
Christian truths embodied in faith, hope and love do not taste
delicious, it is only in their adulterated form that they excite
the palate, and this is why Oskar does not want them on the
menu.

Because Grass, through Oskar, concentrates on faith, hope and
love, it is easy to overlook the fact that this key section of the
novel has other affinities with the thirteenth chapter of Corinthians. The first verse of that chapter runs: "Though I speak with

the tongues of men and of angels, and have not charity, I am become as sounding brass or as tinkling cymbal" (*English Authorised Version*). It is no coincidence that the musician, Meyn, opens the chapter, 'Faith, Hope, Love'. With his trumpet, which he plays "too beautifully for words", Meyn does indeed speak with the tongues of men and of angels. He may need the inspiration of the gin bottle to do this, but he is not without love, keeping and caring for his four cats, one of whom he has even honoured with the name of the great German political hero, Bismarck. It is when Meyn joins the SA that things go wrong. He is sobered by disaster and abandons the gin bottle. Love of his art and of his cats is replaced by a ruthless self-love, and his music suffers: "his playing was no longer too beautiful for words because, when he slipped on those riding breeches with the leather seat, he gave up the gin bottle and from then on his playing was loud and sober, nothing more" (*The Tin Drum*, p. 198). Meyn's art has become as sounding brass, and this symbolises the emasculation of all artistic talent which tried to serve Nazism. That Meyn is representative is made clear when Markus's store is attacked and Oskar notes that "They all looked like Meyn the musician, they wore Meyn's SA uniform, but Meyn was not there, just as those who were there were not somewhere else" (p. 202). Meyn tries to kill his four cats and is fined and expelled from the party. Only then does his musical talent return. Oskar views this fact with alarm because Meyn out of uniform is no longer so easily identifiable as a man with tendencies which made him embrace the Nazi philosophy. At the end of the chapter, Meyn appears once more. "There was once a musician, his name was Meyn, if he isn't dead he is still alive, once again playing the trumpet too beautifully for words" (p. 206). The fairy-tale aspect of the chapter is not resolved in a happy ending. Meyn, the musician, the breeding-ground for Nazism, is still in existence, practising his art with a skill which deflects the listener from the grim truths which lay behind it.

Oskar, then, is capable of more than cynicism. His satire does have a moral basis in this chapter, his protest is one in which compassion and humility can be detected. But he does not preach any alternative faith to the one he denounces. His reply to the horrors of the Third Reich is a critical humanism, a distrustful vigilance. By revealing the inadequacy of conventional morality against the forces of Nazism, he re-defines the area of conflict. It is a willingness to identify and proclaim the enemy that is important: not a reliance on Christian ideals to fight that enemy once he has been allowed to develop his strength.

Oskar's stature as a character is increased appreciably by this chapter. He reveals a moral awareness and a willingness to discuss religious and political values. Paradoxically, the chapter also helps to explain why he has stayed at his infant height. It is better to remain a dwarf than to grow up to be a Nazi and a philistine. It is better to assume the uncomplicated innocence of a child than to become an adult in a world where the consequences of one's beliefs are too horrific to consider. Above all, it is better to be a freak and a complete outsider than lose one's individuality: a deformed three-year-old is in no danger of being acclaimed as the Ayran Dream. Oskar's championing of individuality is not only a response to Nazism. His protest is against uniformity of any kind. Nothing rouses his moral indignation more than the subjugation of the personality in the group. He is at pains to point out that his enemy is "the symmetry of rostrums" and with drum or voice he wrecks meetings of the Reds and Blacks, Boy Scouts and Spinach Shirts, Jehovah's Witnesses, the Kyffhäuser Band, the Vegetarians, and the Young Polish Fresh Air Movement. His rebellion is against the "cut and colour" of uniforms, against any organisation which exacts blind faith in its creed, and which reduces that creed to a series of slogans. Like John Stuart Mill, Oskar believes that "Whatever crushes individuality is despotic, by whatever name it is called" (On Liberty, ch. 3). For in surrendering his individuality, a man relinquishes that most valuable part of his personality: his critical faculty; he gives up what Oskar prizes—his healthy capacity for doubt.

The Tin Drum is, at bottom, a hymn to individuality, and Grass counters the flatness and sameness of Nazi Germany by introducing a host of highly individualised characters. He indicates the enormous loss which takes place in human terms, when any organisation imposes uniformity from above. Even when his characters are most symbolic—Meyn, Leo Schugger, Oskar himself—they remain recognisable human beings, each with his own eccentricities and subtleties. Oskar's own individuality is related

73

directly to the tin drum. To dispose of the drum is a matter of great moral concern to him, therefore, because it will entail a lessening of his individuality. On the other hand, it will be a gesture towards integration into a world which now seems more worthwhile. For Nazism is dead. Matzerath has choked himself in his cellar, just as Hitler has burned himself in his bunker. At Matzerath's funeral Oskar begins to revalue the social and political situation. Poised between two generations—his presumptive father and his presumptive son, Kurt—he examines his future. Should he or shouldn't he cast away the drum, the instrument of protest that was so much needed before?

Oskar decides that he can no longer evade responsibility for the consequences of his actions. He acknowledges that he caused Matzerath's death and concedes that "in all likelihood" it was the German grocer and not the employee of the Polish Post Office who was his real father. This admission dispels one self-deception but leaves another secure. Oskar still persuades himself that Kurt, Matzerath's son, is the fruit of his own supposed union with Maria. It is important that he believes this because it inspires thoughts on the father-son relationship. Oskar can see that he has been a severe disappointment to Mazerath, rejecting all his father's plans for him in the most dramatic way. It was Oskar who soured relations between his father and his mother by pretending to fall down the cellar, an event which "transformed our harmless, good-natured Matzerath into a guilty Matzerath" (*The Tin Drum*, p. 63). Oskar's own experience of "parenthood" has given him a sympathetic insight into his own father's suffering. For Kurt has signally rejected Oskar's ambitions for him, destroying all hope of "dynasty of drummers" by battering the tin drum which he is given at the age of three into scrap metal. Kurt does not want to follow in Oskar's footsteps. During the Russian invasion of Danzig, Kurt again demonstrates his apartness from Oskar and his association with "normal" adults, by putting up his hands when a group of Russian soldiers comes into the cellar. Oskar cannot understand Kurt's action. Why cannot his son stay true to his individuality as Oskar does, or as the ants do, allowing no invader to deflect them from their characteristic mode of self-expression? Oskar is learning to come to terms with Kurt's indifference to him, relating it to his own feelings for Matzerath

—"Perhaps he, too, could express only by homicide the childlike affections that would seem to be desirable between fathers and sons" (p. 404).

Like a weird version of Prospero, Oskar determines that he will abjure his rough magic and bury the source of his art, his drum, in the earth, deeper than sound can plummet. He begins to grow visibly and suffers the violent pains of growth. The physical distance which he puts between his former and new self is matched by the geographical distance which he, Maria and Kurt put between Danzig and their new abode in Düsseldorf. Oskar's critical condition during this period is reinforced by the fact that Bruno takes over the narrative. Oskar picks up the story in May 1946, the date when he was discharged from Düsseldorf City Hospital to embark on "a new and adult life" (p. 422). By the end of Book Two, then, the rebellious dwarf has been replaced by an Oskar with a distinct realisation of his responsibilities, an Oskar with no tin drum.

That Oskar is alive to his duties is shown by the way he attempts to provide for Maria and Kurt, taking on the role of Maria's surrogate husband willingly. How close he approaches the respectabilities of adult life may be judged from the fact that he even entertains the idea of marriage to Maria. This gesture of faith in the state and validity of holy matrimony is quite extraordinary in view of his earlier attitudes towards the Church. Oskar, the self-appointed secular Jesus, is now attracted to the notion of a Christian marriage service. Leading up to his proposal, he assures Maria that he "liked nothing better than to bear a heavy responsibility" (The Tin Drum, p. 460). After weeks of evasion, Maria gently, but firmly, turns him down.

Oskar's renunciation of the drum not only renders him more vulnerable to the setbacks and sufferings of everyday life, but has an adverse effect on the novel itself. The writing in the first few chapters of the Third Book has nothing like the tension and force and ambiguity of the earlier books. Lacking the fulcrum of the tin drum, the inventiveness of the author seems to fall off and many of his effects are unsuccessful. For one of the foremost properties of the drum is its vitality, its affirmation of life. Without it, Oskar drifts towards death, or rather, towards associations with artists who are in some way in the service of death. He works for Korneff, the stone-cutter, whose work adorns graveyards. He makes the acquaintance once more of Leo Schugger, now carrying out his functions in Düsseldorf under the name of Willem Slobber. He models for Raskolnikov, the artist who is haunted by guilt and atonement. He befriends Klepp who is recognisable by his "smell of a corpse smoking a cigarette" (p. 501). Appropriately, it is through the agency of the mad artist, Raskolnikov, that he is re-introduced to his drum. Raskolnikov has an intuitive feeling that Oskar lacks something and tries to fill "the vacuum" with all manner of things for "with his surrealist imagination he was never at a loss for an object" (p. 473). At length, the artist's instinct leads him to the object which has now become a source of fear to Oskar: the drum. He makes a melodramatic protest, but Raskolnikov insists that he holds the symbol of guilt. Oskar is painted as "Jesus the drummer boy, sitting on the nude left thigh of Madonna 49" (p. 473). Possession of a drum has an immediate effect on his relationships. Though continuing to support Maria and Kurt, he moves out of their lodgings, asserting his individuality by taking a room in the Ziedler household.

The drum is not brought back into active service at once. Indeed, Oskar assures his landlord, Ziedler the Hedghog, that "it is very unlikely I shall ever drum again" (*The Tin Drum*, p. 481). For a while, his energies are concentrated on the mysterious Nurse Dorothea, that embodiment of all the nurses who tend, mother and excite him throughout the novel. Then he visits the room of a fellow-lodger, Klepp, who has been lying in bed for five days with Oblomov's Complaint. "This corpulent, indolent, yet not inactive, superstitious, readily perspiring, unwashed but not derelict flutist and clarinettist" (p. 501), has much in common with Oskar. When he announces that he was born by mistake, Oskar feels "a strong sense of kinship" with him. He even forces himself to eat some of his host's foul spaghetti and, astonishingly, finds it so delicious that it becomes his "culinary ideal". Their discussion, and the various objects in the room, conspire to touch off a spark in Oskar. "It was as though all my old, battered, exhausted drums had decided to celebrate a Last Judgement of their own. The thousand drums I had thrown on to the scrap heap and the one drum that lay buried in Saspe Cemetery were resurrected, rose again, sound of limb; their resonance filled my whole being" (p. 506). Oskar undergoes a kind of religious conversion, rushes to fetch his drum, and uses the instrument as a means of confession, drumming up his past history in strict chronological order from his genesis beneath the light bulbs to his exodus from Danzig. It is only the death of Matzerath which he conceals from his listener, returning at the end of his musical account to his main theme—"Kashubian potato fields in the October rain, there sits my grandmother in her four skirts" (p. 506). Transported, Klepp joins in with his flute, and the two play for several hours, rediscovering themselves and the potency of their art. Klepp leaps from his bed, admits fresh air to the room, and washes himself in a manner that amounts to purification. Oskar the Drummer and Klepp have been resurrected. They decide to start a jazz band together.

Once Oskar and the drum are re-united, the old vigour begins to flow in the prose again. The drum is needed as much as ever to combat the complacence of post-War Germany, epitomised in the city of Düsseldorf. Oskar's poem on the Atlantic Wall has been prophetic—the trend is completely "towards the bourgeois-smug". That the drum retains its former powers is shown triumphantly at the Onion Cellar. This episode is thrown into relief by the preceding chapter. 'On the Fibre Rug'. Here we are reminded that a drumless Oskar is an impotent Oskar, even though he is closeted with Nurse Dorothea and a convenient aphrodisiac. From sexual failure he moves to musical acclaim in the Onion Cellar. This is one of Grass's most imaginative conceptions and it allows Oskar to shed his inhibitions again and return once more to a role he has played with such wicked brilliance—that of the satirist. So far in the novel he has satirised the growth of the Third Reich and mocked its victims as well as its creators. He has poured scorn on the Catholic church and exposed what he sees as the total inadequacy of Jesus. He has ridiculed the great mysteries of birth and death and scoffed at the intimacies of the marital bed. He has even derided war itself, presenting it as a tedious interruption: as nations clash in battle, his concern is with the wartime shortage of drums; as the Russians invade Poland, he notes that "sugar that trickled out of the sack had lost none of its sweetness while Marshal Rokossovski was occupying the city of Danzig" (*The Tin Drum*, p. 395). At the Onion Cellar, Oskar finds a new target for his satire—the *Wirtschaftswunder*, the economic miracle of post-war Germany and the affluent quietism which is its concomitant.

The Onion Cellar is a deliberately primitive establishment which caters for "businessmen, doctors, lawyers, journalists, artists, theatre and movie people, well-known figures from the sporting world, officials in provincial and municipal government, in short, a cross section of the world which nowadays calls itself intellectual" (p. 523). With their assorted female or male companions, these people, equipped with shaped wooden boards and paring knives, sit on wooden crates covered with onion sacks and set about peeling onions with the assiduity of true penitents. As the onion juice flows, it provokes the desired response in the German middle class—"It did what the world and the sorrows of the world could not do; it brought forth a round, human tear. It made them cry. At last they were able to cry again. To cry properly, without restraint, to cry like mad" (p. 525). For this privileged way of shedding their guilt, customers are charged twelve marks eighty. Tears are followed by words and the customers exchange frank "self-accusations and confessions" in an ecstasy of purgation. The young as well as the adult patronise the Onion Cellar, and produce the most violent weeping as they consider their relation to the older generation. "Oskar was glad to see that love, and not just sexual frustration, could still wring tears from the young folks" (p. 527).

There are two features of the Onion Cellar which sharpen the cutting edge of its satire. In the first place, it is a night club, a traditional source of entertainment for the middle classes where one might expect rich food, good wine, attentive service, light music, warmth, cleanliness and extravagant comfort. The Onion Cellar rests its popularity on the fact that it is a negation of all these things. It provides only perfunctory service and the music it offers, instead of making its customers relax and enjoy their stay, eases them on their way so that their places can be taken by others. What it is selling, at high prices is the opportunity to indulge in an act of communal relief. In an affluent society governed by the cash nexus, even tears become a marketable commodity.

The second feature of this night club which strengthens its satirical thrust is its setting of a cellar. Notwithstanding alterations, the Onion Cellar is a real cellar, "quite damp and chilly under foot". The wartime associations of cellars as places in which to hide and take shelter have already been summed up by Oskar's "Like everyone else, we began to live in a cellar" (*The Tin Drum*, p. 386). But there are other properties of a cellar which are relevant here. It is a storeroom for items which are too bulky or unsightly to be left about a house. It is the fundamental part of a building and can symbolise a return to basics. It has a dark out-of-the-wayness which makes it sinister: it is the place where Greff, the homosexual greengrocer, goes to hang himself; it is, in folklore, the kingdom of the "little hunchback"; it is an unknown and therefore feared area. In *The Tin Drum* cellars are of especial significance to Oskar. With the aid of cellar steps, he provides an explanation for his physical peculiarities. As leader of the Dusters, he uses a cellar to house the thefts from various churches. And where he does not tell us specifically of cellars, he often isolates the cellar's quality of beneathness. His story begins beneath the four skirts of his grandmother and he frequently returns to them. His grandfather is allegedly drowned "under the raft". His own birth takes place beneath two sixty-watt light bulbs. His sexual education begins beneath a table, as Jan's foot explores his mother's thighs. His main drumming of protests takes place under rostrums. His preoccupation with Nurse Dorothea leads him to squat in her Clothes Cupboard, beneath her clothes. And, as we have seen, his moral sense is awakened at a series of burials, as bodies are placed beneath the earth. When he forsakes his drum, he lets it form its own cellar underground.

It is only appropriate that Oskar's return to effective drumming in public should take place in a cellar, beneath the watering eyes of its habitués. When matters get violently out of control at the Onion Cellar, it is Oskar's drum which saves the day, returning his listeners to the world of their lost childhood and asserting its superiority over the power of the onions. Oskar has to wait until another graveside scene before he is given a chance to display his talents in front of a wider audience. At the funeral of his employer, Schmuh, who has been sparrowed to death in his Mercedes, Oskar is approached by Dr. Dösch of the concert bureau. Dr. Dösch admits that Oskar's drumming took him back to the bliss of childhood at the Onion Cellar, and wants to promote a tour for the hunchback. Not only does Oskar's drumming have a therapeutic effect, it is "a terrific stunt". To think things over, Oskar takes a trip with Lankes the artist and they end up on the Atlantic Wall of Concrete where they first met. The occasion marks another display of moral concern on the part of Oskar. He drums a protest against the Concrete Eternal, the symbol of German war defences and post-war rebuilding alike. And he criticises Lankes strongly when the latter rapes the young nun, "the little girl who was supposed to be the bride of Christ" (*The Tin Drum*, p. 550). Revolted as he is by Lankes's callousness, Oskar learns something from his companion's readiness to turn the possible drowning of the nun into a saleable painting. Lankes's success in creating art out of his relations with nuns convinces Oskar that he, too, must exploit to the full his talents. "The time had come to transmute the pre-war and wartime experiences of Oskar, the three-year-old drummer, into the pure, resounding gold of the postwar period" (p. 551). The choice of a metaphor of material wealth here is highly apposite.

Though Oskar now makes his name and his fortune on tour, he has to do so within the terms of the capitalist system which offends him so much. His protest becomes absorbed and ceases to be a protest at all. Oskar the Drummer is a mere entertainer, unique as his entertainments might be. When he recovers his glass-shattering voice "I made little use of it: I didn't want to ruin my business" (p. 556). Later, he is embarrassed by this period in his life when "Oskar and his drum had become healers of the body and the soul. And what we cured best of all was loss of memory" (p. 556). The commercial world which raises him up brings him down, as he is sued for breach of contract by Dr. Dösch. The death of his mentor, Bebra, and the marriage of Klepp send him into a state of profound depression.

It is at this stage that Oskar finds the ring finger which he claims has belonged to Nurse Dorothea. This finger is the symbol of his lost potency. It is the "eleventh finger" which first declared its independent existence during fizz powder experiments with Maria. It is his third drumstick which has no more strength to drum. He keeps it as a reminder of his past achievements, preserving it in a jar of alcohol, or perhaps just drinking in order to remember. That he is forever cut off from his former glories, as the ring is cut off from its hand, is shown by the fact that he is separated from the finger. The love and marriage which are also symbolised by the finger are now equally beyond him. Oskar feels the decline in his powers and the bed in the mental hospital becomes his goal. Indirectly, the finger points the way, acting as part of the evidence against him in his trial for the murder of Nurse Dorothea. Oskar would rather be an imprisoned criminal than live in a world in which his drum is powerless to protest. Not that the drum has lost all its old skills. In one last desperate performance, it saves the life of Victor Weluhn by drumming up "Poland is not lost", thus routing his enemies. This unselfish act brings the novel full circle. Oskar has rescued Victor Weluhn in the same way that his grandmother rescued Joseph Kiljaiczek. While Oskar's music called up the history of Poland, Anna Bronski's spirts made the fleeing Joseph invisible beneath the four partitions of Poland.

Oskar's story is now over and the drum which has helped him to tell that story is exhausted by the effort. As the drum weakens, the influence of its counterpart, the Black Witch, swells. While the drum was carried before him, Oskar was able to keep the Black Witch behind him. Now she creeps up, kisses his hump and then comes to face him. The end, literally, is within sight. Oskar, for long the consort of those distant relatives of the Black Witch—Rasputin, Meyn, Leo Schugger, Raskolnikov, Bebra, and so on—now achieves a closer relationship with her than they. The apostle of vitality becomes the bridegroom of death: the artist with drum and voice now surrenders all his individuality to the final silence of the grave.

The Tin Drum, then, is far more than an exceptional debut: it is a fully-realised work of art. In the turbulent sea of its language, the themes and purposes of the book are miraculously saved from drowning by Grass. Like a contrary Canute, he can command the waves, can impose his authority on the loftiest surge. Again, he constantly beachcombs along the vast shore of his work, arranging what he finds into intriguing, related patterns. Objects dominate the novel. They control, influence, symbolise or in other ways reflect the behaviour of its characters. The tin drum itself is pivotal and the importance of other objects is affirmed in the table of contents. Very few of the chapter headings contain the

81

names of the figures who people the novel. For the most part, it is a case of wide skirts, light bulbs, photograph albums, windows, schedules, rostrums, card houses, ring fingers, walls, preserving jars, scrap metal, clothes cupboards, tombstones, firestones and fibre rugs. These objects are joined in the story itself by many others of equal significance. They are representational details of that environment which Oskar first assesses, then rebels against, then reconciles himself to, then re-examines critically, then flees from. And in the course of it all, the drum does take him and us towards a measure of light and of truth.

Oskar the satirist, the clown, the picaro, the innocent, the secular Messiah, the practitioner of black arts, the folklore dwarf and the autobiographical figure are all contained in Oskar the historian who has taken on a challenging task: the writing of a report on the character and history of the German people in the twentieth century. It is not an objective report. It is wildly subjective, totally irreverent, and frequently cruel. And yet it has the power to effect moral responses in its author. Oskar may operate largely in a value-free sphere of his own creation, but has several moments when he makes moral judgements either in word or deed. One of the messages of his story is that which Seneca delivered nearly two thousand years earlier: "The knowledge of sin is the beginning of salvation" (*Epistle* 28). The recognition of wrong is the first step towards right. It is with such a recognition of wrong in Germany and the Germans that *The Tin Drum* is actively concerned.

The book has the defects of its virtues. Linguistic brilliance sometimes distracts from a serious point that is being made; the sheer number of characters sometimes diffuses the interest; the surrealistic flights are sometimes counter-productive; and the astonishing range of choice which is offered to the reader in the way of ideas and symbols and insights is occasionally too great to be assimilated. Also, as we have seen, there is a loss of power in the opening chapters of the Third Book so that, structurally, the novel resembles the coffin of Oskar's mother, which was tapered at the foot end. But these are minor reservations and dwindle into impertinence when we consider the strengths of *The Tin Drum* —its intelligence, its assurance, its wit, its vigour, its uninhibitedness, its invention, its tirelessness, its delineation of character, its bravery, its poetry, its profusion, its universality, its narrative magic. There is also the extreme care of its construction and a masterly skill in concealing that construction. *The Tin Drum* is an astounding demonstration of what it is possible to do within the novel form. It is the product of a rich, rococo imagination, a giant Gothic clocktower, extravagantly decorated, enclosing an impossibly complicated but delicate mechanism, and deeply, professionally, in love with time.

Let us end with a passage that is highly characteristic of the book. It shows a love of ambiguity and an urge to synthesize opposites. It presents us with what is, at one level, a rather revolting sight, but what becomes, at another, a beautiful and mysterious experience.

She, Roswitha, lay with me and was frightened. Oskar, on the other hand, was not frightened, and yet he lay with Raguna. Her fear and my courage brought our hands together. I felt her fear and she felt my courage. At length I became rather fearful, and she grew courageous. And after I had banished her fear and given her courage, my manly courage raised its head a second time. While my courage was eighteen glorious years old, she, in I know not what year of her life, recumbent for I know not the howmanieth time, fell a prey once more to the fear that aroused my courage. For like her face, her body, sparingly measured but quite complete, showed no trace of time. Timelessly courageous and timelessly fearful, Roswitha offered herself to me. And never will anyone learn whether that midget, who during a major air raid on the capital lost her fear beneath my courage in the buried Thomaskeller until the air-raid wardens dug us out, was nineteen or ninety years old; what makes it all the easier for Oskar to be discreet is that he himself has no idea whether this first embrace truly suited to his physical dimensions was conferred upon him by a courageous old woman or by a young girl made submissive by fear.

(*The Tin Drum*, p. 328)

This passage offers us an Oskar who is at his most freakish, and yet who makes the reader identify easily with him. It shows Grass displaying his lyrical gift. In a cellar.

3

Cat and Mouse

His Adam's apple like a barrel, with a pair of bronze goitres hanging down from it, fine pieces which matched and were shaped like an hourglass.

Rabelais, *Gargantua and Pantagruel* (1532–4)

Now the birth of Jesus Christ was on this wise: When as his mother Mary was espoused to Joseph, before they came together, she was found with child of the Holy Ghost.

New Testament, *St. Matthew*, ch. I, v. 18

The appearance of *Cat and Mouse* (1961) confounded the many critics who had declared, on the evidence of *The Tin Drum*, that Grass's prose talent suffered from the common German maladies of complexity and prolixity. Beside its predecessor, *Cat and Mouse* looks taut, frugal and disconcertingly lucid. Written during a period of rest from work on *Dog Years*, it hangs like a superb miniature between the vast oil paintings of the two major novels in the trilogy, concentrating and intensifying their experience. It has a precision and severity which is in the best traditions of the German *novelle*, and is executed with a consummate artistry. Though it does not conform to a purist's definition of the *novelle*,[1] it clearly belongs with the finest of the genre in this century. If *The Tin Drum* enabled Oskar Matzerath to hold his own in the company of Hans Casthorp, Joseph Knecht and K., then *Cat and Mouse* admits its hero to the ex-

[1] E. K. Bennett and H. M. Waidson, *A History of the German Novelle* (revised edition, 1961).

clusive society of Gustave von Aschenbach,[2] Tonio Kröger and Gregor Samsa.

Once again the title and the design on the book-jacket are integral parts of the work. The cat who sprawls across both sides of the cover is no fireside decoration. It is an act of criticism upon the book, selecting and displaying all the salient features of the text. The cat looks solid and self-assured, at once a contented, domesticated animal and a creature of fierce independence. It wears its ribbon and medal as if they have been awarded by competition judges, and yet is aware how provocative it is being in mocking Germany's most revered military honour. To the nine lives bestowed upon it by popular superstition, the cat has added the Knight's Cross, a medal usually bought with the deaths of human beings. The iron nestles comfortably against the fur, just as the metallic surface of the writing nestles against the feline grace of the author's invention. The cross itself attests the presence of the religious element, while the phallic tail speaks up for the sexual motifs. The absence of the mouse is emphatic.

It is tempting to see the cat as a symbol of those forces which were crystallised in National Socialism, but there is more to it than that. It is a supernatural being, the familiar of the Black Witch. It stands for those permanent aspects of the human psyche which leads men to single out and persecute the abnormal. It represents a malign fate which marks out its victims and controls their destiny with a sadistic relish. It is the eternal predator, the incarnation of evil. The mouse in the title is Joachim Mahlke and it is typical of Grass's subtle mind that the character who is eventually swallowed by the cat is one who has swallowed a "mouse" himself. In contrast to the black of the cat, the mouse of Mahlke's Adam's apple is painfully white and defenceless. It is what a cat finds irresistible—a moving target.

Thoroughness informs Grass's approach to his symbols. There is a strongly naturalistic quality about the way he permits his cat to behave in the *novelle*. When a cat catches a mouse it takes it to open ground or to some area from which it cannot possibly escape. It then tempts the mouse with promises of release that

[2] In *Death in Venice*, Mann, too, has an eye for physical peculiarities: "a strikingly large and naked looking Adam's apple rose out of the open collar" (Penguin edition, p. 67).

are immediately revoked by its paw. Between successive free pardons, the mouse is weakened and maimed more and more. Even when it is dead, it affords considerable pleasure to the cat who will toss it in the air, use it as a football, or walk away from it in order to turn and pounce yet again. Only when its play value has been exhausted will the mouse be dined upon. Grass makes his cat and mouse follow this established ritual. From the moment that Mahlke's Adam's apple attracts the care-taker's cat, he has been trapped. Though he is shown apparent escape routes—the sea, the minesweeper, the Iron Cross—they lead him back to his death. He is toyed with pitilessly until the only freedom of action he has left is the capacity to commit suicide.

The family likenesses are evident from the start. Like *The Tin Drum*, the *novelle* is set in Danzig, explores the world of ado-lescence, and tells its story retrospectively. It has its Oskar, its Störtebeker, and its Lucy Rennwand, who appears here and in *Dog Years*, as Tulla Pokriefke. Father Wiehnke from the Church of the Sacred Heart also walks across the pages of *Cat and Mouse*, which again includes the catholic religion, the war and National Socialism among its targets for satire. The potentialities of pro-test are not neglected, and the role of the clown is once more filled. The protagonist is acquainted with impotence. These similarities have been trimmed to fit into the smaller scope of the *novelle*. Action is limited to wartime Danzig for the most part, and the work gains from this sharper focus; the weakest parts of *The Tin Drum* are those which are set outside Danzig and after the war. The world of adolescence is the entire world of *Cat and Mouse*, and its population is strictly limited so that its central figure, Joachim Mahlke, can be observed without distraction. A lonely, taciturn character, Mahlke is unsuited to the task of narrat-ing his story as Oskar did. The narration is left to Pilenz, whose motives are not entirely unrelated to those of Oskar Matzerath. The tin drummer is recounting his past as part of his cure in the mental asylum. Pilenz, prompted by Father Alban, is also under-taking an act of confession. Psychoanalysis finds common ground with religious guidance. It is instructive to compare these two approaches with a third—that taken by Siegfried Lenz in his fine novel, *The German Lesson* (1968). Here, too, the past is viewed

86

ironically through adolescent eyes. Siggi Jepson, in a penal institution for juvenile delinquents, is writing his essay on 'The Joys of Duty' as a punishment that is meant to have cleansing effects. His guard, Joswig, is the counterpart of Bruno in *The Tin Drum* and Father Alban in *Cat and Mouse*. All three narrators introduce us to an individual at odds with a totalitarian society. All three unnerve us by describing the social attitudes which were so conducive to the rise of National Socialism.

What isolates the members of this trio from one another is their respective moral stand-points. Oskar is only fitfully in touch with the moral sphere; as a rule, he refrains from any kind of moral judgement, as unworried by the weekly adultery of his mother as he is by the systematic rape of Lina Greff. Pilenz does have moral scruples. Though he is in league with the cat, and is responsible for making Mahlke aware of his pecularity, he is able to respond seriously to moral considerations. For Pilenz is racked with guilt and undertakes his narrative in the first instance as an act of atonement. Custom may have neutralised his reactions to his mother's promiscuity—"One of the heads of the labour police at the railroad car factory was eating with us" (*Cat and Mouse*, p. 189)—but it has not dulled his awareness of his part in Mahlke's history. If Pilenz's tale is told partly by way of extenuation, that of Siggi Jepson is set down wholly by the way of justification. *The German Lesson* examines the various refinements of the concept of duty. Where Pilenz is handicapped by the absence of a father, Siggi is constrained by the presence of his. Jens Jepson, "The northernmost policeman in Germany", has to impose the Nazi ban on the paintings of his lifelong friend and neighbour, Nansen. He obeys Berlin to the letter, insisting that he is only doing his duty. Siggi ignores his duty to his father in favour of a higher duty, to the artist, rescuing and hiding the paintings from the authorities. The war ends, the ban lapses, Nansen is acclaimed internationally. But the Rugbüll policeman still conceives it as his duty to destroy the paintings. Siggi therefore puts his duty to the art itself above everything else, stealing the paintings from their creator in order to protect them from his father. Ironically, it is for this "crime" that he is arrested. With great moral certitude, Siggi recounts what happened, converting an essay which should have taken him a few hours into a major statement which takes him many months. To complete this work, to discharge his duty to himself, he stays in solitary confinement. When he faces the Governor at the end of the novel, he has undoubtedly won a notable moral victory.

Pilenz may not win a moral victory but he puts what he has done into a clear moral perspective. The former altar boy is now parish hall secretary and his reading habits indicate his cast of mind—"I read Bloy,[3] the Gnostics,'[4] Boll,[5] Friedrich Heer,[6] and often with profound emotion the *Confessions* of good old St. Augustine" (p. 110). These authors are a far cry from Oskar's beloved Rasputin and Goethe, and suggest a different set of values altogether. Pilenz's affectionate reliance on St. Augustine is especially interesting. The *Confessions* record the spiritual struggle of a young man in a world full of temptation. With engaging freshness, the book tackles those problems which are eternally relevant, such as the question of good and evil, the difficulty of belief and the nature of God. Pilenz does not pattern his *mea culpa* on St. Augustine's but there are features of his narrative which recall the *Confessions*. In Book One, for instance, St. Augustine talks about the sins of infancy and youth, admitting how he loved games much more than study. He deals with theft and its attractiveness. He speaks of the quality of friendship and love. Like Pilenz, he, too, suffers from toothache. In Book Nine, he explains how God tormented him so much with toothache that he was rendered speechless. He was cured when he urged men to pray to God, an urge which he communicated by writing on a tablet. Pilenz, by contrast, is "cured" by distraction, when he sees the caretaker's cat about to pounce on Mahlke's Adam's apple. In this dental context, one remembers the description of the snowy owl which had "Mahlke's parting in the middle

[3] Leon Bloy (1846–1917): influential French Catholic writer.

[4] Gnostics: widespread pre-Christian spiritual movement, claiming a higher and secret knowledge, revealed by arcane tradition. They attacked, and were attacked by Christianity. For them, salvation of the soul was achieved by means of their special knowledge and not by the death of the Saviour.

[5] Heinrich Böll: famous novelist, Roman Catholic, critic of the last war. Winner of the Nobel Prize for Literature, 1972.

[6] Friedrich Heer: Austrian historian, expert on the history of ideas, leading Catholic writer.

and the same suffering, meekly resolute look, as of a redeemer plagued by inner toothache" (*Cat and Mouse*, p. 28).

But there is another side of St. Augustine's character which links him with Pilenz and this is his love of theatrical performance. "Then, too, I was enraptured by plays represented upon the stage, which were full of images wherein my own miseries were expressed. . . ." (*The Confessions of St. Augustine*, Book Three). St. Augustine cannot understand how men can wish to see "sad and tragical events" which they would not willingly "suffer in their own person". These remarks anticipate a major element in the relationship between Pilenz and Mahlke. Pilenz is the spectator: Mahlke is the performer. Pilenz observes Mahlke's tragic story, sometimes sympathetically, sometimes callously. Mahlke plays his role to its inevitable end. The invisible line between spectator and performer is never crossed. Pilenz may claim that "I alone could be termed his friend, if it was possible to be friends with Mahlke" (p. 110), yet he is ready to join, even lead, his classmates in laughing at Mahlke. And in coining the name 'The Great Mahlke', and repeating some of his feats with awe, Pilenz further isolates Mahlke from any possibility of a normal friendship. As he notes early on—"And as for his soul, it was never introduced to me. I never heard what he thought. In the end, all I really had to go by was his neck and its numerous counterweights" (p. 42).

Like Oskar, Mahlke is an artist who depends entirely on an audience. He is a self-styled clown who approaches his role with a lugubrious dedication. Even when he is engaged in the most private act of all, that of prayer, he is aware of being watched. Throughout he is "always, with or without effort, gathering applause" (*Cat and Mouse*, p. 31), constantly in need of the reassurance of approval. Everything about him compels attention. Dressed in the handed-down clothes of his dead father, he strides towards the Church in "monumental solitude", but the enormous safety pin which holds his scarf in place announces his associations with the finest traditions of clowning (Grock, Chaplin), and draws a crowd: "men, women, soldiers on furlough, children, singly and in groups, grow toward him over the snow. . . . And the eyes of all who approach him are focused, Mahlke is probably thinking, on that comical, very comical, excruciatingly comical safety pin" (p. 57). Not surprisingly, when Mahlke returns to Danzig as a war hero, Pilenz employs a theatrical metaphor for the old school, describing it as "the familiar backdrop". For it is in the Conradinum that many of Mahlke's most telling performances occur, and it is the applause of the school which he covets above almost any other.

Unlike Oskar, Mahlke is unable to make contact with any fellow-artists. He remains steadfastly alone, and the greater the crowd around him, the more this apartness is accentuated. Oskar consciously rejected the society in which he found himself as a "clairaudient infant". He took active steps to become a total outsider. Mahlke is a born outsider who takes active steps to conform to social norms. He is a natural victim whose desperate attempts to be accepted within society become increasingly poignant. While Oskar strove to preserve and display his individuality, Mahlke wants to surrender and submerge his individuality in the mass. The tin drummer opposed and despised the Nazi regime: Mahlke refrains from making any moral judgements upon it. He is perfectly willing to put his abilities as an artist at the disposal of the Third Reich, which is something Oskar would not have done. The dwarf may have worked with Bebra in the propagandist Theatre at the Front, but only in order to satirise it. Oskar's was an "inner emigration" of the type exemplified in real life by the novelist, Ernst Jünger,[7] a decision to remain within the sphere of National Socialism and to attack it from inside. Like Jünger, Oskar does not feel that his artistic responsibilities have been hopelessly compromised. Mahlke, by contrast, is not troubled by any moral obligations to his art. As soon as he steals, and rehearses with, the lieutenant-commander's Iron Cross, his artistic integrity is doomed. "For the first time the Adam's apple which, as I still believe—though he had auxiliary motors—was Mahlke's motor and brake, had found its exact counterweight" (*Cat and Mouse*, p. 112). Since the Cross can only be obtained by embracing the philosophy of the Third Reich, and by killing its enemies, Mahlke has no qualms about doing just this. The medal alone

[7] Ernest Jünger: the most important writer to remain in Germany after 1933. A military hero from World War One, Jünger became a writer who was preoccupied with death, total war, and the depersonalisation of modern man. His *On the Marble Cliffs* (1939) is an exposé of National Socialism.

will cover and compensate for his enlarged Adam's apple but it must be earned in the proper fashion. A stolen Cross will not serve the purpose and this is why he returns it. When he is expelled, his yearning for the Cross takes on a new dimension. It will gain for him once more the respect and approbation of the school. *but ....*

Grass's mockery of the war is largely, and appropriately, confined to the context of the school. It is there that the inculcation of militaristic values takes place. It is there that Party members like the principal, Dr. Klohse, flourish; it is there that unfortunates like Oswald Brunies, the German teacher, are arrested and removed in the interests of the state. A representative of each of the armed forces is introduced—an Air Force lieutenant, a naval lieutenant-commander, and an Army sergeant called Joachim Mahlke. Each has won the "coveted lozenge", and each has a goal beyond military honour. They wish to return to deliver a lecture to their school, to show how far they have come since they left it and at the same time to acknowledge the strength of its influence upon them. They want to impress their former teachers, do a valuable propaganda job for the government, and perform before an audience. It is this aspect of it which appeals to Mahlke—the chance to give a privileged performance. When the Air Force lieutenant speaks to the school, Mahlke is not aware that he is a parody figure, trapped in Air Force slang. What he can see is a performer who has earned the right to appear before this particular and very special audience. He is at once inspired *— it doesn't inspire him* and depressed. The road to the Iron Cross seems to lengthen all the time—"Now they need a bag of forty if they want the medal. In the beginning and after they were through in France and in the North, it only took twenty—if it keeps on like this. . . ." (p. 73). Mahlke has taken the speaker at face value, but Grass makes sure that the reader does not do this. He underlines the close relationship between the world of the school and that of the war by letting the lieutenant compare the shooting of goals in the school football team with the destruction of enemy aircraft: "Maybe Mr. Mallenbrandt remembers: either I didn't shoot a single goal or I'd shoot nine in a row; that's how it was that day: six that morning and three more in the afternoon" (*Cat and Mouse*, p. 70). The war hero still defers to his physical education teacher:

the relationship between military excellence and the school gymnasium is hammered home. Little wonder that Mahlke reserves his "particular zeal" for physical education sessions; or that the lieutenant-commander needs to join in with the boys in the gymnasium and exhibit his skills on the trapeze.

This second speaker at the Conradinum provides Grass with the opportunity for further satire. The lieutenant-commander begins mechanically, with "a very colourless survey such as one might have found in any naval manual", but he soon becomes more colloquial and, in turn, more lyrical—"swaying like a train of priceless, dazzlingly white lace, the foaming wake follows the boat which, swathed like a bride in festive veils of spray, strides onward to the marriage of death" (p. 92). This may amuse the "pigtail contingent" in the audience, but it reveals also the lieutenant's warped attitudes. If his physical feats impress Mallenbrandt, his prostitution of language and use of literary allusions can only sicken Dr. Brunies, his former German teacher. Mahlke leaves before the lecture is concluded. He has not been offended by the absurd attempt to make the horrors of war a subject for eloquence. It is the sight of the Iron Cross which has made him tremble, and reinforced his desire to own one for himself. When he steals the Cross, he is helping to mock the military values it symbolises. The great naval hero, who has fought so hard to win his medal, has allowed it to be lifted from a school changing-room. The gymnasium which dispatched him to his honours has been the setting for his disgrace.

Mahlke is transformed once he has stolen the Cross. He has found a new aim in life. This does not prevent him from clowning with the medal, dangling it over his outsized penis, but failing to entertain Pilenz with his "circus number". When he saw the medal on the lieutenant-commander's neck, Mahlke was unnerved and perspired: when he has it in his possession for the first time, he is "wild with glee", showing a most uncharacteristic lack of inhibitions. It is not only his artistic integrity which has been vitiated by the theft. He now enters a period of progressive moral decline. In *The Tin Drum* Oskar moved slowly and uncertainly towards a consciousness of moral issues, whereas Mahlke moves steadily in the opposite direction. He forfeits all of the moral probity which he shows at the beginning of the story. Compared

92

to Pilenz, Schilling, Kupka, Hotten Sontag, and his other classmates, he is a boy of unusual maturity and fastidiousness. He
does not join in the eating of the seagull droppings which encrust
the barge. He displays magnanimity in disposing of the various
objects which he gathers in the course of his diving, retaining
only a few of them. He removes the condom from the handle
of the classroom door, where it has been placed by way of a
practical joke against the half-blind Dr. Treuge. He risks his life
to save that of a younger boy who is in difficulty in the water.
And he conspicuously avoids the sessions of public masturbation
in which the others indulge. When he does masturbate for them,
it is not a sign of degeneracy. He does it in order not to have
to do it again. He submits to the fascinated gaze of the boys, to
timing, to measurement, and to the tactile assessment of Tulla
Pokriefke, because he knows he will place himself beyond the need
to do so again—"Joachim Mahlke was never obliged to repeat or
better this performance, for none of us ever touched his record,
certainly not when exhausted from swimming and diving; sports-
men in everything we did, we respected the rules" (*Cat and
Mouse*, p. 47). Mahlke, too, has an exaggerated respect for the
"rules" and it is partly this which persuades him to take part in
the masturbation ritual. It is an act of conformity, of oneness
with the others. At the same time, it sets him even more apart
from them. They view masturbation as an end in itself: he sees
it as a means to an end. Though he finds it distasteful, he is prepared to prove his superiority in this field as he has done in that
of swimming and diving; or, later, as he does in the field of
military endeavour. He is performing before an audience yet again
and declares himself a professional among amateurs.

Some critics thought that the scenes involving masturbation
were examples of Grass's fondness for obscenity,[8] and one German state even discussed the possibility of placing *Cat and Mouse*
on the list of those books which were dangerous to youth.[9] To
adopt this attitude is to misunderstand the intention behind these
scenes, and to subscribe to the notion of "Pornograss", an appel-
lation which is as nonsensical as it is unjust. These critics ought
to consider the story which a writer of Grass's abilities could pro-

[8] Alte Kameraden, No. 1, 1962, quoted in *Text und Kritik* I/Ia, p. 94.
[9] State of Hesse, quoted in K. L. Tank's *Günter Grass*, p. 86.

duce if obscenity were his aim. That story would bear no relation whatsoever to *Cat and Mouse*, lacking its subtlety, its perception, its poetic vein and its fundamental morality. The masturbation scenes in the *novelle* are an essential part of the detailed realism of the adolescent world which is being evoked. Pilenz is projecting himself back into the time when study at school seemed far less attractive than swimming, diving, going to the cinema or taking part in sexual experiment. To give an accurate picture of adolescent preoccupations, Grass cannot omit this aspect of the boys' education. Again, the treatment of masturbation is in no way designed to arouse the reader. It takes place when "we decided to give our swimming trunks a rest and sprawled naked on the rusty bridge, with very little idea what to do with ourselves" (*Cat and Mouse*, p. 43). In other words, it is symptomatic of boredom, of that great vacuum in the boys' lives which they have no imagination to fill for themselves and which is later exploited by the Nazi government. In showing us a group of boys masturbating beneath the judging eye of Tulla, Grass is giving us a symbol of something which is one of the main themes of his work—the pitiful wastage and self-abuse of German youth at that point in time.

It is the mouse of Mahlke's Adam's apple which sets in motion the change in his moral values. Shocked into a recognition of his abnormality by the caretaker's cat, he does everything he can to be accepted by the others and to distract attention from the mouse. He learns that he can excel the others in almost everything, and this gradually leads him to adjust his attitudes. While he may distribute much of what he finds beneath the water, he has no intention of sharing with anyone the radio shack which he locates. He disguises the entrance, imports into the shack all of his most precious possessions, and takes an increasingly selfish viewpoint of his submarine retreat. He plays music to the others on his old gramophone, but only to impress them with the privileges which his superior diving skill has brought him. His altruism evanesces into a series of concessions made to the boys.

Mahlke's motivation is fairly consistent. Oskar Matzerath's motives, it will be remembered, were highly ambiguous and subject to change. Siggi Jepson, however, always acted in response to his intuitive feelings about the nature of duty. Mahlke obeys three promptings: "And perhaps, in addition to Virgin and mouse, there was yet a third motive: Our school, that musty edifice that defied ventilation, and particularly the auditorium. . . ." (*Cat and Mouse*, p. 48). These motives lead Mahlke to join with Oskar and Siggi in a conscious act of rebellion. Oskar's rebellion is spectacular and comprehensive. Siggi rebels against his father and the uniformed authority which the Rugbüll policeman represents. Mahlke rebels against the cat. While Oskar and Siggi achieve a considerable measure of success in their rebellion, Mahlke's ends in total failure. He attempts to negotiate with the cat and appoints the Virgin Mary as a kind of mediator, briefed to reconcile cat and mouse. What handicaps Mahlke is his inability to recognise the cat in all its manifestations. The school is one of the most powerful cats in the story, and Klohse, Mallenbrandt and Pilenz are its most effective agents. Mahlke does not discern this, partly because of the religious undertones of the school which help to disguise it. Mallenbrandt, the physical education teacher, also teaches religion. The gymnasium and the chapel are one and the same thing in Mahlke's mind—"Our neo-Gothic gymnasium preserved its air of solemnity just as St. Mary's Chapel in Neuschottland, regardless of all the painted plaster and ecclesiastical trappings Father Gusewski could assemble in the bright gymnastic light of its broad window fronts, never lost the feel of the modern gymnasium it had formerly been" (p. 96). To Mahlke, physical and spiritual devotions coincide. The image which best sums this up is that of Mahlke wearing the silver Virgin round his neck to "succour him amid gymnastic perils" (p. 16). His dedication to the gymnasium is even more ironic when one recalls that Mallenbrandt, its secular priest, has "written a rule book to end all rule books for the game of Schlagball" (p. 16). It was on a Schagball field that Mahlke is first made aware of his mouse.[10] It is a mania for playing to, and winning by, the rules which is Mahlke's downfall.

As in *The Tin Drum*, the religious and political themes overlap. Oskar protested against the Church as strongly as he did against political organisations. He rejected all established dogmas and mocked those who accepted them uncritically. Oskar's atti-

[10] cf. 'A mouse cannot usefully interpret the moral duty of a cat" (*The Demonstration* by David Caute, p. 62).

tude towards the church was characteristically equivocal: "I must admit that the floors of Catholic churches, the smell of a Catholic church, in fact everything about Catholicism still fascinates me in some inexplicable way . . . and that Catholicism never ceases to inspire me with blasphemies which make it perfectly clear that I was irrevocably though to no good purpose baptised a Catholic" (*The Tin Drum*, p. 137). Like Mahlke, Oskar at first comes under the influence of the Virgin Mary. He cannot even "wait for a streetcar without thinking of the Virgin Mary" (p. 138). But it is Jesus Christ who is to hold the greatest fascination for Oskar.[11] When he first visits the Church of the Sacred Heart and sees one of the three coloured sculptures of Christ, he is struck by its "embarrassing resemblance" to his presumptive father, Jan Bronski. Politics and religion coalesce here as the Polish side of his family is linked with the Saviour. This scene is echoed in *Cat and Mouse* by the finding and wearing of the Matka Bosta Czestochowska, a symbol of Polish Catholicism Dr. Klohse forbids Mahlke to wear this "Polish article", banning it on political rather than religious grounds. The Black Madonna eventually joins Mahlke's other treasures in the radio shack, which, of course, is part of a former Polish minesweeper.

Confronted with a statue of the three-year-old Jesus, Oskar is amazed by its resemblance to him: "I take a good look at Jesus and recognise my spit and image. He has my stature and exactly my watering can, in those days employed exclusively as a watering can. He looked out into the world with my cobalt blue Bronski eyes and—this is what I resented most—he had my very own gestures" (p. 141). Oskar puts the statue of Jesus to the test, placing his drum around its neck and folding his hands in prayer. Will this image of a potential protester drum a protest? The miracle does not occur and Oskar considers that he is a "realer Jesus than he is". He takes back his drum and then assaults the glass all around him with his voice. Now, a miracle does take place. The glass is proof against his voice. He weeps bitterly because "Jesus had failed, because Oskar had failed" (p. 145). He acknowledges the existence of God but has lost all faith in Jesus. There are, however, consolations. "I was irritated over that plaster Boy

[11] cf. the constant reference in *The Tin Drum* to the "athlete on the Cross".

Jesus who wouldn't drum; on the other, I was pleased that the drum was now all my own" (p. 146). The experience has served to heighten his feeling of individuality.

If Oskar isolates Jesus Christ in order to condemn him, Mahlke singles out the Virgin Mary so that he can worship and exalt her. All his religious impulses are directed to her service, and as he confides to Pilenz: "Of course I don't believe in God. He's just a swindle to stultify the people. The only thing I believe in is the Virgin Mary. That's why I'm never going to get married" (*Cat and Mouse*, p. 169). As the protagonist in a story with strong visual elements, Mahlke, like the tin drummer, has a fondness for photographs. The room to which he invites Pilenz is "full of the usual juvenile bric-à-brac, from the butterfly collection to the postcard photos of movie stars, lavishly decorated fighter pilots and Panzer generals" (p. 28). Mahlke's pride in Poland is shown by the medal which bears the bronze profile of Pilsudski,[12] and by the presence of the Black Madonna. The snowy owl and the gramophone are also on display but the centre-piece, as far as Mahlke is concerned, is the colour print of the Sistine Madonna. When he discovers the radio shack under water, Mahlke begins to move these various items into his new, secret hideout. The books are the first to go, then candles, a stove and food follow. But it is when Mahlke takes excessive pains to preserve the coloured print of the Sistine Madonna during its submarine journey that Pilenz realises "why he was knocking himself out, for whom he was finishing the former radio shack" (p. 81).

Oskar believed that he had exposed the falsity of Jesus Christ, and sought to replace him as an effective voice of protest. He is called 'Jesus' by the members of the Dusters gang and he organises a systematic series of thefts from the city's churches, gathering all that is stolen into a cellar until he has built a travesty of a chapel. Mahlke does not seek to replace the Virgin Mary, but there is no doubt that she is the main feature of his radio shack. Pilenz does not believe the shack was a chapel to the Virgin because "most of the rubbish that found its way there had nothing to do with her" (p. 93); he thinks that Mahlke has simply moved

---

[12] Pilsudski, a great political leader, was made chief of the state of the New Republic of Poland in 1918; and was given the supreme honour of being appointed first Marshall of Poland.

his room from Osterzeile to a new setting. Mahlke's actions suggest that the Virgin Mary has increased her influence upon him as a result of her shift of location. He dives to reappear with the Black Madonna round his neck. After a second dive, he comes up whistling, and Pilenz alone, as the only other Catholic on the barge, realises that Mahlke is in fact whistling one hymn after another to the Virgin. As always, Mahlke gives a faultless performance and the other boys even ask for an encore of the *Stabat Mater*, though "nothing could have been more remote from their interests than Latin and liturgical texts" (*Cat and Mouse*, p. 93). The form of Catholicism attracts where its content would repel. Mahlke the artist has made sound woo where meaning rebuffs. His performance begins with "aggressive good humour" and then becomes at once an entertainment and a celebration.

In Mahlke's eyes, the Virgin Mary never fails him. Oskar found Jesus totally wanting. Even when the statue does, miraculously, play the drum after the war, Oskar does not concede the powers of the boy Jesus. The drumming is no longer a relevant act of protest: Jesus has made a futile gesture. The Virgin Mary is the one constant in Mahlke's world and yet, in some ways, she is treated as unfairly by him as her son is by Oskar. For in concentrating all his fervour upon the Virgin Mary, Mahlke wrenches her out of the context in which she belongs and projects on to her all his needs and fantasies. She becomes his ideal of a woman in all her phases, and Mahlke sees her by turns as a mother, a wife, a sex-object, a source of comfort, an adviser, a protector, an uplifter of his soul and a blessed peacemaker between the eternal mouse and the eternal cat. She accompanies him through every stage of his moral decline, a process that is signalled by the downward move of the Sistine Madonna from the attic in Osterzeile to the radio shack beneath the water. Mahlke's Virgin Mary is a "realer Virgin" than the one who is part of the larger complex of the Catholic religion. He can control, and be controlled, by her. When he accepts the Nazi creed and fights the enemy, she has no reservations about joining him. His visions in the tank are inspired by the Virgin Mary, and Pilenz is the first to admit that "the Virgin Mary had made you invulnerable" (p. 160). In fact, the reverse has happened. The Virgin Mary, by ceasing to be the figure as understood in the setting of the Catholic church, has made him vulnerable. When he wins the Iron Cross with her help, he has been delivered into the paws of the cat.

As in *The Tin Drum*, war itself is jeered at by being reduced to an offstage interruption. Oskar described the Russian invasion of Danzig by way of the sudden popularity of Lina Greff with the "Ivans". In *The German Lesson*, the actual ending of the war takes place during a biology lesson on the reproductive systems of the fish. In *Cat and Mouse* the war is a distant and not disturbing noise. The boys show the same keen, uncomplicated interest in it that they would show in a major international sporting event; and, as we have seen, the school fosters this idea of the battle-ground as no more than an extension of the gymnasium. They memorise details of Polish shipping and insist on knowing everything possible about losses and victories. When Mahlke returns on leave and autographs the copybooks of some truant schoolboys, they make him write out his rank, the number of tanks he has "knocked out", and the exact location of the victories. They ask for a photograph, and press him for more information. The effects of the war within Danzig are also played down and dealt with in disingenuous asides by Pilenz. When one of his teachers is removed, he observes that "probably for political reasons—Brunies was a Freemason—he was arrested at school" (*Cat and Mouse*, p. 55). And a whole social phenomenon is encapsulated in his casual remark that "It did strike me as silly when early in 1940 he put in a petition to have his name changed—less than a year later he called himself, and had others call him, Father Gusewing. But the fashion for Germanising Polish sounding names ending in *ki* or *ke* or *a*—like Formella—was taken up by lots of people in those days. . . ." (p. 124). A direct political action is treated as a matter of fashion, of no more significance than the pompoms which Mahlke popularises.

The fact that Pilenz is narrating Mahlke's story enables Grass to keep the war at arm's length, so to speak. Mahlke's wartime exploits exist only by report, and his whole army career is conveyed to us by soldiers' gossip rather than by direct experience. This distancing of information allows Mahlke's progress to assume legendary proportions. Viewed from the standpoint of what he has left behind in his training camp—his epic affair with the commander's wife, his *Stabat Mater* carved in the latrines, his awed contemporaries—he really is the Great Mahlke. As a corrective to the reader's being overpowered by the legend of Mahlke, Grass also views the boy through the eyes of his aunt: "And now they've put him in the tanks. He'll be safer than in the infantry and dry when it rains" (p. 142). While the war itself is relegated to a minor role, its consequences for the individual are anything but ignored. The two war heroes who speak at the Conradinum are both examples of the pernicious effects of war on human values, and Mahlke is an even more fulgent example. In *The Tin Drum*, Oskar marked the progress of the war by the successive deaths of his family and friends. In *The German Lesson*, Siegfried Lenz epitomises the consequences of war in the picture of the legless Albrecht Isenbuttel, back from Leningrad, lifted with difficulty by his wife, Hilde, on to a handcart which she drags away; no word is spoken and Nansen gently supplies the caption to the picture—"They can see enough". In *Cat and Mouse*, it is the case of Sergeant Mahlke which provides the sharpest criticism of the war and the attitudes which lay behind it in Germany. Pilenz rushes to meet Mahlke when he learns that the hero has returned to the Conradinum, and is surprised not to find him in the auditorium. When he does catch sight of him, his eye travels immediately to the famous neck but the Great Mahlke is "mouseless—for from his neck hung that very special article, the abracadabra, the magnet, the exact opposite of an onion, the galvanised four-leaf clover, good old Schinkel's brain child, the trinket, the all-day sucker, the thingamajig, the Iwillnotutter it" (*Cat and Mouse*, p. 159). Grass is pouring scorn on the Iron Cross here by deliberately not mentioning it by name, and by treating it not as a supreme military honour but as an effective shield for a young man's Adam's apple. Mahlke is convinced that he will be invited to lecture to the school and has prepared a talk that will be "short but full of action". He is even making suggestions about seating arrangements and feels himself in a strong enough position to announce that he will not ask Dr. Klohse to introduce him but will insist on the proctor's doing so.

Mahlke is on the brink of the achievement which means more to him than anything and is arrogant in his confidence. Within seconds, he changes. He sees the stuffed cat in the case and he is lost. The cat seems to creep towards him for "Stuffed cats are

100

able to creep more convincingly than live ones" (p. 162); and the mouse wakes up in fear. Nothing can save Mahlke now. Pilenz may remind him of his father, the locomotive driver, who won a posthumous medal for bravery and whose example has always inspired his son, but to no avail. The war hero made invulnerable by the Virgin Mary is simply a "schoolboy in uniform on his way to a solemn conference" (p. 163). The mouse goes into Dr. Klohse's study to be interviewed by the cat, and Pilenz enjoys his "moment of superiority". Klohse has purred over him and shown a "pointed interest" in him before he has even turned to Mahlke, the winner of the Iron Cross. Pilenz's "nasty little triumph" is yet another moment of betrayal, and though he may try to intercede on Mahlke's behalf with Dr. Klohse, he cannot atone for his treachery. The army sergeant has found out that a revered national decoration takes second place to the discipline of one small school. The highest military honour cannot erase his one schoolboy peccadillo. Mahlke, who has shown an immense capacity for renouncing things throughout the story, has to stand before his former Principal and be told that he must "learn renunciation". This advice about one religious virtue is especially ironic in view of the fact that it is another religious virtue—confession—which has brought Mahlke's theft of the Iron Cross to light. Dr. Klohse twists the knife in a subtly impersonal letter. He claims that he was not free to act as his heart desired and that "in the interests of the school, he must request manly cooperation in conformity to the old Conradinian spirit; he would gladly attend the lecture which Mahlke, soon, he hoped, and without bitterness, would deliver at the Horst-Wessel School; unless he preferred, like a true hero, to choose the better part of speech and remain silent" (*Cat and Mouse*, pp. 166–7).

What makes this letter so venomous is its constant harping on the interests of the school over the individual, the reminder that Mahlke was expelled, and the ludicrous suggestion that he should exhibit the old Conradinian spirit of an institution which has just humiliated him. Klohse advocates silence now in the same way as he urged his students to observe a "manly silence" on the occasion of Mahlke's expulsion. The cat is playing with the mouse in earnest here. For the first time the mouse retaliates. Ignoring Pilenz's appeals to "reason", Mahlke lies in wait for Klohse on four successive nights and at last finds his former Principal alone. The setting is almost romantic—a quiet lane, nightingales, the night-scented roses; then the realistic element intrudes when we learn that the lane is "conscientiously blacked-out" as a wartime precaution. Mahlke seizes the schoolmaster by the shirt collar and, following the latter's advice, "chose the better part of speech, heroic silence" (p. 168). He slaps the Principal's face making a noise that is "alive and eloquent", delivering in this action a lecture against all the things which have conspired against him and which are symbolised by Klohse. As he does this, he is holding the man in the area of his Adam's apple, and thrusting him against a "forged iron fence" which is the counterpart of the forged Iron Cross. Characteristically, Pilenz tries to apologise for himself as much as for Mahlke. This is yet another instance of what one critic calls the "equivocating Narrator",[13] for and against Mahlke, defending his friend but putting his own skin first.

Mahlke has made a valid act of revolt but he is unable to realise this. They race from the scene of Klohse's disgrace and Mahlke talks incessantly about metaphysical problems. Though the Virgin Mary has led him to his predicament, and though his exacting of revenge is an act of defiance against her, he is very anxious to attend Mass on the following day. Indeed, it is at this moment that he reaffirms his faith in the Virgin Mary and in her alone. He also tells Pilenz that his leave has in fact expired. In order to comfort Klohse in the Baumbachallee he has even broken regulations and is absent without leave. Pilenz urges him to return to his camp with a plausible excuse but Mahlke simply says that "I've just had enough" (p. 174). Two of the arenas in which the legend of the Great Mahlke grew—the school and the army—are now closed to him. A third arena remains and it is Pilenz who suggests it. Refusing to hide Mahlke in his cellar because it "struck me as unhealthy", he searches in his mind for alternative places and remembers the barge. "For a while the word hung in mid-air. 'In this filthy weather?' Mahlke said. But the thing was already decided" (*Cat and Mouse*, p. 175). They row out in the boat, with food which Pilenz has obtained from Mahlke's aunt. "No rain, but forehead trickling. Every muscle

[13] James C. Bruce, 'The Equivocating Narrator in Günter Grass's *Katz und Maus*', *Monatschefte*, vol. LVIII, 1966 (University of Wisconsin).

tense. . . . No cat offshore. But the mouse scurrying" (p. 182). The stomach ache which Mahlke has from eating too many goose-berries is yet another evidence of the insatiable mouse which is always hungry.

That he cannot understand the implications of his act of rebellion is shown in the way that Mahlke rehearses the lecture he would have given to the school. In contrast to the performance which Mahlke would have given—pithy, controlled, dramatic—this lecture consists of "chopped words" coming from "intermittent groans". All the factors in his life are placed side by side in ridiculous juxtaposition. He talks of his father's "courage and self-sacrifice", of the Virgin Mary and her positive assistance during tank battles, and he addresses Dr. Klohse directly in order to clarify a point—"Yes, Dr. Klohse, it's hanging in our hall beside the brushbag. And she didn't hold it over her breast, no, lower down. I had the locomotive in my sights, plain as day. Just had to hold steady between my father and Labuda. . . . Proofs? She held the picture, I tell you. Or in mathematics. Suppose you're teaching maths. . . ." (p. 183). Mahlke's claim for paternal and religious support on the battlefield are made even more absurd by this attempt to find—as the Air Force Lieutenant attempted to find—a parallel in school terms for the barbarities of war.

When he strips off before diving, Mahlke makes a final avowal of his desire to come to terms with the cat. He folds his uniform carefully, keeping to army regulations despite the fact that he is, technically, a deserter. His red gym pants are a last "vestige of our school tradition". He hums part of his favourite litany. The war, the school and the Virgin Mary are thus all deferentially acknowledged before he plunges into the sea. He wears no Iron Cross round his neck and as he disappears, weighed down by two cans of pork, we know that the mouse has gone unprotected to the ultimate confrontation with the cat. Pilenz, who has already deliberately discomforted Mahlke with stories about his mother, adds another betrayal. He keeps his foot over the tin-opener, without which Mahlke's food supply is useless. He repents and leans over the side of the boat yelling "Can o-pen-er!", but Joachim Mahlke is a model of that manly silence so beloved of his former principal. Pilenz may ask for someone to supply him with a "good ending", but this is a selfish demand, designed to relieve him of his guilt. Mahlke's death is the only ending to the story, because he can take his rightful place among the true community of the war—that of the squandered youth.

Certain critics have argued that Mahlke is a character with Messianic qualities, a redeemer who fails in his appointed task.[14] In this context, Pilenz must take on the guise of a Judas, betraying the man he follows, and waiting in vain for a resurrection from the waves. But Mahlke is not a Christ-figure. What links him with Christ is what links Oskar with the three-year-old statue of Jesus—a physical resemblance. Mahlke does not take on any Messianic role because this would emphasise his apartness from the others and his major concern is to conform. He may be united with Christ in the pointlessness of his suffering, but not beyond that. Grass makes it very clear that the exclusiveness of his religious fervour has a warping and completely irreligious effect. In Mahlke we are not given a wartime redeemer with a centre-parting: we are given a figure of tragic dimensions whose story reflects what it meant to be young and German at that point in time. In this sense, bearing in mind the centrality of the school, it might borrow a subtitle from Siegfried Lenz and be called *A German Lesson*.

For all his uniqueness, Mahlke is patently representative of his generation. He may enjoy a mythical status among his schoolfriends, but not elsewhere: "There was nothing unusual about being transferred from the Young Folk to the Hitler Youth, and Member Mahlke remained a colourless unknown quantity in the official youth organisation" (*Cat and Mouse*, p. 34). This is partly a comment on the depersonalisation of these Nazi organisations, but it is also a reminder that Mahlke can pass unremarked as a typical Member. His tragedy is the tragedy of all German youth, urged by statute and the persuasive arguments of Baldur von Shirach to submit to social and political conditioning in the name of the Third Reich. Mahlke stands for all those who dedicated their futures to purposes which were corrupt and therefore corrupting. His moral regression, his confusion, his gullibility, and his

[14] Karl H. Ruhleder: 'A Pattern of Messianic Thought in Günter Grass's *Cat and Mouse*', *German Quarterly*, 39, No. 4 1966; E. Friedrichsmeyer: 'Myth, Paradox and Obscenity in Grass's *Die Blechtrommel* and *Katz und Maus*', *Germanic Review*, 40, No. 3, 1965.

self-deception are emblematic. His death is not an act of re-demption, a deliberate withdrawal from the society which has debased him. It is the logical outcome of the values which have come to dominate him and his contemporaries: it is proof positive of the appalling and unnecessary wastage of promise and talent.

Comparisons form queues. One could compare *Cat and Mouse* endlessly with the other works in the Danzig trilogy. One could relate its observations upon the artist in society to such novels as Hesse's *The Glass Bead Game*, or Musil's *A Man Without Qualities*, or Thomas Mann's *Doktor Faustus*. One could measure its insights into a young man with an embarrassing physical deformity alongside Somerset Maugham's *Of Human Bondage*. Or one could explore further similarities between it and *The German Lesson*, another story which has its complement of gulls, its artist, its cellar, its ships, its schoolboy persecution, its photographs, its deserter, its innocent victims, its circus, its lyricism, its deep intelligence and its demonstration of the power of silence. Because these comparisons suggest themselves so readily, it might perhaps be interesting to look to a less likely source, that of Shakespeare's *Antony and Cleopatra*. Conceived for radically differing purposes and audiences, the play and the *novelle* are conjoined by the theme of betrayal and the relentlessness with which they pursue that theme. The drama of love which has no love scenes, and the story of war which has no war scenes, find common ground in their loyalty to treachery as a major theme.

Antony is seasoned in betrayal before the action of Shakespeare's play begins. He has betrayed his wife, his soldiers, and his friends by his relationship with Cleopatra, and has failed in his duties as a Roman by "going native". He goes on to betray Cleopatra in word and deed, to be party to political betrayals in Rome, to betray his new wife, to betray his country, and to betray himself in the most signal way by attempting suicide. Yet he is only one link in the chain of betrayal. Like him, Cleopatra, Octavius, Lepidus, Enobarbus, and many other characters both betray and are betrayed. In a world of shifting fidelities, betrayal becomes the norm. At another remove, Antony even betrays his audience's expectations: he is no tragic hero who rises to a noble end, but a failed warrior who dwindles into his death.

Cat and Mouse, too, has its chain of betrayal, forged appro-

105

priately out of iron. The story opens with the betrayal of Mahlke by his schoolmates, and he is subsequently betrayed on more than one occasion by Pilenz. He is betrayed by the school itself when he is expelled and when, later, his lecture is not permitted. He is betrayed by his father into dangerous ambitions of winning medals. He is betrayed by his mother and aunt in front of Pilenz, when they pursue the topic of Mrs. Pilenz's promiscuity and Mahlke, a "mild but firm chairman", has to remind his family that such an unseemly discussion is itself a betrayal of the memory of his father. He is betrayed by his Polish ancestry, which is no protection against the dictates of the German government. He is betrayed by the commander's wife in the Reich Labour Service. He is betrayed by war itself which tempts him with promises of honour which turn out to be false. He is betrayed by the society whose values he so readily accepts in order to escape the attention lavished upon the outsider. And he is betrayed by the Virgin Mary who saves him from marriage and death only to guide him into ignominy and shame. Mahlke dives in search of the radio shack which is presided over by the Sistine Madonna. Like Antony, he dies without dignity before the woman who has enslaved him.

Mahlke, too, has his own capacity for betrayal, though it is for the most part unwitting. He betrays his school by stealing the medal. He betrays school, society and the older generation by assaulting his former Principal. He betrays Army regulations by his affair—albeit a reluctant one—with the commander's wife; and by his desertion. He betrays his Catholicism and his priest by his over-concentration on the Virgin Mary, which in turn constitutes a betrayal of the mother of Christ herself. He betrays his schoolmates by denying them any true friendship. He betrays Poland by fighting in the German Army. He betrays his father by re-enacting in his tank battles the exploding of the train which cost him his life. He betrays Tulla—"A hot number, you can take it from me". He betrays his family by bringing some of his own shame upon them, he betrays his artistic potential, and he utterly betrays himself. He even betrays Pilenz, the self-appointed Boswell, by refusing to surface and make possible a happy ending to the story. Antony was a mighty soldier whose devotion to Cleopatra led to his being humbled in battle: Mahlke is a renowned swimmer and diver whose devotion to the Virgin Mary leads him to his death beneath the waves. Both are willing victims of what they seek to love and serve. Both are betrayed by the sea.

To press this analogy much further would be to take it into the huge areas of dissimilarity which exist between the play and the story; but there is one final mark of similarity which we can note. *Cat and Mouse* no less than *Antony and Cleopatra* is a work which is distinguished by the care and subtlety of its structure. Within their respective narrative frameworks, both build up a delicate and beautiful poetic structure out of recurring motifs, repetitions and verbal echoes. In the *novelle*, sexual imagery vies with sacerdotal, and the symbols of militarism, of school life, of the cat and of the mouse roll on throughout the story with, and like, the sea. Pilenz draws attention to this technique: "It is pleasant to pirouette on white paper—but what help are white clouds, soft breezes, speedboats coming in on schedule, and a flock of gulls doing the work of a Greek chorus?" (*Cat and Mouse*, p. 114). Pilenz's story answers its own question. Its narrative tension derives from that most dramatic of situation implicit in its title; its structural tension comes from the interaction of its outer form upon its inner poetic world.

Notwithstanding the narrator's misgivings, the story has a wonderful sense of completeness, of wholeness. It begins with a yell of fear from Mahlke and ends—as the story of Oskar ends—with the protagonist's lapse into silence. It begins with a cat and a mouse, and ends with a cat alone. It begins with an involuntary start of revolt and ends with an unprotesting capitulation. Energy has become impotence; creativity has waned into self-destruction. *Cat and Mouse* is outstanding for many things—the firmness of its control, the deftness of its comic touches, the cunning of its imagination, the clarity of its argument, the relevance and integrity of its themes. It is full of fine moments; but none is more moving or assured than the scene in which Mahlke dives for the last time and becomes one with other Polish casualties beneath the sea. With and without irony, Grass allows his hero the important freedom of sponging his own redeemer's countenance off the blackboard of the story.

4

Dog Years

> There thou mightest behold the great image of authority: a
> dog's obeyed in office.
>
> Shakespeare, *King Lear*, Act IV

> Each man has his Jew; it is the other. And the Jews have their
> Jews. And now, now above all, you must see that you have
> yours—the man whose death leaves you relieved you are not
> him, despite your decency.
>
> Arthur Miller, *Incident at Vichy* (1964)

Afterwards begins beforehand. The content of *Dog Years* (1963)
is prefigured in the title and in the design on the book-jacket.
Once again Grass has provided a front cover which is both
starting point and destination, and invitation to read on and a
warning of what we shall find. *Dog Years* is as much a novel about
the relationship of dog to man as Jack London's *The Call of the
Wild* (1903). In the opening paragraph of the book, the narrators
discuss who should begin and insist that ownership of the dog
is the key factor—"After all it was your dog. But before my dog,
your dog and the dog descended from the dog" (*Dog Years*, p. 3).
From this point on the dog dominates. At the heart of the novel
is the fable of the shepherd dog who was presented to Hitler by
the party leadership of the Danzig District. This animal brings
schoolboy fame to Harry Liebenau and links a humble, working-
class family with great affairs of state—"Prinz, our Prinz, listened
to conversations and worried about his master with canine fidelity. For the Führer feared for his life" (p. 154). When that life
approaches its end, canine fidelity gives way to an instinct for
survival. Prinz, the quintessential German dog, betrays his master
who has commanded the loyalty of the German people. He flees

from Hitler, eludes capture, finds and adopts a new master, and responds readily to the changing of his name to Pluto. Myth and motion pictures are his twin spheres. He is a hound of hell and a Disneyland favourite. This simultaneous existence in the underworld and in the child's imagination is something which Prinz is already used to; he has been present when Hitler has made some of his vilest decisions, and was popular in film newsreels with that same former master, who "Loves dogs and is always kind to dogs".

The dog is a symbol of totalitarianism; it is thus appropriate that Prinz's conception should take place under police supervision. It stands for National Socialism and its gratuitous violence. At the same time it represents a nation's misplaced, dog-like faith in its master. It is an embodiment of evil and its comprehensive blackness sets it alongside Oskar's Black Witch and Mahlke's cat. It is the scourge of culture and will savage the swallow-tails of a concert pianist. It is the animal element in the human, that force within us which is still in touch with the wild and which needs to be constantly watched, schooled and kept on a leash. The dog's origins are firmly noted in the drawing on the book-jacket, where the Alsatian is part-wolf and part domesticated animal. The open mouth suggests aggression and bestiality, while the inflamed tongue is penis, excrement, finger and sausage all at once. The face is made by the shadow of a human hand, and is thus a man-made illusion designed to frighten—like a scarecrow. Yet that hand itself is another illusion, a skeletal hand, a memory of a real hand, the hand of a writer.

This death's head on the front cover is more than a symbol of Germany's past. It anticipates that union of human and dog worlds which occurs most signally in the characters of Tulla Pokriefke and Walter Matern. A whole host of political, economic and parochial details are given as marking the time when Tulla was born, but the most telling detail is reserved till the end—"When Tulla was born, Harras, her uncle's watchdog, was one year and two months old" (*Dog Years*, p. 113). From the beginning Tulla's life is measured in dog years. She has a natural affinity with the dog, who joins her deaf-mute brother, Konrad, to form "her real retinue". The corpulent Amsel may earn himself the title of "Artist and dog-tamer", but the bony Tulla has a deeper and more dangerous control over the animal. She and the dog are inseparable for "she could do what she liked with Harras; and she did with Harras whatever entered her head" (p. 140). If she cannot compete with Jenny Brunies as a girl, she will defeat her at dog level by getting Harras to attack Felsner-Imbs, the piano teacher. When Konrad is drowned, Tulla reacts with a piercing five-hour scream, like a dog howling over a dead puppy. She has already been established as a creature who inhabits a world of smells, and shortly after Konrad's death, she makes the brief journey between the human and animal aspects of her character and moves into the kennel with Harras. Her life is now measured in dog-kennel days.

Walter Matern is an even more dramatic example of a human who behaves like a dog. Our first sight of him is when he is on the Nickelswalde dike, grinding his teeth—"He alone is standing. Except maybe for the dog" (*Dog Years*, p. 6). That dog, outside or inside him, stays with Walter Matern throughout the novel. At school he defends Eddi Amsel against the attacks of the other boys, then willingly takes on the role of a guard-dog when Amsel makes his scarecrows, "ensuring the peace necessary to his friend's bird-repellent labours" (p. 35). Matern may not understand the aesthetic principles of scarecrow-building, nor can he share in Amsel's creative work. But he shows a stern fidelity towards Amsel, allowing the latter to make him so completely a "flunky" that the word becomes a taunt among his schoolmates. If he and his friend run along the dike, Matern always trots, obediently, in the rear. His dog-like servitude, we are reminded, was "an act of love", Harras the dog follows Matern in heeding Amsel's every word, but the bond between dog and boy goes much further than this. Matern is even susceptible to the same sounds and seasons as the animal.

There stood Walter Matern in the background. Disreputably dressed; a costumed proletarian in a problem play, who has learned social indictments by heart, who in the third act will become an agitator and ring-leader, and who nevertheless fell a victim to our buzz saw. Like our Harras, who time and time again, under certain weather conditions, accompanied the song of the buzz saw—never that of the lathe—with a rising and falling howl out of a vertically held head, so the gloomy young man from the Nickelswalde reacted directly to the buzz saw. He did not, to be sure, move his head into a vertical position, he did not stammer anarchist manifestoes, but in his old familiar way underscored the sound of work with a dry grinding of the teeth.

This grinding had its effect on Harras: it drew his lips above his scissors bite.

(*Dog Years*, pp. 162–3)

The certain seasons referred to here are the dog-days, the *dies caniculares*, generally reckoned to run from the beginning of July until the second week in August, and regarded by the ancients as the hottest and unhealthiest part of the year. The dog-days were thought to be the direct cause of madness among dogs, and offered no advantages to the human animal either. Benvolio in *Romeo and Juliet* is alive to the dangers of "these hot days" when "is the mad blood stirring". And few South Europeans have been able to welcome the influence of the dog-star. In *Dog Years*, Grass extends the annual period of dog-days until it spreads over more than two decades. Instead of remaining a seasonal feature, the stirring of the blood becomes a permanent condition: and since a dog year is seven times the length of the human year, time is intensified unbearably during *Dog Years*. In Matern the madness of the day finds expression in the relentless grinding of his teeth and in his fierce but joyless dedication to a succession of causes. He devotes himself grimly to his blood brotherhood with Amsel, to sport, to Communism, to National Socialism, to Catholicism (with a Mahlke-like preference for the Virgin Mary), to acting, to drinking, and to a quasi-religious creed of vengeance. His anti-fascism is displayed most strikingly in his later treatment of Harras. He goes down on his knees in front of Harras and "assumed the attitude of the dog. Human cranium versus dog's skull, with a child's head's worth of hair in between. On one side growling: rising, falling, yet restrained; on the other side a grinding more of sea sand than of gravel and then in rapid fire the word: 'Nazi Nazi Nazi Nazi!' " (*Dog Years*, p. 242). Matern becomes a dog in order to revile the dog. Or, to put it another way, only a victim of Nazism can call it by its true name. Later, on another visit to Langfuhr, Matern adds disillusionment with the Catholic Church to his anti-fascism. He accuses the church not only of helplessness in the face of Nazism but of collabora-

GÜNTER GRASS

tion—"For to our Harras who alone remained available Walter Matern was saying: 'You black Catholic hog!' Hymnally he spewed up his guts: 'You Catholic Nazi hog! I'm going to grind you up into dogballs. Dominican! Christian dog! I'm twenty-two dog years old, and I still haven't done anything to earn immortality . . . just wait!'" (p. 244). If Harras stands for National Socialism and the Catholic Church, Matern's words are an impassioned plea on behalf of all German youth.

It is when the war is over, and Matern is released from a Prisoner of War camp, that his dog-like traits assert themselves most strongly. He is impelled by an icily hysterical anti-fascism and sees himself as an avenging angel—"I come to judge with a black dog and a list of names in my heart spleen and kidneys. THAT DEMAND TO BE CROSSED OFF" (p. 369). There is no mention of Matern's own guilt. It is for the crimes of others that he seeks retribution. He is accompanied by the dog, Pluto, who is at once an embodiment of his own animal self; of Harras, the dog from the older generation whom he poisoned; of evil, and, being Hitler's former dog, of the very things which Matern is committing himself to extirpate. Like and with a dog, he ruthlessly tracks down his prey; then he marks his territory with the scent of his venereal disease. Ironically, it is from Cologne, a city which has given its name to scented toilet water, that Matern goes forth about his priestlike task of pure pollution round Germany's human shores. The men's lavatories in the Catholic Central Station are apt headquarters for Matern. With the smell of urine in his nostrils, Matern can react like a dog; he has learned the lesson which the narrator of Kafka's Investigations of a Dog (1931) sees as the essence of all dog-knowledge—"Water the ground as much as you can". On six feet, Matern and Pluto go back into the past in search of names. Since Matern himself is guilty of many things of which he accuses these people, his travels into the dog years of his past might well take their text from the Old Testament—"As a dog returneth to its vomit, so a fool returneth to his folly" (Proverbs, XXVI, 11).

The Danzig Trilogy conforms to the laws of simple arithmetic. In the first work, The Tin Drum, a single figure of a dwarf dwarfs everyone else. In the second work, Cat and Mouse, it is from the equivocal relationship of narrator and main character that the story gains much of its edge. In the third work, *Dog Years*, it is the number three which is crucial; Grass exploits triangularity. To begin with, there are three narrators who have come together to form an authors' consortium at the suggestion of one of their number, Brauxel. It is Brauxel who begins, dividing his literary work like a model mine-owner, into a series of Morning Shifts. This "sober-minded man at home in a free-market economy" began life as Edouard Amsel, became Eddi Amsel, then Hermann Haseloff, then Goldmouth, then Brauxel. He knows only too well what is extracted, at risk, from mines—"Coal, iron, potash, scarecrows, the past". The second narrator is Harry Liebenau, a failed poet who is now working in radio broadcasting. His story is couched in a long series of Love Letters to that most unlovable creature, his cousin, Tulla Pokriefke. Using the most intimate literary form, Harry retails information about some of the greatest racial and moral outrages of the century; and though he is the only one of the narrators who uses a first-person narration, he emerges least clearly as a rounded and convincing character. Like Pilenz, he is primarily a spectator, who accounts for his stance in terms of a progressive reading-list: von Treitschke, Savonarola, Luther, Martin Heidegger. Grass does not permit us to imagine that this is in any way an ascending progression.

The third narrator is the actor, Walter Matern, a grisly, humourless and remorseless character worthy of Dostoevsky. With typical self-importance, he styles his contribution 'Materniads'; and though he complains to Brauxel about deadlines and work schedules, he sticks to his task with his usual unremitting fanaticism. It is during the Second Materniad that one of the most memorable uses of a triangular relationship occurs. Throughout *Dog Years*, Grass groups characters or motifs or actions or events into threes. Amsel, Matern and Senta form the first trio which we see on the Danzig skyline and thereafter the trinities multiply, like gulls, in flight: man, dog, scarecrow: Tulla, Harry, Harras; Tulla, Harry, Jenny Brunies; Tulla's three spits into the empty baby carriage; Tulla, Harras, Konrad; Tulla and the two possible fathers of her child; the three canine assaults on Felix Felsner-Imbs; Amsel, Hamlet and Dorian Gray "posing jointly"; the order from the SA sturm for the Grinder to take three men

113

for guard duty and give three loud grinds as soon as he leaves the town hall; Jenny, Haseloff and the Mercedes; the ballet in three acts with three main characters; the love letters which Harry sends three times a week; Matern, Pluto, the list of names; the three freshly-ironed shirts with which Matern leaves Aachen; Matern, Karl Moor and Franz Moor; the obscenity in the confessional box between man, woman and dog; Matern Snr., Matern Jnr. and Pluto; the three main speakers in the radio discussion; Matern's "tension-charged triangle—Central Station, cathedral, Radio building"; Matern, Goldmouth, Pluto; the three-legged lady table at which Matern and Goldmouth sit to discuss the past; the three shifts which the men work in the mine; and the Holy Trinity in the name of which, Matern denies believing in God.

There are many other instances but one of the most extraordinary is the scene in which Matern calls on former Sturmführer Jochen Sawatzki and ends in bed with husband and wife together. In its lyrical treatment of a grotesque situation, the following passage recalls the subterranean embraces between Oskar and the Lady Roswitha.

> Matern prefers to lie on the left. As host Sawatzki contents himself with the right. To Inge belongs the middle. Oh, ancient friendship, grown cold after two and thirty beer-house brawls, now rewarmed in lurching marriage fortress. Matern, who came with black dog to judge, explores Ingepussy with affectionate finger; there he meets his friend's goodnatured husband-finger; and both, friendly affectionate goodnatured, as long ago on the Burgerwiese, at the Ohra Riding Academy or the Kleinhammerpark bar, join forces, find a cosy nook, and take turns. She's having a fine time; so much choice and variety; and emulation spurs the friends on. . . .

> (*Dog Years*, pp. 374–5)

In the ensuing sexual free-for-all, it is Inge, wife, woman and common denominator between the men, who improvises upon her name to provoke and christen the perversions they explore together. Understandably and appropriately, she finishes up as "Dogtiredinge". Grass is not indulging in obscenity for its own sake here. Immense concern for detail has gone into the scene, which contains some of the major themes and stylistic devices of the novel. The crisis of identity, which afflicts Oskar in *The Tin*

Drum, Mahlke in *Cat and Mouse* and Starusch in *Local Anaesthetic*, is dwelt upon once more. Who is doing what to whom? Is Matern the man with a dog and a list or a sensualist who simply "wants a chance at the buttered side?" How can one distinguish between the three characters when each "is the other's phenotype", when what they are doing blends them into a bizarre oneness? The search for identity is built into the thematic structure of *Dog Years* and underpins much of the name-changing and travelling and role-adjusting. Allied to confusion of identity, indeed, stemming from it, is the impossibility of weighing and allotting responsibility. Where does the guilt lie for what is happening in the Sawatzki bed? With husband, wife, or guest? With potato schnapps or with the sickly-sweet smell of syrup brewed from sugar beet? Or must it rest with the need to celebrate the occasion? Matern has arrived with a very clear notion of how guilt is apportioned. He may lose sight of his purpose in the heat of the moment and yet, paradoxically, he is fulfilling that purpose by punishing Sawatzki through his wife. In the wider context, this scene demonstrates how Nazism and its impulses can make a mockery of the sacred ties of marriage and friendship, how it can distort the laws of hospitality, and how it can degrade the act of love.

Afterwards begins beforehand. Dark deeds have their consequences, as Grass emphasises in the dictum—"NEVER SLEEP THREE IN A BED—OR YOU WILL WAKE UP THREE IN A BED." Never sleep with Nazism or you will wake up with Nazism. Past actions leave an indelible mark on the soul. Matern may gloss over his own guilt but it informs everything he does and has made him what he is. To a man who has betrayed and beaten up a Jewish friend, the betrayal of another friend and the violation of his wife may seem like a form of recompense. Matern is judging with a corrupted judgement. He, Sawatzki and all the other former Nazis remain culpable, despite his host's disclaimer —"To hell with the final solution and the final victory routine. It's finished and good riddance. Forget it. Forget all that crap. . . ." (*Dog Years*, p. 373). Grass sardonically prefaces this justification of a selective memory with the observation that Sawatzki "doesn't forget to put briquettes on the fire" (p. 372). Domestic comfort is a relevant consideration while the fate of a whole race is not. Sawatzki may believe he can ignore his past but that past will not ignore him. The sexual encounter between man, wife and guest is not a means of forgetting the Nazi past but a way of representing it in microcosm. In the general tangle of arms and legs and identities it is not difficult to imagine the letters which form Sawatzki's name being shaken up also and landing on the pillow to be only a consonant's change away from the word 'Swastika'. It is that same pillow which Inge hugs to her as she sleeps, a symbol of the daughter who is to grow up from such unseemly origins.

Another theme which is investigated in this scene is the debasement of the language and the sickness of knowledge under National Socialism. In the Sawatzki's room with its three club chairs and its oil painting of 'Goats' to act as a visual cipher of the lechery that is to follow, there is a bookcase with an encyclopaedia in thirty-two volumes—one for each of the teeth knocked out of the head of Eddi Amsel. Grass flips through the volumes alphabetically to show the corroding effects of the Third Reich upon the basics of communication. He singles out such words as 'Afterbirth' to describe the death of the hundreds of thousands of young German soldiers; 'Beerhouse Brawl' to remind us that Nazism grew up in beer hall society (in *Cat and Mouse*, Mahlke, striving unwittingly towards the Nazi code, learns to dive with a beer bottle filled with sand); 'Eau de Cologne', a product which Matern markets so assiduously; and 'Laughing gas', a cruel description of the gas chambers. It is interesting to place this alphabet alongside the one which occurs in the 'Eighty-Eighth Sterile Materniad'. Time has now passed, the economic miracle has set in, and everything is seen in commercial terms. At the Sawatzki's "the trend is dull", though as a gesture to bourgeois conformism, Jochen now speaks "correct German". The encyclopaedias yield a new alphabet with words like 'Business', 'Currency', 'Goods', 'Pearls', and 'Textiles' controlling the tone. The Nazi past has been disguised beneath the economic present, and bourgeois values are the order of the day, even down to the obligatory maid. Little wonder that Grass terminates the list with Z for 'Zombie'. That the Sawatzki's life is now dedicated to the New German Affluence is emphasised in the reference to O for 'Oskar', who is still performing at the fashionable Onion Cellar.

The three-sided sexuality at the Sawatzki household is presaged in the first alphabet under S for 'Square'—'Take it from me three is more fun than four' (*Dog Years*, p. 374). It is not out of a sense of fun that Grass presses the number three into service, but for a serious purpose. That purpose is instinct in the narrative approach which is taken. In *The Tin Drum* and in *Cat and Mouse*, respectively, a single, omniscient or near-omniscient narrator told his story chronologically from a declared point of view. Oskar let Bruno and Vittlar relieve him of his duties for short periods, and Pilenz presented us with information through the mouths of others if he himself was not a first-hand witness; but, by and large, the tin drummer and the parish hall secretary were firmly in control and offered us coherent and unified pictures of reality as they saw it. *Dog Years* has no such coherence or unity. By giving us three different perspectives, Grass ensures that the reality which we are invited to examine is fractured and contradictory. This in itself is a direct result of the nature of the material under review. Such is its force and horror and complexity that no one mind can assimilate and describe it. While a solo narrator could not be relied upon, two narrators might produce diametrically opposed views which balanced each other, in the way that Rasputin balanced Goethe, or the Iron Cross balanced the Adam's Apple. An odd number, three, is essential because it guarantees imbalance and inequality. It carries the promise of that fragmented and uncertain and inconsistent "reality" which Grass sets out to discuss. Truth is a shared commodity. A wealthy Jewish mine-owner must compete with an indecisive, failed poet and a fanatical radio actor. It is left to the reader to shade in those areas of the narrative triangle where the pure reality seems to lie.

Variety of narration allows Grass to administer correctives or add codicils. In the passage from the Second Materniad which involves three in a bed, he juxtaposes two narrators subtly and effectively. The orgy ends, the men sleep, all three have "won". Grass engineers a shift to Amsel's perspective with ease and smoothness. The tree-sawing noise which the men make as they snore becomes the felling of the whole Jäschkental Forest, where the Gutenberg Monument stands. As the trees fall, Steffensweg becomes more and more visible. In one of its villas lives Eddi

Amsel, who is passing an artists's judgement on the Sawatzki bed by building three life-size scarecrows—"one represents a sleeping SA man; the second represents a sleeping SA Sturm-führer; the third signifies a girl splattered from top to toe with sugarbeet syrup which attracts ants" (*Dog Years*, p. 375). Amsel's aesthetic viewpoint counterpoints the teeth-grinding directness of Matern's account. Grass effects a transition back to the situation in the bedroom with speed and naturalness. He has Amsel building a fourth life-size scarecrow—"a black mobile twelve-legged dog. To enable the dog to bark, Eddi Amsel builds in a barking mechanism. And then he barks and wakes up the snorer, the grinder, the ant-maddened syrupfigure. It's Pluto in the kitchen. He demands to be heard. The three of them roll out of bed without saying good morning" (*Dog Years*, p. 376). They are awakened to an awareness of being three-in-a-bed. The twelve legs of the scarecrow dog correspond to the twelve headless knights and twelve headless nuns about whom Amsel loved to hear from Grandmother Matern; and the colour and ubiquitous-ness of the dog is also caught in the artist's representation. Grass achieves yet another ironic comment on what has taken place by moving from the interior to the exterior of the Sawatzki house-hold and framing it like a Christmas card—"Snow is falling for reasons of de-Nazification: everybody is putting objects and facts out into the severe wintry countryside to be snowed under" (p. 376). Seasonal whiteness cannot hide the blackness of Nazism. When the work of de-Nazification is in the hands of ex-Nazis like Matern then the results are revolting.

The three narrators who reconstruct *Dog Years* for us are paralleled in the 'Second Materniad'. When Jochen, Inge and Matern give their different versions of what happened in the bed, whose do we believe? Is the child Matern's or Jochen's? All three were totally involved in the bedroom yet none gives a wholly reasonable or accurate account. Like Amsel, Liebenau and Matern, they quibble, differentiate, modify. Inge appears by turns as a woman betrayed by her husband, her friend and herself; as German womanhood outraged by Nazism; and as Germany itself, torn between the man to the West of her and the man to the East, siding with one of them and then defecting to the other and his companion-dog. The issues which are enlarged upon elsewhere in the novel—freedom, guilt, human susceptibility, betrayal—are all encapsulated in the Ingestory. So, too, is Grass's most characteristic stylistic feature which Klaus Wagenbach has rightly called the "artistic stuttering rhythm". Only the Vistula, the river of time which is evoked at the start of the novel, flows evenly and inexorably. The prose itself is deliberately chopped, checked and interrupted in a way that makes it quite unlike some of the mellifluous flights in *The Tin Drum* or some of the poetic felicities in *Cat and Mouse*. Sentences are short, barked, repetitious and entirely in keeping with the subject-matter.

This use of the language further sectionalises the view of the past which we are being given, and reminds us that none of our three historians can adequately recapture that past—in Ranke's phrase—as it actually happened. Since the language denies itself freedom to flow and surge, the reader is forced to slow down and halt and ponder. Simple and laconic as the sentences are in themselves, when they are placed next to each other in such profusion and at so many varying angles, the final effect is of a vast, intricate carpet, triangular in shape. Viewed in its totality, the prose seems rich and matted, while the most vivid patterning on the carpet is provided by the imagery. The purpose of *Dog Years* is clearer and bolder than that of *The Tin Drum*, and it is assisted in the pursuit of that purpose by its more precise imagery. The central image, as we have seen, is the dog and it finds its dialectical opposite in the scarecrow. The strife between dog and scarecrow, like that between cat and mouse in the *novelle*, propels much of the work. To see this contest solely in terms of National Socialism against Art is to miss many of the subtleties which Grass introduces, for his imagery is never static and one-dimensional; it is dynamic and many-sided, able to influence plot and character and yet capable of adapting itself in response to those same things. Like the dog, the scarecrow has several values; and just as the dog has its genealogy so does the scarecrow have its history neatly split up into stages.

If Matern's life can be measured in dog years, that of Eddi Amsel must be gauged in scarecrow years. "From the very start it was his vocation to invent scarecrows" (*Dog Years*, p. 24), and such is the quality of his art that his birth is invested with supernatural significance. Birds sense that an enemy is being marked by name in the church below and five hundred of them, not counting the sparrows, flee in terror—"anguish darkened numerous bird hearts of varying sizes" (p. 27). To begin with, then, Amsel's art is intuitive. It is only later that ideas are "grafted" on to Amsel from such sources as Otto Weininger's book on *Sex and Character*. It is from Weininger that Amsel first gleans the notion that "The scarecrow is created in man's image". But whereas a scarecrow is a functional object for most people, designed to frighten away birds, it is purely a means of expression for Amsel, who insists on many occasions that he has nothing against birds. Indeed, he bears a bird's name—in German, Amsel means 'blackbird'.

Amsel's gifts duplicate those of Grass. The scarecrows echo *Dog Years* itself in being extraordinary in their reflection of authorial powers of observation—"Though all these transitory edifices revealed industry and imagination on the part of the architect, it was Eduard Amsel's keen sense of reality in all its innumerable forms, the curious eye surmounting his plump cheek, which provided his products with closely observed detail. . . ." (*Dog Years*, p. 31). These early scarecrows are experimental and built without design. They have "no enemy in view", but art and reality joined with such effect creates its own opposition. Panic spreads among birds. As the scarecrows themselves become human and live, the birds reply with a formal human protest, using a metaphor drawn from calligraphy—"They write their terror in a birdscript that grows steadily steeper, narrower and more jumbled" (p. 35). Aroused to the commercial potentialities of his work, Amsel starts to build in earnest. He takes a more systematic approach and records his findings in a diary. Here he writes down his basic precept—"Models should be taken primarily from nature"; or, in its later, amplified form—"Everything that can be stuffed should be classified as nature: dolls, for instance" (p. 41). In the first phase of his scarecrow-building, Amsel takes his models from people and from nature, reproducing in artistic terms what he sees around him. The honesty and clarity of his vision prove to be fatal handicaps. When he unites the human world and the natural world in a synthesis of Grandmother Matern and willow tree, the result is so frightening to birds, animals and people that Amsel has to destroy it. From the reactions to the three-headed willow tree, he learns a vital lesson —"Thus it was brought home to the artist for the first time that, when his works embodied a close enough study of nature, they had power not only over birds of heaven, but over horses and cows as well and were capable of disorganising the tranquil rural gait of Lorchen a human being" (p. 48). What Amsel does instinctively with his "half willow half grandmother", Brauxel does knowingly in his later manufacture of magic spectacles. Scarecrow and glasses are a means of ruthless self-appraisal. They present people and reality in a cold, uncomfortable and true light.

The second phase of Amsel's art is altogether more self-conscious. After reading Weininger's book, he makes a concerted effort to "surmount the Jewishness within him". His devotion to Weininger's ideas is parallel by Matern's later enslavement to Heidegger. To prove his Germanness, Amsel becomes obsessed with Prussian militarism and explores mythology with an almost Wagnerian thoroughness. Like Mahlke, he is an outsider who is desperately trying to align himself with the rules. If Weininger states that Jews cannot sing and have no aptitude for sport, then Amsel must join the choir and make himself into a fine faustball player. Yet like Mahlke again, the more he tries to lose himself in the mass, the more he stands out. On the same schlagball field where Mahlke's terror was awakened, Amsel is marked out as a victim. Schlagball is the German school sport *par excellence*, and for Mallenbrandt, who makes a brief appearance in *Dog Years*, it was also "a way of life, a philosophy" (p. 95). While Matern can shine as he plays schlagball within the strict rules of the game, Amsel can only waddle about the field "as though waddling through purgatory. . . . He was the team's weak spot. He was tracked down and hunted. . . ." (*Dog Years*, pp. 95–6). As on the schlagball field, so in society at large.

For a while the second phase of Amsel's art meets with success. Grass includes a newspaper article which is both a parody of its own mock-lyricism and an indication of the way in which Amsel's art is interpreted for the purposes of the state—"For we have the impression that in the very midst of a civilisation that is levelling everything in its path, the Nordic heritage is here flowering afresh and anew! the spirit of the Vikings and Christian simplicity in an East-German symbiosis. Especially a group of three figures. . . ." (p. 58). The critic is ecstatic in his praise of what suggests to him the Crucifixion group on the mount of Calvary. Grass deflates the whole over-blown passage in the following paragraph—"let no-one suppose that Amsel fashioned this group with its childlike piety—only one thief was sketched in the diary—with a view to divine reward: according to the diary, it brought in two gulden twenty" (p. 58). It is business acumen which separates Amsel from Mahlke. He may be forced into a particular course of action, but he will always seek the means to exploit that situation commercially. It is this aspect of his character —his readiness to haggle—which helps to alienate Matern. The scarecrows which honour and celebrate the old Prussian gods are more than symbols of art and sources of income. As the uniforms in which they are dressed become more and more recent in time, they come to represent the ideals and aspirations of National Socialism. They are at once a pictorialisation of the current ideology and an attack upon it.

Amsel has developed his own dialectical mode, restating an ideology in order to discredit it. Like Oskar, his protest is not limited to National Socialism: he despises all ideologies which demand unquestioning allegiance and which subdue individual and artistic liberty. Like Oskar, too, his art takes the form of an 'inner emigration', thriving under the very conditions designed to eliminate it. Mahlke's compromise with National Socialism was disastrous: Amsel's is not. It ensures his survival and maintains much of his integrity as an artist. But he does not elude censorship indefinitely. In a shop window on Milchkannengasse he sees some zoological items which inspire him to undertake his most ambitious project so far. This return solely to nature for his models is prompted by the sight of an eagle above a lamb, of Prussian militarism poised to strike the defenceless and the innocent. Amsel determines to create "something paradoxical . . . a scarecrow in the form of a giant bird. It is Amsel's last for many years" (*Dog Years*, p. 81). The Great Cuckoo Bird is a tribute to the dialectical nature of his art: it is an exaggerated version of the very thing it is built to drive away. It is set up "tarred, feathered and superman-high", the ridicule of tarring and feathering being meted out to a figure of dimensions admired by the master race. The Great Cuckoo Bird spreads terror and superstition, and produces the final omen which sees Grandmother Matern into her Catholic grave. At length this scarecrow and all the others are destroyed by fire.

The burning of the scarecrows corresponds to the Nazi book-burning which took place at the same time. Again, it anticipates the scarecrow hell with which the novel ends. Amsel's artistic impulse is not put out by this destruction of his work, but re-kindled. Watching the blaze, he resolves "in his heart and diary that later, one day when he is big, he will revive the idea of the Great Cuckoo Bird: he will build a giant bird which will burn, spark, and blaze everlastingly, yet never be consumed, but continue in all eternity, forever and ever, by its very nature, apo-calypse and ornament in one, to burn, spark, and blaze" (p. 85). Amsel's aim is to raise his craft to a level where it makes political restriction as impotent as it is irrelevant. Persecution is also inspiration. In destroying his art, National Socialism is creating it anew.

In 'Morning Shifts', Amsel traces the movement of his scare-crows from the realm of art to the realm of ideology. In 'Love Letters', Harry Liebenau assesses this development from another point of the triangle, clarifying it with detail. He describes another element of Amsel's art—his ability to transform his own person into a whole series of shapes and characters. With the aid of the dogbitten swallowtails of Felsner-Imbs, Amsel puts himself in the company of Oskar and Mahlke as natural entertainer:

Amsel looked terrifying; Amsel aroused pity; Amsel the hobbler; Amsel the dodderer; Amsel in wind and rain, on sheet ice; the merchant on the flying carpet; roc, the fabled bird; the caliph turned stork, the crow, the owl, the woodpecker; the sparrow at its morn-ing bath, behind the horse, with the dog; many sparrows meet, scold each other, take counsel, entertain and thank the audience for applauding. Then comes Amsel's swallowtail divertimenti: the un-leashed grandmother; the ferryman has a toothache; the parson fights the wind; Leo Schugger at the cemetery gate; teachers in play-grounds. . . .

(*Dog Years*, pp. 180–1)

The order in which the lightning performances is given is signi-ficant. Amsel begins as himself, arousing sympathy for his physical defects or for his struggle against an adverse environment. His commercial leanings take him into the area of folk-tale where he is the merchant on the flying carpet and where he can consort with fabled birds. Having made an association with birds, he gives a whole range of gentle portraits. He concludes with images of death: Grandmother Matern released from the impotence of paralysis, brandishing her spoon; Charon with toothache; the church assailed by nature; Leo Schugger in his customary habitat; and, finally, teachers in playgrounds, the rehearsal rooms for the battlefields which are so important a feature of *Cat and Mouse*.

After his performance in the Imbs music room, a suitable artistic ambience, Amsel becomes more political in his approach. He has no intention of scaring crows, but is drawn nevertheless to to the building of life-size scarecrows. Fellow-feeling for the bird world cannot prevent him from becoming its enemy. Being a victim of National Socialism cannot deter him from frightening the other victims. For he will not accept the Nazi doctrine of a race and a people. To him a crowd is always a collection of individuals; in the Third Reich "they were all individualists who had camouflaged themselves as a mass society" (p. 182). Playing on Amsel's name, Grass notes that "And to his eyes blackbirds were never, not even in snow-covered gardens, identically black and yellow-billed" (p. 182). As a result of these opinions, Amsel's art becomes more consciously political. Harry Liebenau signals this in his statement that "Eddi Amsel built no scarecrows to ward off the sparrows and magpies with which he was familiar; he built with no adversary in mind, on formal grounds. At the most he wished to convince a dangerously productive environment of his own productivity" (*Dog Years*, p. 182). His art will attest its presence in a totalitarian regime and commit itself to subverting that regime. The politicisation of his work does not bring satisfying results at first. He undergoes a period of stasis—"His art remained stagnant. Weininger's text remained paper. Perfection proved tedious. Sparrows were unmoved. Crows yawned. . . ." (p. 187). Nature once more provides him with his model. Walter Matern has a fist fight in his garden with a platoon leader of the Hitler Cubs. The ensuing brawl, which is a miniature version of Nazi violence, gives Amsel's art a focus—"Amsel had found his way back to reality; from that day on he stopped wasting his talent on fashion plates, hothouse plants, studio art; avid

with curiosity, he went out into the street" (p. 188). His mania
for uniforms now becomes the dominant feature of his art. He
builds nine scarecrow SA men, and models them on mythical
heroes to show how Nazism patents and distorts the figures from
the past. The scarecrows are given a mechanism which enables
them to salute and march as mechanically as real storm troopers.
To complete the parody, Amsel himself becomes Hitler in order
to receive and acknowledge the salute. From being a mock-leader
of the Nazis, Amsel becomes a real-life victim when nine actual
'scarecrows', led by Walter Matern, beat him up.

A third phase of Amsel's art is reached in the scarecrow ballet,
which is conceived in the summer of 1944. Amsel, who is now
ballet-master Haseloff, has just returned from occupied France.
In keeping with the tripartite nature of the novel, he has three
possible titles for the ballet—*The Scarecrows, The Revolt of the
Scarecrows,* or *The Gardener's Daughter and the Scarecrows.*
Grass cleverly presents the ballet to us through the eyes of one of
its dancers, Jenny Brunies. She describes it with an amalgam of
childish enthusiasm and professional insight which throws its
political purpose into relief. She cannot understand why what is
pure art to her should be censored on political grounds. The ballet
is a choreographed version of the main themes of *Dog Years.*
Its three characters of gardener, gardener's daughter and scarecrow are representative of society, art and politics; and it is the
interplay of these in which Grass is primarily interested. The
gardener is the cowed and exploited German society of Amsel's
youth; his daughter, played by Jenny Brunies, is a symbol of
culture; and the scarecrow who concludes the ballet with a
macabre solo—"Herr Haseloff is toying with the idea of dancing
this role"—stands for political ideology.

The ballet is a monument to the adaptability and resourceful-
ness of Amsel's talents. That it is based on ideas "with which he
has been fiddling since his childhood" confirms the steadfastness
of those convictions which we saw borne in upon him. A new and
deeper politicisation of his art is attained in the ballet, and it is
noteworthy that in the three possible titles the only constant
factor is the scarecrow, which personifies ideology. Amsel-Hasel-
off associates himself more completely with totalitarianism in
order to subvert it more thoroughly from the inside. Like Bebra's

Theatre at the Front, his ballet company fulfils the purpose allotted to culture by Nazi dogma: spreading propaganda and raising the morale of the soldiers. True to its dialectical nature, the ballet at once reflects this subordination of art and utterly rejects it. These subtleties are not visible from the air and bombers make no distinction between the ballet company and the rest of the German war effort. Bombs fall during rehearsal and wreck stage, props, and hopes for the ballet. As ever, Amsel survives, but Jenny, with whom he has two bonds—absence of parents and suspect origins, is injured in the air raid. The toes of both feet are crushed and have to be amputated. Jenny will never practise her art again. German culture has been one of the grotesque casualties of German political ambitions.

Such is the multiplicity of ideas and incidents in *Dog Years* that, in lesser hands, they could easily disintegrate the novel. Grass holds them in check by the firmness of the narrative line, and by the intensity of the relationship between Amsel and Matern. If *The Tin Drum* revolved around the isolation of its hero, then *Dog Years* turns upon the axis of the love-hate relationship of its two main characters. It is epitomised in the penknife which appears at the start of the book. This is the weapon which has been used in their ceremony of blood-brotherhood, which Amsel gives to Matern, which Matern throws into the river, and which the river, as a proof of the circularity of time, obligingly washes up later in the story. The commitment to blood-brotherhood is ironic in view of the racist theories which later become prominent. Amsel, though only half-Jew, is branded with the name "Sheeny". This contemptuous name and the violence which accompanies it for the Jews is foreshadowed in the scene where Amsel and Matern find a cellar in the high school. It is beneath the changing rooms of the gymnasium, "which, in Franciscan days, had been a library" (p. 74). The boys descend into a sewer which is alive with rats, and which anticipates all too exactly the parable of bones as related by Harry Liebenau. In the course of that parable, Störtebeker speaks of his "ordered prey . . . almost tenderly and with mild didacticism: 'The rats can endure without the ratty, but never will there be rattiness without the rat'" (*Dog Years*, p. 304). This axiom conjoins the theory of Otto Weininger with its Nazi corollary. According to Weininger, he Jew can and should live without his Jewishness; it is a state of mind which must be conquered and subdued. According to Nazi philosophy, the most effective way to eliminate Jewishness is to exterminate the Jews. As a Jew, Weininger insists that the cure for Jewishness lies within the individual Jew. As anti-Semites, the Nazis claim that the "cure" must be in their hands. Amsel and Matern grope in the subterranean tunnel towards an appreciation of this fact. The mine-owner who is to write the bulk of his 'Morning Shifts' below ground and the actor who is to kill a dog with rat-poison are on the verge of recognising the difference between a Jew, albeit a partial and highly self-critical one, and an Aryan. At first they are happy with their underground exploration. Matern thrills to the "theatrical ambience" while Amsel has found his true milieu. Oskar liked to be beneath his grandmother's skirts, and Mahlke liked to be beneath the skirts of the Virgin Mary when she was beneath the sea in the radio shack. Amsel's desire for a womb-like beneathness is even stronger because it is the basis of his art—"Brauxel, who operates a mine, is able to express himself with particular virtuosity below ground".

When he finds a skeleton, Amsel dissolves the blood brotherhood in an instant. The skeleton is at once scarecrow, mound of bones, Hamletesque reminder, death's-head and omen. Seeing Amsel playing with the skull, Matern grinds his teeth with sinister eloquence before calling "Sheeny" and beating Amsel to the ground, an action he is to repeat later in a more formal setting. Matern is obeying his reflexes here. He is not striking Amsel for his Jewishness. There is nothing specifically Jewish in what Amsel is doing at this point, not, indeed, at any point in the novel. He is responding to the fact that Amsel is, quite simply, a Jew. He is ignoring the Weininger prototype of a young man trying to surmount the Jewishness within him. Instead he is applying the Nazi definition of a Jew and responding with aggression. Fear makes Amsel defecate, and even this has a symbolic significance. Amsel is trying to rid himself of his past, to excrete the Jewishness of his origins. This concept of the past as the waste matter of the present is discussed at the beginning of the 'Twenty-fourth Morning Shift', in which the scene under scrutiny takes place. "Who, having relieved himself after breakfast, is standing here contemplating his excrement? A thoughtful anxious man in search of the past. Why keep ogling a smooth and weightless death's-head?" (*Dog Years*, p. 73). Brauxel is forced to consider the painful and pungent facts of his youth. Oskar Matzerath took a similar view of the past when he talked about "this mind of mine which persists in excreting syllables"; and Pilenz is haunted by Mahlke's 'Stabat Mater dolorosa' in the latrine of the Labour Service while he relieves himself, and while "the maggot-ridden dross of my age accumulated behind and under me. . . ." For all these three narrators, the past cannot be flushed hygienically away.

The friendship between Amsel and Matern survives the incident below ground. Together, they are transferred from the Sankt Johann High School to the Conradinum, with its Dr. Klohse, its Mallenbrandt, and its sweet-sucking Dr. Oswald Brunies. To compensate for his failure on the Schlagball field, Amsel undertakes other feats and achieves recognition for swallowing and regurgitating seven salamanders. This act reinforces the point made in the scene below ground. Ugly and distasteful facts of one's past cannot be hidden within. They must either be excreted or vomited up. In the case of the salamanders, Amsel's token alignment with the violent and nauseating code of the other boys is something worthy of applause. But Amsel does not become one of their number. As in Mahlke's case, his feat sets him further apart. He is betrayed again by Matern when the latter leads the group who beat him up and knock out all his teeth. But the friendship even continues beyond this point. However grossly one friend treats the other, they still have to go on living in the same world. If a penknife which has been hurled into the Vistula can be retrieved—"You saw me. I had to throw"—then a blood brotherhood which is hurled into the most destructive situations will somehow pull through. The exact nature of the friendship will be adjusted by changes of name, dentures, profession and purpose; but the fact of the friendship is irremovable. Amsel, the victim, emerges in the superior position, even employing the older generation—Miller Matern—from which the other springs. Matern, the aggressor, ends up as the loser. Like Pilenz he is a persecutor who takes on the task of an expiator; like Pilenz, his narrative moves him insensibly towards a recognition of his own guilt. Fittingly, it is the miracle glasses—"products of Brauxel

128

and Co."—which make him see the truth. Only the victims of our treachery can make us aware of that treachery.

In the final chapter of *Dog Years* the novel comes full circle. It began with the bedrock of Amsel's childhood experiences (this double meaning of 'First Morning Shift' as the lowest, fundamental layer on which all subsequent experience rests is clearer in the German words, 'Erste Frühschicht'). It ends with 'The Hundred and Third and Bottommost Materniad', a descent to the deepest and most basic elements of the human imagination. Amsel comes face to face with Matern. Scarecrow meets Dog. Art confronts Reality. As befits an artist's workshop, Brauxel's mine has rich seams of literary allusion. It recalls Dante's *Inferno*, with its successive circles of hell. It reminds us of Blake's *Marriage of Heaven and Hell* with its Memorable Fancies and its devilish proverbs, insisting with Blake that "All deities reside within the human breast". Again, it has affinities with Wolfgang Borchert's *Stories from a Primer*, in which the senselessness of war is satirised, and which ends with a poetic glimpse of the year 5000 when "the crows still caw and the dogs still lift their legs" and when sometimes, "sometimes you meet a man". (It is no coincidence that Matern recites the part of the "raving Beckmann" from Borchert's *The Man Outside*, the archetypal drama about crisis of identity in the post-war world.) Brauxel's mine also calls to mind the Magic Theatre which makes its appearance at the end of Hesse's *Steppenwolf*. This mesmeric fantasy persuades Harry Haller not to commit suicide and leaves him determined "to begin the game afresh. . . . I would traverse not once, but often, the hell of my inner being." In its stress on the need for self-analysis, Hesse's book has a special connection with the concluding chapter of *Dog Years*.

Virgil's *The Aeneid* also has a special connection with Grass's mine. In Book Six this greatest of Roman epics gives a picture of the Underworld which has many correlatives in the Bottommost Materniad. There is the same progressive system of areas of damnation, the same unsettling noises, the same warnings about human folly, the same symbols of torment and sorrow, the same predilection for famous figures from national mythology. Virgil, like Grass, relies on the power of the number three, giving us Cerberus, the three-headed dog, a threefold wall about the battlements, the three sons of Antenor and the spirit of Deiphobus thrice-invoked. Grass, like Virgil, keeps up the momentum of his tale, frequently apostrophizes, and inserts short extracts of dialogue by way of explanation. Where the author of *Dog Years* chooses a different route from the poet of *The Aeneid* is in the monitory and prescriptive nature of his underworld. Virgil's epic has a powerful moral didacticism because it is an instruction in the heroic. Grass's novel is an instruction in the anti-heroic, in the norms of human existence; as such it is more exact and far-reaching in its moral and political didacticism. Even at his most propagandist—as when he is extolling the glorious destiny of the Roman people—Virgil's technique remains illustrative. He describes rather than teaches. Grass, though allowing the visual element its usual primacy, does not neglect the homiletic—"There is no contradiction between playfulness and pedantry; the one brings on the other" (*Dog Years*, p. 3). In the underworld as conceived by the Roman poet there is a source of hope, a target and reward for those who would lead a truly heroic or pure life. In Elysium or the Happy Place, Virgil depicts—

> the green and genial
> Glades where the fortunate live, the home of the blessed spirits.
> What largesse of bright air, clothing the vales in dazzling
> Light is here! This land has sun and stars of its own.
> (Virgil, *The Aeneid: Book VI*, Lines 638–41, trans. by C. Day Lewis)

The German novelist has no such image of light and warmth, and colour and freshness to offer. His underworld encompasses all. It is at once the source and the final resting place of every human endeavour.

Like Aeneas, Matern has his guide to the underworld; like his predecessor, he encounters the spirit of his father. Approaching the mine, he finds that it lends itself to theatrical metaphor—"Who would want to build cathedrals when the sky is held up by stage-sets like this! This is Brauxel and Co. . . ." (p. 535). Before his descent, Matern must remove all trace of individuality by dressing in a regulation uniform. Through the partition between his bathroom and that in which Amsel is changing, he gets his first shock. When he asks after his dog, Amsel replies "Pluto's with me. Where else would he be?" (p. 536). Amsel insists that the dog has come home—"Every dog comes from below and has to be lowered again in the end" (p. 537). When Matern complains that the dog has never been down a mine before and will be uncomfortable in the atmosphere down there, he is assured that Pluto will get used to it. He will have to since he is now company property. The dog has been commandeered by the scarecrow to complete the picture which Matern is about to see.

Opposites abound in the evocation of the Brauxel mine. In a cradle of strict realism—Grass worked in a potash mine and has forgotten no detail—the wildest surrealism is rocked vigorously. It tilts to and fro between the natural and the supernatural, the historical and the imagined, the human and the bestial, the man-made and the devil-created. Classical mythology is processed by modern technology. Philosophy, the love of wisdom, allies itself with the most ruinous ignorance. In the vast underground capitalistic enterprise which operates on a scale, and with a success, commensurate with the West German economy itself, all man's needs are accommodated. No aspect of the human condition is left unexplored; and the scarecrows which began in the domain of art, then moved into that of politics, now infiltrate the whole gamut of human activity. Man is satirised for being the devil-porter in the hell of his own making. In the first of thirty-two stalls, the Church is mocked for its part in the degradation of human ambition. Heinrich Schrotter, who tends the vats where fabrics are degraded, is mindful of the proverbial advice about supping with the devil and employs a long spoon-billed pole. What is occurring here is not just the recycling of clothes but the systematic corruption of all the people and the occupations represented by the different materials. In some cases the moths of time do the work of destruction: in other cases, additional methods are used so that the fabrics are burned and torn out of all recognition. Only then, when they are "fully degraded", are they machine-stitched and re-used. These clothes are the apparel of scarecrows and the scarecrows are the mirror image of man. The moral and intellectual clothing which men wear is made from abused and humiliated materials. By his choice of the *schmotte* trade to introduce us to the products of the mine, Grass reminds us that it is a line of business in which the Jews have had a traditional interest.

131

Matern's only comment is that "This is hell, indeed", but his tour of inspection has only just begun. In the seventh, eighth and ninth stalls he is exposed to "the three cardinal emotions and their echo effects" (*Dog Years*, p. 543). First comes weeping, that commodity which Oskar put on the market so effectively at the Onion Cellar. But here, the weeping is tearless. The urge to cry is overwhelming, the means non-existent. "Each circle has set itself a different tear-promoting yet desert-dry task" (p. 544). Grass is here satirising false grief over past crimes. It is as futile as it is attention-seeking. Simply by being raised to the level of a discipline—and therefore redolent of those other "disciplines" of Nazi Germany—weeping becomes imposed and based on no real emotion. Laughter, too, is a crude manufactured artifice. It is the cold, cynical and unregenerate laughter of the German people, who laugh mechanically to order—"here laugh the company, the regiment, the army, the loons, homerically the gods, the people of the Rhineland, all Germany laughs at, with, in spite of, without end: German scarecrow laughter" (*Dog Years*, p. 545). Unable to feel or show genuine guilt, the Germans compound the felony by laughing sardonically at what they have done. There are exceptions, the most notable being Matern whose mindless anti-fascism is catered for in the ninth stall. Here are displayed the emotions of hate, rage and roving revenge, which are as indiscriminating in their targets as the political attitudes they oppose. Matern is told not to worry about being in a minority—"Hate, rage, and roving revenge will be back in style one of these days. A cardinal emotion that promotes the grinding of teeth can't be a passing fad. To abolish revenge is to take revenge on revenge" (p. 547). Everything is seen in terms of its marketability.

In the subsequent stalls, political, legal and economic authorities are cruelly exposed, and all philosophical, sociological and ideological achievements are jeered at in the militant obscurity of Heidegger's language. Matern wants to run from this attack on his favourite writer but he cannot and must stay to learn that "The scarecrow comes-to-be in errancy, where, erring in circles, it fosters error" (p. 552). The particular stocking-capped scarecrow, who wrote *Time and Being* has spread the error out of which he himself grew, infecting the German intellect in the same way as the veneral Matern infected the German bloodstream. In the passages

132

which assault those who corrupted the mind of Germany with their quasi-philosophical solemnities, Grass achieves some of his most sustained and virulent satire. He matches the intellectual decay with physical and moral degeneracy. In his underworld, Eros rules with a stern hand. Love has been banished and lust is so uniform as to have lengthened into perpetuity. Orgasm is permanent and therefore devoid of any satisfaction. The rutting scarecrows are eternally erectile and symbolise the monstrous and joyless wastage which lies at the centre of private life. Matern, who has himself foreshadowed this relentless intercourse in his roving revenge, is not aware of the irony in his remark that "Life, real life, has more to offer. I know. I've lived it!" (p. 550).

The experience below ground affects Matern deeply. By the time he reaches the thirtieth stall, where the graduation ceremony takes place, his customary self-control gives way to a sense of shame. He cannot bear to see scarecrows dignified by these pseudo-scholastic celebrations. He has to turn away as the 'soulless automats' take the oath to the firm of Brauxel and Co., promising never to deny their origins or to depart from their allotted purpose. Matern is shocked when they conclude with "So help me God", unable to cope with this final travesty of scarecrows, who are created of man and in the image of man, being programmed to acknowledge the supreme Creator. In the last two stalls, packaging and distribution takes place. After production, sales and profit. Matern has it brought home to him that the scarecrow hell is no after-life which is geographically apart from reality. It is an ante-chamber to that same reality, a factory for the automated ideas, creeds, emotions and moral attitudes which are so much in demand. All these things will take their appointed place in what Matern always believed was "Life, real life". By returning to the commercial aspects of the Brauxel mine at the end of the inspection, Grass emphasises the scale and power of Amsel's art. He has developed an enterprise which produces all the warped values of which he was once a victim. He has become an entrepreneur of total degeneracy in order to mine and undermine it. His business monopoly represents an artistic triumph. But it also means that his art has had to become more committed, more overt, more admonishing.

The difference between the artistic and ironic perception of

Amsel and the simplistic view of the visitor, Matern, is summed up in their respective mottoes for the mine. Amsel's is 'Glück auf'—'good luck!': Matern's is "Abandon hope all ye who enter here!" In fact, the hell from which Matern has come and in which he has been a devil-expiator is far worse than anything below ground. Amsel rightly points out that "Orcus is up above". In the mine, everything is revealed for what it is, and produced to certain standards: in the real world, the purposes of hell are not so plain nor the layers of human experience so neatly segmented into stalls. To see is to understand. To look into the scarecrow inferno is to look at oneself. This is the message which Amsel is putting across. Ruthless self-appraisal is the only hope. The path to salvation is the path of painful self-knowledge. The great mysteries enshrined in the titles of two influential books—the mysteries of time and being and sex and character—are things which each man must seek to explain for himself. Weininger's self-loathing and Heidegger's arrogant word-spinning are equally irrelevant.

Even Matern begins to realise this in the concluding paragraph of the book. Returned to the surface without his companion-dog, he goes to take his bath. The narrative slips into the first-person and the hitherto detached mine-owner, Brauxel, slips into 'Eddi'. As they splash about in their respective bath-tubs they are once more akin to the two children whom we met in the 'First Morning Shift'. But the friendship has altered under the pressure of the circumstances. Amsel is very much the stronger partner and it is he who sets the standards. If he whistles, then Matern must follow suit—"But it's difficult. We're both naked. Each of us bathes by himself" (*Dog Years*, p. 561). Once they have taken off the mine uniforms, they are individuals again. They cannot react to life and its problems in exactly the same way. Each must cleanse himself separately. Each must look into himself and take stock of his own private hell. The Brauxel mine showed the enormity of the task facing the man who was prepared to confront his own mirror-image. In urging each individual to undertake this task, Grass is advocating a personal heroism which links his name once more with that of Virgil.

A novel of such encyclopaedic range as *Dog Years* attracts a corresponding range of comparisons. It has been analysed beside

Thomas Mann's *Doktor Faustus* as a study of the artist in an alien society. It has been compared with Uwe Johnson's fine *Speculations about Jakob*, which does for Communism what Grass does for Nazism—criticises it from inside. It could be studied in conjunction with Siegfried Lenz's *The German Lesson*, which also treats of the impact of the war on the adolescent mind. Like Amsel, Nansen the painter adapts his art to evade censorship; he tells the Rugbäll policeman that he will paint pictures with so much light in them that they will be invisible. Another work which is brought to mind by *Dog Years* is Martin Walser's play *The Rabbit Race*, which is also an examination of the insidious influences of Nazism. In the clarity of its symbols and in the sharpness of its irony, Walser's play has definite points of contact with Grass's novel. Alois, the hero, is a former communist, like Matern. He goes into a concentration camp to have his Marxism purged and volunteers to be sterilised in the interest of German science (though not, as his frustrated wife keeps pointing out, in the interests of their marriage). Through impotence comes strength because the operation has left him with a counter-tenor voice of remarkable qualities. But is it a natural German voice or is it a biological accident? The rabbits which Alois keeps are the counterparts of the rats in *Dog Years*. Alois is allowed to keep his angoras by the commandant of the concentration camp. The rabbits are called after the names of exterminated Jews as "such-and-such a name is free", which enables the commandant to order another Jewish death when calling for a rabbit for his table—"give us Benjamin, Isadore or Solomon . . ." After the war, an international Song Festival is held at the Oak Ridge Restaurant, another venue which is plagued with a foul smell if the wind is in a certain direction. Alois is banned from singing and decides to lay the guilt where it belongs. He kills his beloved angora rabbits and hangs the skins on the national flags which surround the festival, chanting a pedigree after the manner of Grass's recital of the dog's history—"Moritz begat Joseph, Joseph begat Eli, Benjamin begat Hildo and Fritz, Fritz begat Lamech . . ." In its lightness of touch, *The Rabbit Race* is very reminiscent of *Dog Years*. Grass sums up the horrors of Stütthof Concentration Camp in the notification of the death of Dr. Brunies—"Cause of death: heart failure". Walser achieves a similar effect when one of his characters, Woizele, says that he is still searching for his three sons who took to the forest—"They must be earning their living as charcoal burners. I've tried to trace them. I've been to the Forest Warden but I can't get any satisfaction from him. He says the last charcoal burner let his kiln out in 1935—but he's lying or covering up for somebody because I remember seeing the smoke from a kiln in 1940" (*The Rabbit Race*, Scene 7). Novel and play cover similar ground but end at different destinations. Alois, whose acts of sane protest are presented as "relapses", voluntarily withdraws into the Asylum at the end to have the vestiges of Nazism drained out of him. At the end of *Dog Years*, Amsel and Matern have no such Oskar-like refuge. They are alive and at risk in a cold and merciless world, and the book closes on a note of warning.

There is one work which must be compared in more detail with *Dog Years*, since its similarities with that novel are many and various. It was in a letter to the *Times Literary Supplement* (17 February 1966) that the resemblances between Grass's novel and Johannes Bobrowski's *Levin's Mill* (1964) were first remarked upon. The correspondent listed ten features which the novels had in common: a precise, geographical setting in an area along the Vistula; violent religious antagonism between Catholics and Protestants, as well as anti-semitism; the mocked eccentricities of minor sects; a mill burned to the ground as an act of hatred (*The German Lesson* has one, too); a bizarre christening which has an effect on subsequent happenings; the insistent and significant cry of a bird; regular excursions into medieval and other historical times; a legend involving robbers; a ghost-figure as a living event; and the telling presence of gipsies.

Clearly, since the novels are set in the same part of Europe and since the experience of the respective authors overlaps somewhat, a number of similarities are unavoidable. But the extent and exactness of the resemblances goes beyond coincidence, and beyond the list enumerated above. Far more striking than any of the features noted so far is the related narrative approach of both novels. In *Dog Years* as in *Levin's Mill* the story is told obliquely and retrospectively. In both cases the reader is firmly distanced from the narrator and reminded repeatedly that he is not viewing events from one sympathetic standpoint. Grass does this by using three different narrators who give changes of perspective and emphasis. Bobrowski does it before the novel begins. His sub-title 'Thirty-Four Sentences on My Grandfather' is an accurate description of both the content and the technique of the novel. For while recounting the tale of Levin's mill, the narrator constantly breaks off to add up the number of sentences so far achieved out of the goal of thirty-four. At one point, he even suspends the action to tell us that a subordinate sentence is so-called because it "lacks two of the characteristics of a main sentence: striking brevity, and, most of all, feeling". As in *Dog Years*, where the narrators argue about approach and delivery dates, we are continually made aware of the mechanics of story-telling. Both novels are thus conscious acts of criticism upon the business of writing, and manage to add a dimension to themselves where they might so easily have been accused of a wearisome exercise in alienation. Bobrowski's thirty-four is the echo to Grass's thirty-two, the number of teeth knocked out from the mouth of Eddi Amsel, and then reinserted in gold. (As the chorus sings in the Discussion—"To us the number isn't new/We keep on hearing Thirty-two".) Bobrowski, too, has a penchant for dental observation. His grandfather grits and unclenches his teeth during Vision Number Three, and he is later joined by another teeth-gritter in Alwin Feller. Later still, the grandfather graduates to Matern-like grinding and gnashing. (Just as *Dog Years* has its Bobrowski, *Levin's Mill* has a Mattern, who makes a brief appearance.) To complete his set of teeth, Bobrowski gives us a sentence—not one of the thirty-four—worthy of Grass himself: "But that was a long time ago, sweetheart, all that decays as quickly as your teeth."

The subject-matter of the two novels also converges. True, their respective focus of events is separated by half a century, for Bobrowski takes us back to 1874. Notwithstanding its historical digressions, *Levin's Mill* is as faithful as a dog to its nominated year; whereas Grass takes us forward into and beyond the war itself. Yet if we look closely at the themes of these two works, they are not as dissimilar as these time-schemes might seem to suggest. 1874 was an especially crucial time in the history of West Prussia, and Bobrowski uses the tiny village of Neumühl as a microcosm of the whole area in much the same way as Grass

137

used Danzig as a microcosm of Germany. In 1874 the Germans were starting to impose their culture, their laws and their religious beliefs upon the indigenous population of West Prussia, which was largely Slav. "They are Germans and that's worse than churchgoers" is one of Bobrowski's many digs at their expense. There is a moment of fine irony when Levin, the Jew, tries to gain retribution by appealing to German—and therefore Christian—law. Like Shylock, in other circumstances, he fails disastrously in this recourse to foreign justice. He goes into self-willed exile and grandfather stays unpunished. At the very end of the novel, having fought Levin with cunning and instinct, grandfather suddenly comes upon a *Gartenlaube* article by one Otto Glagau, who provides written ratification of the old man's behaviour—"No longer may tolerance or miserable weakness prevent us Christians from taking preventive measures against the extravagances, excesses and effrontery of Jewry". Grandfather, that model of intolerance and ruthlessness, does not pause to note that Levin is a patent enemy of extravagance and excess. The fact of his Jewishness is enough. This quotation has a direct link with Amsel's reading of Weininger's *Sex and Character*, whose thirteenth chapter helped to feed anti-semitism.

There are still further similarities. Both novels deal with the vicious influence of new German aspirations upon the intellectual, spiritual and physical life of the whole community. Both treat of betrayal. *Levin's Mill* has its own idiosyncratic Grandmother Wendehold to rival the eccentric Grandmother Matern. Changes of name are commented upon as pointers to political developments—"Pilchowski, who moved to Osterode and called himself Pilch, which is just as Polish but not as conspicuous". Casual obscenity is frequently introduced—grandfather, like Brauxel, is caught meditating in the lavatory and "considers between the plops". As in Grass, animals abound: dogs, cats, chickens, rats and a wolf all make their contribution to the story. Nor is the Grassian love of food missing. A whole meal, including jellied eels, is described and we are even given hints on how to bake hedgehogs. Music, too, is used to excellent effect and there are moments when the structure of the narrative recalls musical composition itself, and places Bobrowski, if only fleetingly, nearer to Thomas Mann. If we add to all this Bobrowski's talent for absurd comedy,

138

his control of a variety of dialects and speech rhythms, his measured flights into prose-poetry, and his love of the laconic, we build up an even more convincing argument for the influence of the one novel upon the other. And yet *Dog Years* and *Levin's Mill* are very different novels.

What distinguishes them most obviously is the highly individual personalities of the authors. Grass and Bobrowski are men of different generations, different temperaments, different attitudes. Their novels were produced in radically different circumstances. Grass wrote *Dog Years* with the supreme advantage of having one epic undertaking, *The Tin Drum*, triumphantly behind him. He was able to avoid some of the weaknesses of the earlier novel as well as to draw on its strengths. *Dog Years* is a book written with unassailable self-confidence by an author at the height of his powers. *Levin's Mill*, on the other hand, is the first novel of a man approaching fifty. That it is so fully-realised makes one regret that its author did not live to make further experiments in the novel-form. Bobrowski's aims are altogether less ambitious than Grass's. He concentrates on a small village at a fixed point in time, while the author of *Dog Years* tackles a whole turbulent era of German history, and includes a study of the nature of the German himself. The sheer dimensions of Grass's novel set it apart from Bobrowski's. Those features which have been listed as common to both novels represent a fraction of *Dog Years*: in *Levin's Mill*, they are its entirety. This is not criticism of Bobrowski. In confining himself to an examination of local relationships, his novel achieves a depth, realism and honesty which recalls Breughel.

There is a fundamental disparity, too, in the moral concern expressed by the two novels. Both may account for present discontents by going back into the past, but there the resemblance ends. The poet's preoccupation with form, shared by Grass and Bobrowski, is dictated by different moral apprehensions. In *Levin's Mill*, the device of the thirty-four sentences breaks down the relationship between the first-person narrator, and the main protagonist, his grandfather. Had the story been seen solely through the eyes of an affectionate grandson, then the grandfather would have emerged as a lovable rogue. By denying the narrator any moral standpoint, Bobrowski shifts the task of moral judgement to the reader. He makes us see the grandfather for what he is—

likeable yet despicable, amusing yet pathetic. In *Dog Years* the moral concern is expressed in more complex and devious ways. Grass purposelessly assaults the ethical standards of his readers in order to break down and re-shape them. His three narrators refrain from direct moral comment with Oskar-like consistency. Harry Liebenau addresses his Love Letters to that incarnation of amoralism, Tulla Pokriefke, and the Materniads are a record of that most perverted kind of moral indignation which drives Matern along the road of hate, rage and roving revenge. None of the characters engages the total sympathy of the reader, because Grass is at pains to present a world of moral uncertainty in which no comforting constants exist. In true dialectical fashion, when he is outraging morality most freely in his scarecrow inferno, he is at the same time evincing most moral concern. For the message which we bring out of the Brauxel mine is an urge to face up to that greatest act of moral courage—to know oneself. *Dog Years* exposes the inadequacy of conventional moral values which are quite unable to come to terms with the horrors it has been describing. A new morality is needed and this can only be found in the rigorous self-criticism of individual man.

Though this discussion of the virtues of *Levin's Mill* may have proved a fruitful mode of access to *Dog Years*, the novel with which it must finally be compared is *The Tin Drum*. Is it a greater or lesser work? The answer must surely be that *Dog Years* marks an advance. Its wit is keener, its comprehension is deeper, its scope is larger, its construction is more subtle and delicate, its themes are presented in a more challenging way, its satire is more caustic, its imagery more controlled, its effect more disturbing. *Dog Years* finds a better balance between its artistic needs and their method of treatment. *The Tin Drum* profited from the central presence of Oskar, whose drum years were the staple of the novel. But when Oskar's drumming lost its power for a time in the post-war period, the novel, too, lost some of its impetus. There is no loss of impetus in *Dog Years*. It accelerates towards the terrifying climax in the Brauxel mine. Viewing events from three standpoints instead of one, Grass is able to achieve far more historical accuracy and artistic truth. The ambivalence of Oskar's position in some ways worked against our acceptance of him as an omniscient narrator. By rejecting the concept of omniscience,

Dog Years gets closer to reality. Its three narrators can qualify and refine and adjust and restate. Paradoxically, this splitting-up leads to a more unified picture of reality than is the case in *The Tin Drum*. Again, there is infinitely more narrative variety in *Dog Years*, and especially notable is the radio discussion about Matern. This is at once a parody on the fashion for discussion as an end in itself, an opportunity to ridicule Heidegger in another form, a reworking of all the themes and ideas of the novel and a demonstration of the inability of the younger generation to cope with the truth about its elders.

There is nothing in the philosophic content of *Dog Years* that is radically different from that of *The Tin Drum*. But its treatment is more assured, and its thrust more purposive. In becoming more overtly political, Grass does not sacrifice aesthetic criteria. *Dog Years* is a superbly-sustained artistic achievement. That it should remain so in view of the stronger politicisation of its arguments is a tribute to Grass's craftsmanship. In particular, it is a tribute to his skill as a storyteller, for what ultimately binds the whole of *Dog Years* together is its narrative. *The Tin Drum* was a magnificent, freewheeling satire. But the third novel in the Danzig trilogy is a finer work because it attempts, and succeeds in, more difficult aims. It brings politics into the realm of art and does not become either documentary or hortatory. It can take its deserved place beside that greatest ideological novel, Dostoevsky's *The Possessed*. The essential concern of the Russian master and the German novelist alike is the politics of salvation. The ruling obsession is with the redemptive powers of confession of past crimes.

Dog Years began with two boys and a dog. It ended with two men alone in their baths, having left the dog in its natural domain. The dog's element is below: man's should surely be above that of the dog? In the years that have been reviewed, man acted through and like an animal. It is now time to recognise and conquer the dog within him. A man can wash himself clean. But the wisdom of ancient Greece must be invoked on the subject of animals—"What has a dog to do with a bath?"

5

The Plebeians Rehearse the Uprising

It was for the sake of others that I started writing biographies; but I found myself proceeding and attaching myself to it for my own; the virtues of these great men serving me as a sort of looking-glass, in which I may see how to adjust and adorn my own life.

Plutarch, *The Life of Timoleon*

Fame grows like a tree with hidden life.

Horace, *Odes*, Book I

Once more the number three is decisive. Shakespeare, Brecht, Grass. Ancient Rome, Jacobean London, Post-War Berlin. A play within a play within a play. Documentary, autobiography, fiction. The state, the citizen, the artist. Revolution, repression, survival. The written word, the spoken word, the acted word. Theory, practice, compromise. A rehearsal, a performance, a criticism. Human tragedy, artistic tragedy, German tragedy. And the whole thing moving from exposition, to development, to dénouement, within the Classical unities of space, time and action. By superimposing these and other triangles upon each other, Grass has, by a kind of geometrical progression, gone on to produce a play which is vastly superior to his earlier dramatic writings. *The Plebeians Rehearse the Uprising* marks a change and a continuation in his work. Its novelty lies in its exploration of a more formal dramatic mode than has hitherto been the case, in the emigration from Danzig as the basic setting, in its departure from a world seen through the eyes of the young, and in its treatment of a specific event at a given point in the post-war period. Its neighbourliness towards the Danzig Trilogy rests on its return to

142

the themes of the role of the artist in a totalitarian society, the nature of the German, and the possibilities of protest; it also rests on the fact that the play represents a further stage in the growth of the author's political awareness. For like Shakespeare's *Coriolanus* and Brecht's *Coriolan*, Grass's play is a drama of political action.

To understand this increasing politicisation of Grass's work, it is necessary to sketch in the situation in which German writers in general, and Grass in particular, found themselves in the 1960's. It was a period of time which differed radically from the fifteen years which preceded it. With the victory of the Allies in the spring of 1945, German political life came to a halt. It was not until the Potsdam Agreement of 2 August 1945 that "democratic political parties" were allowed to form and hold public meetings. The Social Democrats were the first to recover, benefiting from the fact that their traditional base, the trade unions, had been encouraged to re-form soon after the end of the war. Again, they had in Dr. Kurt Schumacher a leader of skill, courage and experience. The old Centre Party found itself facing a dilemma: should it be revived in its old form as a predominantly Catholic Party, or should a new Christian Party be founded which relied on Protestant and Catholic support? In his memoirs for this period, Konrad Adenauer recalls that—"The discussions on the problem of a new Christian party which took place among members of the former Centre were often difficult and frequently painful".[1] Notwithstanding this, a new party was formed and held its first meeting in December, 1945. It wanted the word 'Christian' in its name to indicate its ethical basis and its opposition to National Socialism; it chose the word 'Democratic' to affirm its faith in a truly representative system of government; and it decided on the word 'Union' to stress the fact that it wished to be a rallying-point for all classes and creeds who shared its ideas. The Christian Democratic Party (CDU) and the Social Democrats (SPD) shared the honours fairly evenly in the first federal elections in 1949. But in 1953 the CDU strengthened its arm to become the dominant party of the 1950's. It may have had to rely on a coalition at each stage, but it became more and more the party identified as the revitalising influence in Germany. The Adenauer Era seemed

[1] Konrad Adenauer, *Memoirs (1945–1953)*, 1966, p. 43.

to be synonymous with recovery, stability and affluence. With the Chancellor himself still firmly in the seat of power, there was no reason to suppose that the 1960's should not witness further consolidation. The real fear which Grass expresses in the Danzig Trilogy is that the *Wirtschaftswunder*, and all that it implied, would carry on unchecked and unquestioned.

But it was not unquestioned. Some of the features of CDU policy were, like the party's leader, showing signs of age. If the characteristic mood was still one of complacence and reaction, there were fast-flowing undercurrents of doubt and scepticism. These were channelled into a veritable whirlpool of dissent by the *Spiegel* affair in 1962. This affair was to prove both cause and symptom of serious political unrest. It began when the news magazine, *Der Spiegel*, published critical opinions on government defence policy, an area of especial sensitivity to every post-war German administration. The article provoked the Minister of Defence, Franz Josef Strauss, to an action which was more characteristic of government officials in the other sector of Germany. He ordered that the offices of the Magazine should be raided and the editor arrested. This high-handed action not only forced his resignation, it provided a focal point for the discontent and disillusion which had been rumbling beneath the surface. The incident did a great deal of harm to the CDU—Strauss was in fact leader of the Christian Social Union, the Bavarian counterpart of the CDU—and seemed to confirm the anxieties which many people had about the government's entrenched conservatism and anti-liberal policies. Adenauer survived for another year as Chancellor and the CDU even increased its strength in the 1964 elections. But stocks and shares in its credibility had nevertheless begun to fall after 1962, and a fundamental re-assessment of political life itself was undertaken. Extremists at both ends of the spectrum gained ground. The new Nationalist Party (NPD) was formed in 1964 while left-wing groups had particular success in university circles. Though many Germans—Grass included—saw the NPD as a neo-Nazi Party, it made an electoral breakthrough in 1966. In the same year an ex-Nazi was appointed Chancellor. Kürt Georg Kiesinger helped to fan the already crackling flames of political debate.

The quickening politicisation of the 1960's did not leave

literature unaffected. Those many writers, like Grass, who had been concerned with the theme of identity at the start of the 1960's, now found a new challenge to their craft. The function of the writer became a key issue once again in Germany, and for some years a debate raged over the nature and limitations of literature and, in particular, what its relationship with politics should be. There were several commentators ready to read the burial service over literature, pronouncing it a moribund and useless diversion. Others advocated a greater use by the artist of factual material. Since the creative imagination had failed to give the ring of authenticity, these argued, then literature should pitch its tents on the more solid ground of documented facts. The first outstanding contribution to the documentary literature of the 1960's was Rolf Hochhuth's controversial play, *The Representative* (1962)[2]. This examines with care and compassion the problem of responsibility for the extermination of Jews in Nazi Concentration Camps. It calls Pope Pius XII to account for not condemning outright Hitler's 'Final Solution', taking the view that those in influential positions who did not fiercely oppose were, in effect, condoning. (A similar attitude is taken by Grass in *Dog Years*, where the Catholic Church is again accused of assisting the progress of National Socialism.) Hochhuth was not afraid to put Adolf Eichmann on the stage, showing him in convivial company as he speculated on the most efficient methods of disposing of his intake at Auschwitz. *The Representative* is an audacious, moving and intelligent verse-play, which discusses its documentary sources in the 'Historical Sidelights' appended to the published version. Other plays in a similar vein soon followed, the most notable being Heinar Kipphardt's *In the Matter of J. Robert Oppenheimer* (1964); Peter Weiss's *The Investigation* (1965) which, like Kipphardt's second play, *Joel Brand* (1965), explores the theme of Auschwitz; and Tankred

[2] It was first produced in Berlin by the great Erwin Piscator, under whom Brecht had worked in the 1920's. In collaboration with Alfred Neumann and Guntram Prufer, Piscator had adapted *War and Peace* for the theatre in 1955. An extract from the narrator's prologue is purely piscatorial, looking back to pre-war German theatre even as it looks forward to the documentary theatre of the 1960's—"For us the theatre is not a place for anaemic, cautious art-for-art's-sake, but the last surviving platform of prophecy, a place in which to proclaim, to judge, to confess, to shock. . . ."

145

Dorst's illuminating account of the Expressionist playwright, *Toller* (1969). To a greater or lesser degree, all these plays called extensive documentary material to their aid; all of them were caustic indictments of twentieth-century inhumanity; and all of them were unashamedly <u>didactic</u>. — to teach

The Plebeians Rehearse the Uprising was in no way a bid to join this company. It is not a documentary drama. Grass is primarily interested in the dramatic situation which lies at the heart of the play and which gives it its sheer theatricality—a quality not always shared by some of the plays enumerated above. In some ways, of course, Grass has been from the start a documentary writer, taking from Döblin and Dos Passos that abiding passion for historical detail and exhaustive lists; and constructing those fascinating and teasing relationships between the factual and the fictional. But as we have seen from our study of the Danzig trilogy, he is essentially a writer with a lyrical talent that flourishes in the kind of imaginative freedom which a straightforward documentary approach would never tolerate. In the context of such plays as those by Hochhuth, Kipphardt and Weiss, it is not surprising that many critics considered Grass's drama to be yet another essay in the current mode. In fact, *The Plebeians Rehearse the Uprising* is no more a documentary study of the events in Berlin on 17 June 1953, than Shakespeare's play is a strict historical reconstruction of the life of Coriolanus. This does not mean that Grass was immune to the political and cultural trends of the 1960's. Since his work has always had a genuine immediacy to the world around it, he responded to new challenges and changes quickly and firmly.

Increased political awareness led to greater practical involvement. At the start of the 1960's Grass was a frequent and stylish resident in the Arts Columns of newspapers and periodicals. As each year passed, he began to make sudden overnight stays in the Political Pages, then spent whole weekends, then longer and more intense periods of time. The problem which he encountered on his travels between the Arts and the Political Features was a familiar one to generations of German writers: there was no intermediate resting-place, no respectable motel for someone who wanted to to register as neither artist nor political activist and who yet claimed to be both. There was the additional problem of luggage. Grass carried his fame wherever he went and desk-clerks at both ends of his journeys began to ask impertinent questions. If he was an artist, what right had he to speak upon political matters? If he was a political activist, why pretend that his work had anything to do with literature? No German writer would have understood this situation more clearly than Bertolt Brecht, and it was fitting that when Grass chose to grapple with the problems of the role of the artist he should use Brecht as his touchstone. *The Plebeians Rehearse the Uprising* is a study of the possibilities of peaceful coexistence between a man's political attitudes and his artistic abilities. The conclusions which it reaches are anything but reassuring.

Grass has not only given us a drama but an account of the genesis of that drama. In 1964, at the West Berlin Academy of Arts, he delivered a lecture to commemorate the quartercentenary of Shakespeare's birth. *The Pre- and Post-History of the Tragedy of "Coriolanus" from Livy and Plutarch via Shakespeare Down to Brecht and Myself* is a title which fits the man—provocative, ironic, presumptuous, comprehensive and in love with pedigree. What are the permissible limits of plagiarism? Grass decides that any amount of literary theft is justifiable if the result transcends its sources; and there is no better example of this than *The Tin Drum*, that glorified receiver of stolen goods which somehow contrives to look fresh, unworldly and wholly original. The example which Grass concentrates on is Brecht's adaptation of Marlow's *Edward II*, claiming that it showed how "a powerful adaptation can breathe life into a play that has gone flat". By contrast, Brecht's version of Coriolanus, after Shakespeare, is a disaster which was undertaken at a time when "the god who protects all thieves of literary property was away". In an entertaining and polemical fashion, Grass goes on to explain why Brecht's *Coriolan* is paradigmatic of bad literary practice. After running at speed through whole galleries of ideas and arguments, he ends up by outlining a play which is forming in his mind, a play which encompasses and highlights the main themes of his speech, a play which "demands to be written".

Grass's Shakespeare lecture would be more convincing if the assumptions on which it is based rang true. Brecht did not, nor did he intend to, show a "lightness of touch" in his handling of

Marlowe. What the young playwright did to *Edward II* was to take it firmly by the scruff of the neck, shake it vigorously so that it lost almost half its cast and some of its incident, and deprive it of the two things which were archetypal Marlowe— the mighty line, and the poignant relationship between Edward and Gaveston. Brecht's Gaveston is allowed none of the Renaissance sensuousness of speeches such as "I must have wanton poets, pleasant wits . . ." His relationship with the king is altogether more direct and realistic. Where Marlowe's Edward was weak and passive, Brecht's is determined and active; he fights to retain both Gaveston and the crown, instead of resigning them with a world-weary sigh. Brecht's king, unlike Marlowe's, develops as a character throughout the play; in addition to the single foil of Gaveston, provided by the Elizabethan dramatist, he is given two other foils in the shape of Mortimer and the Queen. Both these are toughened and enlarged as characters, so that the play does not—as in Marlowe's version—sag after the disappearance of Gaveston. Mortimer and Anne appear in a final scene which takes place after Edward's appalling death. They face their victim in the shape of his son, young Edward, and pay for their betrayal. Young Edward concludes the drama with a prayer which has a sardonic side to it in view of his mother's treachery—"And grant us, God, that also/Our lineage shall not perish in the womb". Brecht is not breathing life into Marlowe's play. He is rewriting it in the most fundamental way, parodying it, countering it, extending its sphere. What he sacrifices in Marlovian poetry, he more than compensates for by his simplification of plot, clarification of themes, finer delineation of character, sly humour and by his cogent portrayal of Edward as a hero.

Was Brecht's *Coriolan* equally successful in improving upon the original? Grass affirms that it is not and urges that Brecht's art is totally subtractive taking away from a great work but giving it nothing of comparable worth. Once again we must examine the assumption from which Grass is operating. He sees *Coriolanus* as a play with a distinct anti-democratic bias, with its central figure standing "between the two classes". According to Grass's reading of the play, the two tribunes, Sicinius and Brutus, are presented as "pusillanimous rebels" from the first; while the plebeians get an even worse press, appearing as "cowardly rats and ignorant dogs". The patricians, on the other hand, emerge as "noble lords and heroes without taint". Such a misinterpretation must be challenged. Far from being an anti-democratic play, it is Shakespeare's most balanced, controlled and dispassionate drama, written with an almost pathological fair-mindedness. What attracted Shakespeare to Rome is what attracted Brecht to *Coriolanus*—the promise of artistic liberty. Shakespeare had exhausted the potentialities of political debate in the Histories; he had to go back in time to gain distance. Also, he had to find a period which was known well enough to have some interest and relevance for his audiences, and yet was not so well-known that considerable manipulation of the facts could not be attempted. From North's translation of Plutarch's *Lives*, Shakespeare could see that the story was too one-sided. Hero and villains were too obviously differentiated. Follow Plutarch to the letter and he was in grave danger of writing a moralising history about the perils of democracy. In fact, Shakespeare went out of his way to improve the case of the plebeians. It may be expressed crudely but that does not detract from its rational basis. For example, Shakespeare makes Coriolanus lose his temper and taunt the citizens whose vote he is soliciting. In Plutarch, the fact that they exile him without such provocation is held against them.

The first scene of *Coriolanus* unites Shakespeare, Brecht and Grass. Shakespeare's opening is masterly. As befits a play about conflict and political action, it opens with violence and confrontation. Armed citizens storm on to the stage and pause to rehearse their uprising, checking their lines, justifying their gestures, and being prompted by the first of their number. Into this man's mouth—Grass's "ignorant dog"—Shakespeare puts the shrewdest assessment of Marcius we are to hear—"Though soft-conscienced men can be content to say he did it for his country, he did it to please his mother and to be partly proud, which he is even to the altitude of his virtue". Menenius arrives, a putative friend of the people who does not rate their intelligence very high if we judge by the Parable of the Belly which he tells them. This would have been familiar to Elizabethan audiences as yet another set-piece on the need for an organic view of government. The rulers of Rome in the fifth century B.C., like the rulers of seventeenth-century England, and of twentieth-century East Germany, required the masses to accept the idea of a structured hierarchy, whether it was based on birth and right, or on election and committee. Everyone, Menenius urges, has his function in the State. Abuse it and there is anarchy; hold to it, and a beneficial harmony results. The temporary calm which has fallen on the citizens is lifted by the arrival of Caius Marcius, who reviles them bitterly. His speeches set the characteristic tone of the play—direct, abrasive, metallic. His brutal verse falls like strokes of a sword after the uninspired prose of the citizens' speeches, or the gentle, mocking verse of Menenius. Marcius brings the news of the concession of the five tribunes and spies the dangers in this for the patricians. The announcement of war intrudes and further divides Marcius from the citizens: he welcomes it, they steal away. At the end of the scene, only Sicinius and Brutus remain. Grass sees them as "two benighted fools" who talk ineffectually about Marcius's courage as opposed to his arrogance. He is underestimating their importance. The play begins with the citizen's view of Marcius; this is balanced by Menenius's view of him; this is tilted sharply by Marcius's own view of himself; this is adjusted slightly by the Roman State's view of him—First Senator and military leader come looking for him especially; and this is then given the necessary corrective of the tribune's opinions. They remind us that the play is not about military excellence, but about naked political power.

Grass's lecture, then, does a disservice to Shakespeare by failing to appreciate the subtlety of his political observation. It does a disservice to Brecht by casting him as a literary house-breaker who comes up against a burglar-proof play. And it does a profound disservice to *The Plebeians Rehearse the Uprising* itself by equipping it in advance with an interpretation which is quite damaging. For since the lecture is self-confessedly the father of the play, it is bound to look as if its virulent attack on Brecht's adaptive techniques is extended and refined in stage terms. This is not the case at all. In the lecture Grass treats Brecht's aggressive didacticism with scorn: in the play he views his position with compassion and no small amount of fellow-feeling. The lecture restricts itself to an analysis of one unfinished adaptation by Brecht: the play offers us something nearer to the full splendour of the man—established talent, revered sage, practical man of the theatre, wily and devious dialectician, husband, human being, madman of method, and, despite all that happens—to borrow Wilson Knight's phrase for Coriolanus—"a great value". In the lecture, Brecht betrays his source: in the play, he is betrayed by his fame. Lecture gives us Brecht on his own; play makes him representative of the artist in general. *The Pre- and Post-History . . .* is at best a Curate's egg: *The Plebeians Rehearse the Uprising* is at worst a witty, pertinent and thought-provoking drama.

The basic premise which gives the play its title and scope is an authentic *coup de théâtre*. For the first time in his dramatic work, Grass has found a form which is a generous host to content instead of one which is a shoulder against the door. There are no Absurdist fantasies here, no lyrical flights across the skies of the image and metaphor. To select is to begin. And to select an idea as brilliant and fecund as that which underlies *The Plebeians Rehearse the Uprising* is to begin with considerable advantages. At a stroke, before the play has even started, the title has connected Shakespeare, Brecht and Grass. Shakespeare's play, within Brecht's rehearsal method, within Grass's play. The distancing effect of the narrative approach to *Dog Years* has found its counterpart on the stage. Each character acts out his story, but each is audience to the other's performance. Once again, Grass is able to argue, reply, simplify, embroider, and shift perspective at will. It is an important freedom because it gives the play much of its tension, and allows Grass to dwell on the interplay between reality and illusion with a Pirandellian relish. At a linguistic level, it enables him to point up the contrasts between Shakespearean verse, a Brechtian idiom (subtly re-created by means of borrowings from Brecht's works), the East Berlin dialect of the workers, the officialese of Kozanka, and the more characteristically Grassian moments, such as the fine speech which closes Act Three— "Benighted children, worshipping a dove". The clever juxtaposing of these different modes enriches the text, adds variety, permits great use of bathos, assists the mobility of the changing perspective, and helps to underline both the universality and particularity of the event which is at the centre of the play.

Grass does not content himself with setting one linguistic mode beside another to achieve an incongruous or serious effect. At a moment of crisis in Act Three, he blends Shakespeare, Brecht

151

and his own individual style into a single speech. Wiebe and Damaschke come purposefully upon the scene to give the revolt of this particular group of workers cohesion and "solidarity". The Boss is amused by this intrusion of a more practical, organisational element into the uprising—"They always come in twos, each the other's witness". Instinctively, he reaches for a theatrical yardstick when they announce their names—"What delightful names! Rather like Rosencrantz and Guildenstern". But Wiebe and Damaschke have no applause for the Boss's own performance as an ironic, temporising Hamlet. They take charge and order the workers to "Hang 'em in the middle of their phoney Rome", a fate which is especially appropriate if one recalls that the ultimate insult which Shakespeare's Coriolanus throws at the Plebeians is that they should hang themselves—"He that depends/Upon your favours swims with the fins of lead / And hews down oaks with rushes, Hang ye!" The Boss is not alarmed by this new development, relating it as always to the world of theatre—"I've always detested this brand of dramatics". Erwin, however, begins to perspire as the noose is put round his neck. If the Boss oscillates between the roles of Hamlet and Coriolanus, Erwin reaches gratefully for that of Menenius and expounds the Parable of the Belly. Ironically, the Boss has already told Erwin that this parable is quite unworthy of its reputation—"Try it, I ask you, on welders and Mechanics/Just try it on a modern cable winder". The exigencies of the moment force Erwin to try it on the road workers, the hod carriers, the plasterer, and their companions:

> The belly spoke unhurried, confidently—
> For one who has good bowels can be patient:
> Well now, my precious members, arms and legs.
> Head upon neck, two thumbs, eight fingers,
> Where would you be, I pray you, without me?
> And the eleventh too would be impotent
> To draw the nourishment from celery.
> I am alpha and omega. I'm
> The main dispatching station that sends out
> Freight trains to your farthest villages.
> And what share falls to me? The offal.
> You know it, I presume. You all have learned
> To wipe yourselves with care. . . .

Shakespeare's Menenius knew that he was home and dry as soon as the citizens agreed to give him a hearing. Despite the First Citizen's warning that he must not think "to fob off our disgrace with a tale", Menenius reduces the heat of the situation by substituting argument for action. He flatters the citizens by coming down to them, appearing to give them a privileged insight into the workings of government. Erwin has no such status to gain him attention. It is the urgency of his protest—"Ye holy demagogues, come help me now!"—which delays the hanging. He gains a hearing for the Parable of the Belly, even though Wiebe, the First Citizen here, tells him that they've had their "bellies full" of parables in church. As he speaks, Erwin emulates the belly he is describing, speaking unhurriedly and with growing confidence. He adapts the parable to the tastes of his hearers, taking care to concentrate on the coarser aspects of the body's functions and exciting the vulgar humour of his listeners. They are not persuaded by the reasoning of his argument; they are simply given time to reassess an action which was rushed upon them by Wiebe and Damaschke. The workers reconsider, the hod carrier takes control, and the nooses are lifted from round the necks of the Boss and Erwin. The Boss makes no comment, but Erwin has to enjoy his moment of triumph in an aside—

> Well, has the fable about the body's members
> Rebelling against the belly convinced you?
> It's nonsense hallowed by tradition,
> Preserved like corpses in formaldehyde.

Having demonstrated the truth of his earlier dictim that "Parable equals gullibility, / We'll gull the masses parabolic'ly", Erwin now patronises the workers, suggesting that they all "trot along home". At the end of Act Two, Erwin poured scorn on Kozanka's position as spokesman for the government. Under threat of execution, he finds himself occupying the same position as an apologist, justifying the ways of the state to men, and warning of severe reprisals. Irony once again has the floor!

Brecht's *Coriolan*, following Shakespeare's *Coriolanus*, begins with action and strife. *The Plebeians Rehearse the Uprising*, by contrast, has a deliberately low-key, undramatic, casual opening.

This first short scene condenses the exposition superbly.[8] Within a matter of minutes, the audience has been introduced to the main themes, to the two major characters (the Boss and Coriolanus), and to the play's terms of reference. It is immediately apparent that this is Brecht's theatre in East Berlin. Desk, tape-recorder, armchair, and filing cabinet are not the usual accessories of theatrical production in any other part of Europe. Again, there is something about Litthenner and Podulla which sets them apart from their equivalents in other countries. They arrive as workers. They saunter on site, check their tools, chat about the day's stint. This notion of the theatre as a place of work, and of work as the only proper and dignified way of life, is quintessentially Brechtian. It is fundamental to the whole structure of the play. It conditions the interpretation which the Boss and his company place on Shakespeare's *Coriolanus*; and it enables the actors, as workers, to sympathise with the uprising. (To emphasise the difference between amateurs and professionals, Grass later has the workers as actors, playing out the heroic actions which took place in the streets). From the start, then, what is being dramatised is a work situation. When the workers enter the theatre, their complaint is primarily against a sudden change in their work situation—an increase in the norms. The Boss, the ultimate professional, seeks to exploit the workers' dissatisfaction to advance his own work. Kozanka comes upon the scene to express his alarm about the danger to the government's work situation. And Volumnia pleads with the Boss to accede to official requests at the end of the play because it is the only way to ensure their getting the new theatre, and improved work situation. All these conflicts over work are contained in, and lit by, the work of a largely unseen but important character in the play, Kowalski, the theatre electrician.

The opening dialogue takes us straight to the crux of the play —to the nature and necessity of change.

PODULLA: Why do we change Shakespeare?
LITTHENNER: Because the Boss says we can.

[8] In the German text, the Acts are divided up into scenes, each scene usually corresponding with the entry of fresh characters. Act One, for instance, has eight scenes. The first scene ends with the entry of the Boss and Erwin, barely a page after the play has begun.

154

As an Hegelian, the Boss would acknowledge that the dialectical process makes change the cardinal principle of existence. As a Marxist, he would believe that the quality of a man's life is determined by the economic system under which he lives; to change his life, therefore, a man must first change his environment. As a playwright, the Boss has already expressed himself memorably on the subject in *The Measures Taken* (1930):

> What meanness would you not commit, to
> Stamp out meanness?
> If, at last, you could change the world, what
> Would you think yourself too good for?
> Who are you?
> Sink into the mire
> Embrace the butcher, but
> Change the world; it needs it.

Grass's play opens with a discussion of artistic changes, dictated by political beliefs. The rehearsal is interrupted by the workers, who want to make specific economic changes. They insist that their demonstration is not a revolution and has no political foundation. Their foreman warns the mason against excess then tells the Boss—"In good order, as we came from our jobs, unpolitically, without flags, not as agitators but as human beings, we're going to march on the government quarter". By the time Kozanka arrives in Act Two, the demonstration has undergone a radical change and now has definite political objectives. The extent of this change is revealed by the appearance and manner of Wiebe and Damaschke, two experienced agitators. Political change of a more decisive kind takes place when Russian tanks disperse the uprising and order is restored. Against the background of these various changes, the Boss himself wrestles with the same problem. Must he change or can he remain himself? If he sides with the workers, he will have betrayed his political employers who have made his theatre possible. If he sides with the state, he will betray the working classes.

It is at this point in the play that we realise his strong affinities with Coriolanus. Like Coriolanus, he suffers from the fatal handicap of being unable to change. If pride brings down the fifth-century Roman, pride in his theory brings down the twentieth-century man of the theatre. Coriolanus learns that military endeavour cannot exist in a vacuum: it has political implications. The Boss is made aware of the fact that artistic achievement can carry with it intolerable obligations to the state. Like Coriolanus, the Boss is vulnerable when he is out of his natural milieu. If Coriolanus's element is war, the Boss's element is the battlefield of dialectical debate. When the workers and Kozanka demand an unequivocal statement from him, they are asking him to repudiate that element. Both Coriolanus and the Boss are betrayed by a Volumnia. Both are consummate professionals in their chosen fields, and treat amateurism and incompetence with contempt. Both become progressively more isolated from those around them as the play proceeds. Both disdain an easy popularity. Both face their crisis at a time when their status is about to be improved. Coriolanus is awaiting ratification as Consul (just as Brutus and Sicinius are awaiting confirmation as Tribunes). The Boss is awaiting his magnificent new theatre (just as the workers are awaiting his signed ratification of their demonstration). Each protagonist has a worthy adversary with whom he eventually sides. Coriolanus has Tullus Aufidius, the lion he is "proud to hunt". The Boss has the dressmaker's dummy which represents Coriolanus. On to this dummy the Boss projects various images so that his Coriolanus is by turns the state, Stalin, political reality, the common enemy, and—the Boss's greatest adversary—himself. Shakespeare's Coriolanus is betrayed by Aufidius, who wishes to replace him ("And I'll renew me in his fall"). Grass's Boss is betrayed by Coriolanus when he is forced to identify with him.

These parallels must not be taken as proof that Grass has simply transformed the noble Roman soldier into the contemporary German intellectual. There are enormous differences between the characters, not least in their view of themselves. Both may cultivate a self-image, whether it be of a military hero or of a Chinese sage, but there they part company. Coriolanus is completely without insight into his own motives—he has no reflective soliloquies, no developing self-knowledge. The Boss, on the other hand, understands himself all too clearly. He is also prepared to admit adjustments in his ideas. In Act Four, when Kozanka seeks his signature, he stands beside the dummy and says bitterly to his company:

First you want me to play the hero; when I wouldn't join the workers in the street, you called me Coriolanus. And now you want me to embrace Kozanka as he embraced Aufidius. What parts you offer me! The trouble is they're too easy to play . . .

Kozanka presses him to sign—"The initials will do"—but the Boss defies him, speaking each word into his face.

BOSS: When the masons talked about victory, they struck me as absurd. It took their defeat to convince me . . .

VOLUMNIA: Watch your step.

KOZANKA: (*challenging*) Of what?

BOSS: . . . for instance, that we can't change Shakespeare unless we change ourselves.

We are back with the question which started the play off, but the answer has been amended. The Marxist conviction has been reversed. Instead of arguing that one has to change the world in order to change oneself, the Boss now decides that one has to change the individual before one can change his environment. This insight leads the Boss to drop the play which is in rehearsal. Finally, he hands Kozanka his signed statement. One cannot imagine Brecht adopting an intellectual position on the side of moralism as the Boss does, but in the terms of Grass's play this is not relevant. What we see in the closing moments is the dilemma of the artist in a totalitarian state. He may want to separate art from politics, and preserve the dichotomy. In practice, this division is as impossible as it is unreal. He will be forced to embrace the butcher, without even the consolation of knowing that he may change the world in doing so. The tragedy of Shakespeare's Coriolanus is that his rare qualities have no true place in the country of his birth; he meets a tragic death, a noble figure brought down ignobly. The tragedy of the Boss is that he survives at the end of the play, and has to live on with the knowledge of what he has done.

The device of the play-within-a-play is not an original one. It has a history as distinguished as that of Coriolanus himself. Three contemporary examples of its use may cast light on aspects of Grass's play. In Peter Weiss's *The Persecution and Assassination of Marat as Performed by the Inmates of the Asylum of Charenton Under the Direction of the Marquis de Sade* (1964), a brilliant initial idea is exploited with flair and with savagery. The audience are invited to watch an audience watching a group of asylum patients performing a play which has been written and directed by one of their number. This play features a confronta- tion between Jean-Paul Marat, the rabid, pre-Marxist French revolutionary leader, and the Marquis de Sade, the scandalous, perverted, calculating voluptuary. The author of the Reign of Terror meets the creator of *Justine*. Weiss lets the antitheses multiply. Action contends with imagination, collectivism with individualism, politics with art, reason with instinct, organisa- tion with freedom. It is a fascinating contest but it exists more in prospect than in realisation. For Weiss never lets Marat and de Sade face each other long enough to state their respective cases. The problem, as many critics have pointed out, is that the *Marat/Sade* has tried to blend two opposing theatrical concep- tions—Brecht's alienation techniques and Artaud's 'total theatre'. The intellectual debate is part of the first, but it is constantly aborted by the second. Time and again, spectacle interrupts dis- quisition; Artaud's "poetry in space" destroys Brecht's world of ironic detachment. *The Plebeians Rehearse the Uprising* suffers from a similar imbalance. Grass's play does not try to unite the Brechtian with the Artaudian theatre, but it does rest uneasily upon argument and incident. The incident is the uprising which is taking place in the streets, and which provokes most of the dramatic action which the play contains—the attempted lynch- ing, the re-enactment of the mason's heroism, the slanging matches and so on. The argument begins around the first scene in Shakespeare's *Coriolanus* and broadens to accommodate each new development. For the Boss, the only value which the dis- turbance caused by the workers has is to provide material for his play. He wants to absorb impassioned political action into theatrical performance. He wants to assimilate the workers' "reality" for the purpose of stage realism. The Boss—like his creator—is altogether too successful in this. Debate all too often freezes action. Grass has difficulty in keeping up a convincing commentary on the events out in the streets because the Boss, by his very inaction, dominates the action. This imbalance between the inner and outer world of *The Plebeians Rehearse the Uprising* is its most serious defect.

Another play which gains great impetus from its basic idea is *The Balcony* (1956) by Jean Genet. It is set in a brothel, a house of illusion where its clients can identify themselves with the authority figures in the Christian state—Bishop, Judge, General—and indulge their fantasies at will. As in Grass's play, there is the sound of revolution outside the enclosed, make-believe world; here, as there, those engaged in theatrical activities are required to take on political roles; and Madame Irma's girls, no less than the Boss's actors, are studied closely in their work situation! Grass, following fact, makes his Uprising fail; Genet, relying on fiction, makes his Revolution succeed and fail. The leading functionaries of the state are all liquidated, but a new problem is posed. Since the people will not sanction the total overthrow of a structure hallowed by time, where can replacements be found for the revered Great Figures? Madame Irma, the brothel-owner, comes to the rescue. While she plays the Queen, the sham General, Bishop and Judge from her Grand Balcony assume those positions in real life and are at once accepted. Genet is arguing that artifice is the basis of all functions; as it is in the brothel, so it is in society. In its treatment of role-playing, the nature of power, theatrical presentation, and the springs of political aspiration, *The Balcony* adumbrates themes of Grass's play. The style and tone of the two dramas may be disparate, but some of their respective images converge. At the end of *The Balcony*, for instance, Roger, who has been playing the role of Chief of Police in front of his "real" counterpart, suddenly castrates himself and becomes a symbol of impotence. As the Boss is about to leave the stage in the closing moments of Grass's play, he is very evidently the prototype of the self-castrated intellectual. The familiar tension between action and impotence, which is common to all three works in the Danzig trilogy, is once again resolved at the expense of the protagonist. A final strand connects Genet with Grass— the relationship between art and reality. In the last scene of *The Balcony* the Envoy tells the team of successful imposters that they must guard against petty jealousy—"We've reached the point at which we can no longer be actuated by human feelings. Our function will be to support, establish and justify metaphors". The speech which concludes Act Three of *The Plebeians Rehearse the Uprising* takes a more lyrical route to the same territory—

159

Here stood a mason, class of '22:
"He's writing something there. Is that for us?"
And there the old Socialist.
"This is our Wednesday, Boss".
What did I say? It doesn't touch me.
The Holy Spirit breathed and I mistook
It for a draught and cried
'Who's come to molest me?"

The artist's dilemma is beautifully caught in this speech. Does he follow art or reality? Must he judge events by aesthetic criteria or can he allow himself to respond with human sympathy? Should he remain loyal to theory or defect to practice? The Boss sets up the alternatives with clarity, power and wistfulness; but he has long since made up the irrevocable choice and his whole career is a monument to it. A revolution in practice cannot turn him from his theories of revolutionary art. As Volumnia says in her parody of Polonius, there is too much method in his method. As the mason points out early in the play, discussion is his "racket". After the self-questioning of his speech, the Boss goes straight back to his tape recorder, glances at a file card, then runs the tape audibly backwards. In this action his strengths and his weaknesses are tersely and dramatically summarised.

A third drama which uses the device of the play-within-a-play in a manner which has a bearing on Grass's work is Tom Stoppard's *Rosencrantz and Guildenstern Are Dead* (1966). Two minor functionaries from Shakespeare's most famous play become of central importance. These Elizabethans who are "passing the time in a place without visible character" spend the long periods awaiting employment by playing games, indulging in philosophical disputations, and speculating about their futures. The resemblances to *The Plebeians Rehearse The Uprising* are numerous. Both plays perch on Shakespearen tragedies. While the Boss has his Coriolanus in the form of a dressmaker's dummy, Stoppard sits Hamlet on his knee like a ventriloquist's dummy. Both Grass and Stoppard risk the perils of quoting extensively from the original texts and letting Shakespeare's language stand beside their own: both survive with honour. Both playwrights are occasional pen-friends with Pirandello (though Stoppard keeps up a much more regular correspondence with the Samuel Beckett of

Waiting for Godot). Both explore endless layers of reality and illusion. Both deal with the craft of play-making and with the profession of the actor. Both keep the major event—uprising, tragedy of *Hamlet*—offstage. Both treat of betrayal, political duty and the demands of doing one's job. Both are helped along by their wit and humour. Both thrive on paradox and ambiguity. Both tend towards becoming dramas of inaction. There is a final point on which the two plays rub shoulders: the question of destiny. Rosencrantz and Guildenstern may discuss various possibilities, but they are as firmly in the grip of an all-deciding fate as the Player trapped by the limitations of literary creation. ("There's a design at work in all art—surely you know that? Events must play themselves out to aesthetic, moral and logical conclusion"; or, again,—"We're tragedians, you see. We follow directions—there is no *choice* involved.") Choice as an optical illusion is a feature of *The Plebeians Rehearse the Uprising* as well. The workers believe they can choose and achieve an alternative way, that they can ignore the stage directions set down for them by the state. But their freedom of action is more apparent than real. Their spontaneity evaporates before a show of military force. In the Boss's case, method has subdued spontaneity and made his actions and attitudes as predictable as those of Coriolanus. Again, as a Marxist, he accepts a socio-political view of destiny. Paradoxically, he is seen at the start of the play trying to alter the course of literary destiny, "upgrading the plebeians and the tribunes" and changing them into "conscious revolutionaries" When the workers ask him to upgrade their revolt and, as they see it, dignify their case with his signature, thereby influencing their destiny, the Boss refuses. He can amend the design that is work in art; but the drama of reality is something in which he cannot and will not interfere.

Grass's poem, 'The School for Tenors', ends with the line —"Curtain, before you understand the applause". When his play was first produced in 1966 at the Schiller Theatre in Berlin, he understood the applause all too clearly. There was a dearth of critical acclaim. It was generally felt that the play was anti-Brecht, portraying him as a failure at a crucial moment in the history of East Berlin. Since Grass had campaigned for the SPD (though not always with the Party's blessing!) in the 1965

F   161

elections, he was accused of having written a narrowly partisan drama, which attacked the political base of Communism by means of discrediting its one acknowledged artistic oracle.[4] Some critics saw in the play an arrogant and presumptuous purpose—that Grass was only trying to smash one icon in order to replace it with a more up-to-date West German model, one which sported a different hairstyle, wore a celebrated moustache, and was unlikely to be seen in the company of a cigar. Very few of the reviews saw beyond the immediate political associations. In speeches and in interviews, Grass had berated the East German intellectuals for staying at home during the Uprising: in the play, it seemed as if Brecht was being made the whipping-boy. The fact that Grass had made the Boss's refusal to act both intelligible and moving was not taken into account. His 'German tragedy' was interpreted too literally by his German audiences.

By a curious irony, the situation in which Grass found himself had been anticipated by Brecht in *The Messingkauf Dialogues*, where the Philosopher argues that:

> The crux of the matter is that true realism has to do more than just make reality recognisable in the theatre. One has to be able to see through it too. One has to be able to see the laws that decide how the processes of life develop. These laws can't be spotted by the camera. Nor can they be spotted if the audience only borrows its heart from one of the characters involved.

(trans. John Willett, 1965)

The documentary affiliations of *The Plebeians Rehearse the Uprising* made many people see it as no more than a theatrical snap-shot of a specific event. The identification of the Boss with Brecht, the whole Brecht and nothing but Brecht, led to the one-dimensional appraisal which the Philosopher is warning against. Grass might protest that his play was a free adaptation of history, but the general laws which underpin it went for the most part unheeded and unobserved.

The American première of the play was given by the Harvard Dramatic Club in 1967.[5] In order to concentrate on the universal

---

[4] Martin Esslin's *Brecht: A Choice of Evils* (1959) chapter VII, gives the best account of Brecht's motives and behaviour at this time. Grass's view is expressed categorically in 'What is the Fatherland?' (*Speak Out!*)

[5] *A Günter Grass Symposium*, edited by A. Leslie Wilson, 1971, p. 24.

theme of the artist's dilemma, the production subjugated the Shakespearean and Brechtian values of the drama. *Coriolanus* was presented as a Chinese opera, and the text was deprived of as many references to Brecht as was possible. The actor playing the role of the Boss took pains to look unlike the Augsburger. Whatever gains this reading may have had, the losses must have been staggering. Without the Shakespearean element, a vital dimension is lost and the key Roman-Jacobean figure of Coriolanus is eliminated. Without the Brechtian element, some of the warmest and most ambiguous areas of the play are forfeited, along with the many accurate and affectionate parodies of Brechtiana. It is one thing to make sure of seeing the wood for the trees: this production seems to have felled most of the forest.

It was left to the Royal Shakespeare Company[6] to solve many of the problems raised by the Berlin production and to restore all of the richnesses which were suppressed at Harvard. The Aldwych version had the advantage of an audience without the intellectual and emotional ties with the Uprising which German spectators were bound to have. But this advantage was neutralised by the preconceptions of the English theatregoer about modern German drama, namely, that it is too long, too laboured, too complex, too political, too high-minded, too melancholy, too humourless, and worst of all, too German. David Jones's production disposed of these prejudices summarily[7]. It allowed Grass's play to state its case with boldness, wit, lucidity and power. The resemblance between the Boss and Brecht was neither concealed nor over-emphasised. Emrys James's Boss had Brecht's clothes, gait and characteristic gestures; at the same time, it cleverly incorporated features of Grass himself, notably the moustache. In this remarkable performance, three interchangeable *personae* were offered simultaneously—a guileful Brecht, an astringent Grass, and a lonely figure struggling to reconcile art with politics without losing his integrity. The character of the Boss was thus

[6] First English professional production of the play was at the Aldwych Theatre on 21 July 1970. Directed by David Jones, designed by Farrah, lighting by Stewart Leviton.

[7] I am indebted to David Jones for discussing his production with me, and for explaining the approach taken during rehearsals. Not surprisingly, Grass himself considered that the RSC production was superior to that at the Schiller Theatre.

explored on its three levels—as a compassionate study of a famous Communist artist, as a self-examination of Grass, and as an exploration of the artist's role in a totalitarian society.

Rehearsals for the Royal Shakespeare Company production included a discussion of the *Study of the First Scene of Shakespeare's 'Coriolanus'*, to which Grass himself refers in his Shakespeare lecture. In this tetralogue, the question which begins Grass's own play is asked and answered—

W: Can we amend Shakespeare?

B: I think we can amend Shakespeare if we can amend him. But we agreed to think only by discussing changes of interpretation so as to prove the usefulness of our analytical method even without adding new text.

John Willett, *Brecht on Theatre*, 1964, p. 252.

At the beginning of his play, Grass shows Brecht as a complete master of his 'analytical method'; by Act Four he has become its servant. Following the example of the tetralogue, one might use a similar exercise in textual criticism. If one tries to decide what did happen to Brecht during the Uprising on the evidence alone of *The Plebians Rehearse the Uprising*, interpretations vary greatly. Brecht will be seen as a traitor, a victim, a scapegoat, a voice of sanity, a Hamletesque intellectual, an egoist, a model of altruism, a hero, and an equivocator who only appeared to side with the government. These readings are not mutually exclusive, and the fact that they can coexist gives the play its richness of texture. Again, the variety of response confirms that this is no slice of documentary realism which gives a fixed, historical viewpoint. It is a Cubist portrait of Brecht-Grass-the-artist, seen from different angles at the same time. It exposes the contradiction inherent in the role of the artist. How can he discharge his responsibilities to so many conflicting interests —to society, to his art, to his audience, to his fellow artists, to his employers, to his family, to himself? For all his cunning and his Protean dexterity in avoiding intellectual defeat, the Boss is not able to find the solution to this problem.

The Berlin Uprising in the background is viewed from competing standpoints as well. As in *Dog Years*, no one version of reality is accepted as being authoritative. Various characters contribute their visions of what is happening in the streets, and the accounts are by turns optimistic, pessimistic, objective, subjective, romantic, realistic, sentimental, sardonic, impulsive, fatalistic. It is left to the audience to piece together its own picture from the collage which is offered. The RSC production widened the range of these versions of the Uprising by individualising the Workers and the Actors. On the printed page, these groups only seem to function collectively; in the theatre, they were made to operate both as groups and as sets of individuals with differing shades of commitment and apprehension. This effect was achieved by casting distinctive physical types and by giving attention to the delineation of each character. Among the Actors, Flavus suffered a sex-change into Flavia; among the Workers, the Machinist, as well as the specified Hair-dresser, was played by a woman. These adjustments aided the individualisation and strengthened the female aura in a largely masculine play. Grouping and movement was thoughtful and inventive, disguising those weaker moments in the play when Grass has the Workers standing about self-consciously with little to do beyond being spectators. The RSC production surmounted another problem set by Grass—that of placing two sets of actors side by side, one professional, one amateur; both played by professional actors. The Boss's professionals rehearse their Uprising with method and purpose: the workers rehearse theirs with zeal and confusion. At the Aldwych theatre, this dividing line was always in evidence and it was the Boss who often indicated it. When he moved among his actors and assistants, he seemed at home. When he stood amid the workers, wearing his cap, he was at once part of the group— a fellow-worker with a common cause—and yet impossibly divided from it. Professionalism isolates. Art lifts above.

In the First Book of his *Odes*, Horace speaks of "Wars hateful to mothers". This phrase has no relevance to Shakespeare's Volumnia, who sees her own son joyfully off to the battlefield. A woman with decidedly masculine standards, she fully earns the taunt of Sicinius—"Are you mankind?" Yet paradoxically, it is only when Volumnia plays the submissive female along with Virgilia that she is able to prevail with Coriolanus. In *The Plebeians Rehearse the Uprising*, none of these values of the character is lost, but there is an added dimension in the fact that she is a distinguished actress who is married to the Boss. When she betrays her husband-son, her plea is coldly practical—"They'll cancel our new theatre. We've been working for months with that revolving stage in mind". Peggy Ashcroft's performance as Volumnia in the RSC production was a revelation. Between her first theatrical entrance, wandering through a gaggle of Roman plebeians with an air of modernity, and her final, sage exit-line ("All right, go to the country. But leave your guile here. We might need it tomorrow"), she explored all the layers of Volumnia's personality. She began by viewing the revolt fearfully, then with romantic exaggeration, then with sympathy, chiding the Boss for "playing the Chinese sage again", then with burning eloquence, then with real commitment, then with doubts, then with remorse, and finally with cool disdain. This Volumnia emerged as a strong, involved, capricious, outspoken, warm, fallible human being. The relationship with the Boss was shown to be deep and understanding on all three levels—the marital, the professional, the level of friendship. Like Emrys James, Peggy Ashcroft managed the transitions between prose and verse smoothly and unobtrusively. These performers also made credible that awkward moment in Act One where the Boss mocks the situation in which he finds himself by quoting from the supplication scene in *Coriolanus*. What could have been embarrassing and even melodramatic became at once a playful parody and a serious signpost to Grass's own supplication scene in Act Four. Immediately after she has answered quotation with quotation, Volumnia addresses the Boss in her most forthright manner—

> But you, though never a proletarian
> Despite your cap, you've got the gift of the gab.
> Lord, what a manifesto you could write,
> With forest glades of exclamation marks!

This assessment is an important corrective to the Actor's view of the man as summed up in his name, the Boss; and the Workers' idea of him as a pivotal figure upon whom the fate of the whole Uprising turns.

In his essay, 'Grass and the Denial of Drama',[8] W. G. Cunliffe argues that the dramatic potential of the revolt is deliberately

[8] *Günter Grass Symposium*, op. cit., p. 60.

ignored, and that the play revolves around inactivity. He calls the work a "demonstration of inconclusiveness" in which no dramatic situation is allowed to come to a head. Yet Grass takes trouble to ensure a dramatic tension throughout the play by setting the rehearsal against the revolt in the way that he does. He may not achieve a perfect balance between the theatrical and the political situation, but their very opposition engenders a series of conflicts. The observed world of the Boss's stage contradicts the imagined and reported world of the streets outside. Inaction struggles against action, discussion against decision, intellect against emotion, method against impulse, equivocation against commitment, delay against advance, the individual against the collective. These tensions are more evident in performance than in a reading of the play, and they lend the work a tautness and excitement that is not attained in any of Grass's earlier dramatic offerings. Mr. Cunliffe's claim that the play's "plot and whole conception preclude any development or real action", must also be challenged. In the context of the RSC production of *The Plebeians Rehearse the Uprising*, this comment seems strange. True, the play does not abound in incident, or peripateia, or suspense, or naked conflict, or speedy forward movement, or tragic dilemma, or any of the other criteria which Mr. Cunliffe appears to find as the proper measure of 'drama'. But it is not a torpid and inconclusive debate that takes place while the resistless forces of history whistle past outside. The revolt may be doomed to fail, but this does not prevent considerable interaction between character and circumstance. And if the Boss does not commit himself, the reasons for his inaction—like the reasons for Hamlet's inertia—are still dramatically interesting. What finally helps the Boss to change his mind and commit himself, is the impassioned description by the Hairdresser of the worker's heroism. The Boss responds to these futile acts of bravery and self-sacrifice when the character of Katrin, from Brecht's *Mother Courage* is invoked. His past, which has been consistently flung at him by Volumnia, superimposes itself on his present. He agrees to side with the workers —"As in my youth, under a sky swept clean . . ." Appropriately, his exit is blocked by Volumnia. No-one has been more vehement in exhorting the Boss to join in the revolt: now, having brought the news that martial law has been declared, Volumnia is only concerned to disassociate the Boss and the theatre from the event. Her earlier enthusiasm for the workers disappears as she escorts them with brisk efficiency from the premises ("We'll take the stage exit. You go through the storeroom"). The Boss is left alone to dwell upon the irony of what has happened. At the precise moment that he made his moral choice, it ceased to have any validity. There is no longer a revolt to support. This moment when a decision is taken and rescinded simultaneously is, in the theatre—*pace* Mr. Cunliffe—undeniably dramatic.

There are two particular features of the play which contribute strongly to its visual and dramatic impact. The first is the use of lighting, which illumines the play in more senses than one. From the start, the lighting is an expression of the Boss's moods. ("In my mind and in Rome it's daylight".) It is a mark of his perfectionism, for even a rehearsal must be correctly and expertly lit. It is emblematic of his God-like status in the enclosed world of the theatre. He controls the elements: the workers are at their mercy. Inside the theatre, the weather for the Uprising is ideal: outside, the sun beats down on the workers' backs and then it starts to rain ("We're soaked. Even our sandwiches"). The frequent commands to Kowalski ("And give us light. Sunday light") are a constant reminder that we are in a theatre, an example of Brechtian alienation which helps to reinforce the identification of the Boss with the director of the Theater am Schiffbauerdamm. (Again, it is surely no coincidence that the Worker who remains silent throughout most of *The Messingkauf Dialogues* is an electrician.) The lighting is also a commentary on the action. When the hack-poet, Kozanka, first appears there is a shift from illusion to reality ("Kowalski, give us the work lights again"). But, most important of all, light symbolises the dissemination of truth. As in *The Tin Drum*, where Oskar's birth was heralded by moths drumming on light bulbs, so here is the protagonist associated with truth and protest.

> Oh yes, I've fought for justice,
> Those words, those flashes of her spirit,
> Were like a light in the darkness.
> > Yes, I lit
> The world.

Significantly, Kolwalski is the last character to speak to the Boss at the end of the play. He reminds the Boss about his vacation and is told to take off as much time as he wants. As Kowalski leaves, the iron door slams behind him with an air of finality. The theatre is closed and dark. The Boss's mood is depressed. He no longer controls the climate in which he works. He no longer lights his immediate world. When the electrician departs, truth is going on holiday for an indefinite period.

The second aspect of the play which must be singled out is the use of the tape recorder. Like the lighting, the tape recorder exists at a functional and symbolic level. It is an essential part of the Boss's working method. Every discussion and rehearsal is scrupulously recorded. It is the enemy of individualism, mechanising human voices, reducing flesh and blood to sound. At one point in Act Two, the workers revile the Boss who takes down their comments calmly on the tape recorder and then uses them in evidence against them. He replays the tape, applying aesthetic standards to the workers' vilification ("How would it be—just by way of testing our invention and improving upon it—to throw in another 'rotten no-good' between 'slimy' and 'underhand'?"). This moment has great dramatic effect in the theatre, as the workers hear themselves for the first time. Grass turns the tables on the Boss and Erwin in Act Three, making Damaschke leave the tape recorder running as the hanging is about to proceed ("The boys at home will want to hear the show"). The tape recorder is also a cipher of history, enabling Grass to point up a theme which he has dealt with in the Danzig trilogy—the simultaneity of time. When the machine is played, past and present coexist, each a comment on the other. Again, the tape recorder permits yet another twist on the play-within-a-play device. Extracted from its part in the drama and played back on its own, it would be a not incoherent radio adaptation of *The Plebeians Rehearse the Uprising*. But it is as a personal accessory of the Boss that the tape recorder must finally be seen. It is a confessional box into which he pours all his professional secrets. It is a live creature with an appetite as voracious as that of Mahlke, and the Boss feeds it endlessly on words and ideas and dialogues. It is his mind in microcosm, a chorus of voices inside his head which accuse him from and about his past. In the last moment of the play, he

169

addresses the tape recorder directly. When he leaves, the machine remains behind as a grotesque cenotaph.

If *Dog Years* can see its face in the waters which turn *Levin's Mill*, then *The Plebeians Rehearse the Uprising* can find some of its features reflected in *The Demonstration* by David Caute.[9] The central character in this work, Bright, is producer, teacher, intellectual, old-style Leftist, actor, writer, and theorist trying to combat action with argument. He is betrayed by those around him, when his manuscript is destroyed; and he betrays both the students and himself by persuading them to accept a compromise. Other resemblances proliferate. A rehearsal is interrupted and replaced by political revolt. A play within a play meets a counterplay. The spirit of Coriolanus is called up in the opening lines ("Like a dull actor now, I have forgot my part", the very speech quoted by the Boss). Reality wrestles with illusion before brutally forcing it to the canvas in the final scene. Aspiration matures into action but ends in defeat. Dogmatic assertion is the prevailing tendency ("Art should not imitate your life, it should translate it"; "Time is a bourgeois freak-out. Be your own clock"; "A revolution is a continuous process of pressure which finally produces a qualitative change in the system"; "An actor who can't stop acting is an insult to the theatre"). A tape recorder has a telling moment. The virtues of carbon paper are acknowledged by the protagonist. Autobiography intrudes. Brechtian techniques—if not Brecht himself—are utilised. Paradox and parody are lovingly employed. Quotations are in fashion ("As Lenin said, a system cracks at its weakest link"). Authority is presented as something grim, intractable, and devoid of humour. Theatre is celebrated.

But it is in the differences between these two sharply intelligent plays that Grass's theatrical instinct can be seen to be the surer. Where he deals with a factual proletarian revolt, Caute deals with fictional student unrest. Where the Boss is wooed by both sides, Bright is sandwiched hopelessly between them. Where one play confines its action to the streets, the other attempts to bring

[9] *The Demonstration* had its première at the Nottingham Playhouse on 19 November 1966. Marius Goring played Bright. With the novel, *The Occupation* (which also features Bright), and the essay, *The Illusion*, the play makes up a trilogy called *The Confrontation*. There is an interesting summary of Grass's play in *The Illusion*, pp. 83–4.

it on to the centre of the stage. It is this feature of *The Demonstration* which militates against it. In Act One, the drama discusses the theory; in Act Two, it offers action. This shift obliges the playwright to attempt a complete change of style and he indicates in a stage direction that the play "is moving from the dramatic to the epic—consequently the effect must be one of surging mass activity and participation". This is easier to announce than to bring off successfully. The Nottingham production did not find the way to present confusion, self-indulgence, and obscenity without itself becoming confused, self-indulgent and obscene. In this context, Bright's melodramatic intervention as Steinblitz ("We who were alive in Germany thirty years ago do not forget that the road to Auschwitz was paved with words") seemed incongruous, especially for a professor of drama! *The Demonstration* fails to achieve a workable synthesis between the dramatic and the epic, and, as a result, becomes curiously listless at the very time when it is supposed to convey "surging mass activity".

Grass does not make the mistake of straddling two theatrical styles. His stage is the Green Room for the real performance which is taking place outside. Because it is unseen, the Uprising can be controlled and altered to suit the demands of the drama. It is from the reactions and hesitations of those in the theatre that Grass builds up his play, and plaits theme upon theme. Like Caute in *The Demonstration*, he is often too discursive and too homiletic. But he has written a challenging drama about the tragic flaw in the German character, and seasoned it with an immense amount of wit, ambiguity, irony and deft comedy. Brecht's Dramaturg might well have been speaking of Grass on the Fourth Night of *The Messingkauf Dialogues*—

> I can understand him. He wants to 'dig deep'. A mixture of the expected and the unexpected, the intelligible and the unintelligible. He wants to mix applause with terror, amusement with regret. In short, he wishes to make art.

And his wish comes true.

6

Local Anaesthetic

Pain compels all things.
Seneca, *Epigrams*, 5, Querela

There are two types of demonstration; there is demonstration
look-look and there is demonstration bang-bang.

David Caute, *The Demonstration* (1969)

For there was never yet philosopher
That could endure the toothache patiently.

Shakespeare, *Much Ado About Nothing* (*c.* 1598)

Self-inflicted pain is the essence of *Local Anaesthetic*. It is the
common ground on which author, characters and readers meet.
For in subordinating himself so completely to his compositional
aims, Grass has had to make several painful artistic sacrifices; in
pursuing their individual courses, his characters are the creators
of their own discomfort; and in pressing on through the novel's
deliberate and sharp pin-pricks, the reader is like a dentist's
patient, enduring pain in the cause of improvement. Yet again the
graphic artist in Grass abbreviates a novel. A finger, recognisably
male, is held out over a flame. Pain is accepted, sought. It is an
inevitable part of the bland world which frames it. In the specifically dental context of the novel, the finger points to the division
of pain, to the habit of nineteenth-century dentists, noted by
Grass, of placing their patients' hands over a naked flame during
the extraction of teeth in order to divide the agony, to de-localise
it. There are other values in the design. The finger belongs to the
hand of the artist, indicating to the world but meeting resistance
and hurt. It is Grass's favourite eleventh finger, the questing penis
which must pay for its pleasure in pain. The religious significance of the candle is clear, too. Truth lights up the world.

172

To attain knowledge and find truth, men must suffer. And there is no respite from suffering because truth itself is pain. The incomplete world which acts as a venue for flame and finger is also the world of the mind, the human skull. Physical, mental and spiritual pain are conjoined.

In 1966, Grass gave an address at Princeton University, entitled "On Writers as Court Jesters and on Non-Existent Courts". His speech dealt with the problems of commitment in art, and contained the claim that he could divide himself into writer and political activist. These two functions were brothers with lives of their own rather than Siamese twins. Grass concluded his speech by grasping the nettle of paradox firmly:

> But there are also a great many writers, known and unknown, who, far from presuming to be the "conscience of the nation", occasionally bolt from their desks and busy themselves with the trivia of democracy. Which implies a readiness to compromise. Something we must get through our heads is this: a poem knows no compromise, but men live by compromise. The individual who can stand up under this contradiction is a fool and will change the world.
>
> (*Speak Out!*, op. cit., pp. 52–3)

These laudable sentiments ran short of oxygen in *The Plebeians Rehearse the Uprising*. The Boss was unable to preserve the freedom of the 'fool'. His status as a great artist compelled him to make a political declaration. He fought hard against his fate but could not resist it. *Local Anaesthetic* does not continue the fight: it concedes defeat. There is no attempt in it to separate the artist from the political activist. They share the same pen, the same purpose, the same dentist.

First impressions suggest that the Danzig trilogy is a long way off. *Local Anaesthetic* has no Danzig setting, no acutely observed adolescent world, no journey across a nation's history, no wealth of episode, no superabundance of character, no value-free moral sphere, no acres of vitalistic prose, no playfulness and irreverence, no sudden, exhilarating descents into the Brauxel mine of Grass's surrealistic imagination. Seneca has replaced Rabelais: the whole tone of things has changed. *The Tin Drum* did not moralise or make categorical statements. Its aim was to show, to provoke, to expose, to question. *Cat and Mouse* and *Dog Years* followed the same pattern, always critical but never dogmatic. Representation

173

was given strict precedence over information. In *Local Anaesthetic*, the situation is reversed. The factual all but obliterates the visual. Spontaneity is suppressed. Range is severely limited. Pace is checked. *The Tin Drum* and *Dog Years* ran furiously across the past: Grass's third novel walks steadily through the present. One of its shoes is critical, the other, on its stronger, right leg, is dogmatic. The locomotion of the novel depends on this balance.

Narrative approach, too, segregates *Local Anaesthetic* from its predecessors. Starusch's first-person narration is no return to the exuberant style of Oskar's memoirs. For all his ubiquitousness, mental and physical, the tin drummer did adhere to a definite chronological scheme. Starusch does not do this. In his mind, past and present are locked in such a desperate embrace that they are virtually indistinguishable. He insists that historical awareness is all. But he does not view history as a process of organic growth that is generated by cause and effect. He sees it as the unending and oscillating interplay between past, present and future. While this idea of the simultaneity of time is not new in Grass's work, the intensity with which it is taken up is unparalleled. It determines the whole structure of the novel, sabotaging coherence and exploding any possibility of conventional linear story-telling. In each of the books in the Danzig trilogy, a figure of action declines into impotence. Oskar, Mahlke and Matern are all fiercely energetic characters who gradually become weaker in body, spirit and purpose. In *The Plebeians Rehearse the Uprising*, too, there is a highly attenuated version of the same development. The Boss begins as a vital intellectual force, secure in the exercise of his art; he ends up being emasculated by the demands of political expediency. Like the respective protagonists in the Danzig trilogy the Boss takes a clear downward path. In *Local Anaesthetic*, there is no such movement from energy to inaction. Because of Starusch's treatment of time, they coexist. He does not need to trace the line from action to impotence: he continuously exemplifies it.

The opening paragraph of the novel proclaims the style and approach—

I told my dentist all this. Mouth blocked and face to face with the television screen which, soundless like myself, told a story of publicity: Hairspray Vesuvias Life Whiterthanwhite . . . ah yes, and the deep freezer in which my fiancée, lodged between veal kidneys and milk, sent up balloons: 'You keep out of this. You keep out of this . . .'

(*Local Anaesthetic*, p. 7).

The nameless dentist is Starusch's audience. Like Oskar's Bruno and Mahlke's Father Alban, he has both a professional and personal relationship with the protaganist. Though only referred to as a specialist in one branch of medicine—'the dentist'—he plays a diversity of roles with unvarying assurance. He is a teacher, educating his patient in the rationale of pain; he is a historian, expatiating on the development of his science; he is a political animal, believing in the perfectibility of man by means of slow, unsensational reformism. He is also a dilettante philosopher, a psychoanalyst, an employer, a husband and father, a symbol of modern technology, and an arbitration tribunal to which the case of Starusch versus Scherbaum can be referred. Above all, he is a person who has found—and who operates exclusively within—his true milieu. Inside the walls of his surgery, he can even assume other-worldly proportions: 'Hurting is not my profession'.

Starusch begins with paradox. He 'tells' everything to his dentist and yet his mouth, the source of speech, is blocked. He therefore has a silent dialogue with the television screen. The television has been installed in the surgery as a distraction but it is quite the opposite for Starusch. It enables him to focus and confront his pain, to condense past and present with bewildering results, and to indulge in free association of ideas in a manner that recalls Grass's poems. In the first paragraph, the television commercial makes him convert his past into a corresponding advertisement. His former fiancée, Linde, pops up incongruously from a deep freezer, attesting the fact that pain, too, can be kept fresh and undiminished by modern methods. But while the television commercial is designed to sell, Linde has only defiance and indignation to offer to her sole viewer. Dentist, story, television, commercialism, pain, the past, Linde, food, imaginative projection. In this brief paragraph Starusch flashes up the main images which are to occupy him. It is, in itself, a deliberately inarticulate and teasing television advertisement for the rest of the novel.

Mobility, as it applies to *Local Anaesthetic*, is also anticipated by Starusch's initial words. The novel has no real mobility in space. It lacks the sweeping movement of the Danzig trilogy, just as it lacks its geographical certainties. Though nominally set in Berlin in 1967, it does not attempt to create a convincing realistic background. The student unrest and the volatile political situation are assumed rather than described. With the exception of the dentist, the characters have none of the advantages of a protective and carefully-evoked environment. They are exposed and vulnerable, deprived of any sense of place or of meaningful movement between places. *Local Anaesthetic* takes another resolute step away from the earlier prose works: it goes indoors. The Danzig trilogy was notable for its sense of space and fresh air and freedom. Exterior settings flourished. *The Tin Drum* had its potato fields and its rafts and its Crystal Night and its cemeteries and its eel sequences and its Atlantic Wall. *Cat and Mouse* had its schlagball field and its wrecked minesweeper and its Baumbachallee and its trams. *Dog Years* had its dike and its river of time and its mill and its walks with dogs and its drowning and its school playground and its gipsy in the bushes and its kennels and its railway lines and its fields of scarecrows. Such settings had thematic relevance. Freedom under an open sky was something which all the central figures enjoyed—or appeared to enjoy—at the beginning of their respective stories. In each case, they forsook that freedom. Oskar retreated to his asylum bed. Mahlke sought the womb-like comfort of the radio shack. Amsel took Matern below ground, as far as possible from light and fresh air; the two of them ended up alone in separate bathrooms. *Local Anaesthetic* starts where these novels left off. It imprisons most of its action indoors, and thereby strictly limits its nature. The brief visits to Kempinski's serve to emphasise rather than to counter the predominance of interior settings. Starusch is totally immobile at the outset. He is in a room, in a chair, in a fixed position in that chair. He spends half the novel there. Even when released to engage in his argument with Scherbaum, he is no free agent. Much of the time he is shackled to a telephone, reporting what has happened to his dentist. *Local Anaesthetic* is controlled by a series of Berlin walls.

Denied mobility in space, Starusch finds alternative mobility in time. He may have to project his thoughts on to a tiny area, the size of a television screen, but their temporal plane is unrestricted. His mind can range at will through past and present and does so at speed. Fact and fantasy can compete in the television film which Starusch is creating, directing, and playing a central role in. This interiorised action which revolves around Linde and General Krings is balanced by the inaction which now characterises Starusch's life and attitudes. It also foreshadows the dialogue between action and inaction which he has with Scherbaum. The first section of the novel concerns itself with the past-present as seen through the eyes of a teacher of German and history, who is obsessed with his youthful delinquency during the Nazi period and his relationship with his former fiancée. In the second part, the younger generation as represented by Scherbaum, is given its voice. Antitheses teem. Starusch feels the lash of the past while Scherbaum is pained by the present. The teacher extols the virtues of parliamentary democracy while the student talks of its failure. The former urges calm inactivity while the latter proposes violent protest. The one blames his country for its global ambitions under Hitler while the other condemns it for its parochialism under post-war governments. The dental patient sees progress as snail-pace reform while the dog-owner sees it in terms of revolutionary action. Even the supportive roles of their respective females are antithetical. Irmgard Seifert is as racked by guilt about her Nazi past as Starusch, but she does not share her colleague's political stance. Instead of adding her weight to the argument against Scherbaum's act of protest, she openly encourages it. Vero Lewand, by contrast, is so committed in her support of her boy friend that she will even seduce her teacher in order to advance Scherbaum's cause. In the final section of the novel the opposites come to-gether to form a workable synthesis. Scherbaum emerges as the personification of this synthesis. Grass's choice of subject-matter obviates the kind of treatment which he used in the Danzig trilogy. When he was launching an assault on Nazism and post-war middle class complacency, satire, surrealism and passionate prose were appropriate. In turning to a more specific theme—the relationship between the generations—he found it necessary to confine himself to irony, realism and an altogether more dis-passionate prose style. As Grass noted in a political speech in 1968, the spirit of the times had changed somewhat drastically—

"Only a few years ago the Federal Republic presented an image of a humdrum middle class society characterised by hand work, security, law and order and political lethargy. And now suddenly the Germans have been seized with unrest".[1] The circumstances which produced and stimulated the Danzig trilogy no longer existed. New issues needed to be confronted, especially those relating to the violence and unrest which Germany experienced in the mid-1960's. In an earlier speech, Grass had told his audience to "Continue to be restless and difficult. The citizen's first duty is unrest".[2] The unrest he advocates here is not the kind of violent protest he refers to in the 1968 speech. Grass has very firm views on the permissible limits of violence and *Local Anaesthetic* states those views uncompromisingly. It also concentrates on the allied theme of the nature of change, which was dealt with in stage terms in *The Plebeians Rehearse the Uprising*. The Boss asks the workers what they are trying to change, how they intend to change it, and why. Starusch interrupts Scherbaum's rehearsal of his individual Berlin uprising to put the same fundamental questions.

The enormous differences between the Danzig trilogy and *Local Anaesthetic* must not be allowed to obscure the fact that there are many lines of communication between the works. It is true that the artist figure is for the first time absent from both title and centre of events. It is true that the language does not have the old sustained galvanic force. And it is true that the imagery is no longer dynamic and multi-dimensional. But Grass has not forgotten Danzig. He gives Starusch the most respectable literary pedigree by making him Störtebeker from the trilogy.[3] In *The Tin Drum* Störtebeker was the arrogant leader of a gang of teen-age delinquents called the Dusters. The gang first threatened Oskar then became his followers. In *Cat and Mouse* the nefarious activities of the Dusters are recounted via a letter to Pilenz from Father Gusewski. A different moral perspective on their crimes is thus given. Störtebeker is presented in the *novelle* as a feared and single-minded youth who dives incessantly, but in vain, to find Mahlke's radio shack. Another side to his character is offered

[1] 'Violence Rehabilitated', *Speak Out!*, op. cit., p. 116.

[2] 'The Citizen's First Duty', *Speak Out!*, p. 80.

[3] Störtebeker was the leader of a fourteenth-century gang of pirates in the Baltic Sea. He was executed in Hamburg in 1401.

in *Dog Years* where Störtebeker is one of the two presumptive fathers of Tulla's child. Since the child is conceived of Nazism, it cannot be born whole. The miscarriage scene ('Luckily Tulla was wearing ski pants') is as gruesome and dramatic as anything in the novel. From being such a deplorable youth, Störtebeker has moved on to become a mechanical engineer with finer feelings and has then elevated himself into Eberhard Starusch, teacher, as friendly and engaging a man as anyone in Grass's work. The Störtebeker-Starusch link feeds both his own personal tension and some of the structural tension in the novel. Starusch never tires of being his own example—

> (What do you think, Scherbaum? That ought to interest your generation. We were seventeen at the time, as you are now. And certain other traits in common—no personal property, a girl shared by the whole group, and absolute hostility to all grown-ups—cannot be overlooked; even the jargon prevailing in this junior class reminds me of our private lingo. . . .) . . . Because a teacher is a reoriented teenage gang leader who—if you don't mind taking me as an example—has felt no other pain than toothache, toothache for weeks. . . .
>
> (*Local Anaesthetic*, pp. 12–13)

Other familiar chords are sounded in *Local Anaesthetic*. Like *The Tin Drum* it has its photographs, its fingers, its aphrodisiac rug, its concrete eternal, its literary allusions (Goethe's *Tasso* replacing his *Elective Affinities*), and its Oskar-like fantasies about murder and other brutal crimes. Like *Cat and Mouse* it has its toothache, its masturbation, its sexual initiation, its radio, its recreated battles, its Redeemer figure, and its eloquent slapping. Like *Dog Years* it has its guilt, its rage, its Hegel, its Schiller, its Borchert, its trains, its prisoner-of-war camp, its dog, its joyless love-making, its river ("Something is flowing evenly; Father Rhine"), and its distant relative of Matern in Irmgard Seifert. Starusch's reflections also pay close attention to a theme which was touched on throughout the trilogy—the role and responsibility of the teacher. Since it dealt with didactic art, *The Plebeians Rehearse the Uprising*, too, examined the same theme. The concept of the Boss as teacher is basic to the play.

Oskar had many teachers. Spurning the more formal methods of Miss Spollenhauer at the Pestalozzi School, Oskar shatters her glasses with his voice and makes her a symbol of blind instruction. He goes elsewhere for his education. From Jan he learns about Poland. From Gretchen Scheffler he learns about Goethe and Rasputin and how to be attentive to women. From his mentor, Bebra, he learns about life and art; from the Lady Roswitha he learns about the delights of love. From the boil-ridden Korneff he learns about stone-carving. His education is unsystematic, erratic, and couched in the violence of his times. The link between the teacher and violence is made clearer in *Cat and Mouse* where the school inculcates the values of the battlefield. Klohse and Mallen-brandt are the archetypal pedagogues of Nazism: their antithesis is to be found in Oswald Brunies, the lover of Eichendorf, who is forced to sit on the platform in the auditorium while a former student recalls his military success, and abuses the language which Brunies has taught him. In *Dog Years*, this exemplary teacher is betrayed by his pupils (rather as Miss Jean Brodie is betrayed in Muriel Spark's novel) and the teacher-thugs have a clear field. The harmless music teacher, Felsner-Imbs, is also humiliated. It is not enough for a teacher to love his subject. He must teach it in accordance with the ends of the state and pro-duce 'good Germans'. Eddi Amsel understands this fact and protests against it by giving his art an educational function. To combat violence, he introduces violent elements into his scare-crows. In the final section of the novel, the manufactured brutality of the Brauxel mind is a blackboard from which Amsel attempts to teach Matern. *Local Anaesthetic* tightens the handshake be-tween the teacher and aggression. Seneca produces Nero. A gang of juvenile delinquents produces Starusch. The history of pain produces the dentist-teacher. The League of German Girls produces Irmgard Seifert, who keeps cannibalistic fish and incites a student to violence. That student is a dog-burner who wishes to teach his fellow Germans by his act of protest but who ends up editing a school magazine. In a didactic novel which itself administers a series of painful shocks no theme could be more apposite.

Most German critics did not welcome Grass's development in the mid-1960's. To them politics seemed to have descended upon his art like winter frost, leaving it cold, featureless, of uniform colour. If *The Tin Drum* reverberated like an authentic voice of protest, *The Plebeians Rehearse the Uprising* was an unintentional essay in Brechtian alienation with a difference, estranging much of the critical sympathy which Grass had attracted. In 1969, his play *Davor*,[4] the stage version of *Local Anaesthetic*, was fairly unanimously condemned as a dull and undramatic tract for the times. When *Local Anaesthetic* itself followed the play, its reception was equally hostile. The novel was not aided by the fact that its author was an active political campaigner for the SPD during the 1969 elections. He appeared to have produced an extended pamphlet on the virtues of reformism. He appeared to be practising the very didacticism which he had scorned in his Shakespeare lecture. In place of an irresponsible dwarf who awakened the conscience of the nation he appeared to have created an Oskar who wishes to make amends for bad behaviour, by taking a teaching diploma which enables him to stifle and absorb protest. The drum had given way to the piece of chalk.

Such reactions are understandable but they do less than justice to Grass's talent. Technically, *Local Anaesthetic* is his most impressive achievement. It strikes a balance between conception and execution that is aesthetically inspiring. It has a control and discipline which give it the precision of the surgical instruments used by the dentist. It limits its number of themes and achieves a deeper and more thorough analysis as a result. The Danzig trilogy tended to shuffle its full pack of themes like playing cards: *Local Anaesthetic* cracks its few themes like a whip. The sharper focus is aided by a radical change in tone and scale. Destructive ferocity gives way to constructive reflection. The epic becomes the anti-epic. The trilogy ran its murderous eye across decades of history, repeatedly asking what the Germans did wrong. Its successor puts the present under the microscope and asks the more difficult question of what the Germans should do now. In trying to answer this political question, Grass does not betray his literary responsibilities. Politics and literature are ingeniously blended.

The narrative thread of *Local Anaesthetic* is deliberately slender. A teacher from a West Berlin school visits a dentist, who has been recommended by a colleague. While attending to the patient, the dentist explains the nature of his treatment and relates it to

[4] *Davor* is a dramatisation of the middle section of *Local Anaesthetic*. In the translation by A. Leslie Willson, which was performed in America, it is called *Uptight*.

the history of dentistry. The teacher is meanwhile absorbed in his own personal history. What jolts him into the present is the announcement by his favourite student that he is going to protest against the Vietnam War in a most signal manner. The student intends to burn his dog on the Kurfürstendamm in front of the cake-eating West Berliners. A debate involving teacher, dentist, colleague, student and student's girlfriend follows. The dog is spared. The teacher undergoes further dental treatment and reflects on his past again. He replaces one unlikely fiancée with another. He adds a postscript on what happened to the student and his girlfriend. Even beside the story-line of *Cat and Mouse*, this looks jejune and unpromising. Yet Grass redeems the narrative in the manner of its telling.

Violence pervades the world of *Local Anaesthetic*. One has to look to a play like Edward Bond's *Lear* to find a contemporary work which is so grounded in violence. In the preface to his play, Bond declares: "I write about violence as naturally as Jane Austen wrote about manners. Violence shapes and obsesses our society, and if we do not stop being violent we have no future. . . . It would be immoral not to write about violence" (*Lear*, 1971, p. v). Grass's novel anticipates the spirit of these sentiments, though not the way in which Bond gives them dramatic edge. *Lear* is violence incarnate. It is full of violent action, violent thought and violent language. *Local Anaesthetic* addresses itself to the same problem as the play—the nature of political change and the moral justification of violence to effect that change—but it chooses subtle understatement rather than graphic illustration. Its violent action and language are minimal. It has none of the brutal excesses that are to be found in *The Tin Drum* and in *Dog Years*. Its greatest brutalities are confined to the imaginative universe of Starusch, though this is only a correlative of his real existence. Its mood is anything but aggressive. And yet violence has despotic rule over the novel from start to finish.

Violence asserts its presence at once. Starusch is visiting his dentist, which implies a kind of sanctioned violence. His class responds to the news with mild laughter, another kind of violence. Starusch considers his violent past in Danzig. He goes on to talk about his work in the Cement Industry, itself a violation of the atmosphere. He describes sexual violence on cement bags. A general is so conditioned by aggression that years after the war he still re-enacts battles in a sandbox. Various ways of killing his daughter are envisaged. Irmgard Seifert and Vero Lewand find an outlet for their innate violence in Scherbaum's proposal to burn Max. The whole political situation in which this proposal is discussed is full of latent violence. Starusch's lecture to dissuade Scherbaum is a history of torture. The dentist's journey back to the dawn of dentistry also takes in many landmarks of violence. It is he, appropriately, who sums up one of the burdens of the novel, when seeing a television film about the murder of Malcolm X, he observes casually that "Violence seems to have a future" (*Local Anaesthetic*, p. 215). By this stage, Starusch has already violated the relationship between teacher and pupil by succumbing to Vero's advances; he has also deprived his new Berber rug of its virginity. Seneca, the intellectual equivalent of the Arantil tablets, supports endurance. Yet not only was Seneca the tutor of Nero, he was also the author of nine of the most horrendous tragedies ever penned. In *Local Anaesthetic*, then, violence is presented as normality.

Pain results from violence. Pain is therefore a permanent and usual condition of mankind. It can be alleviated but never removed. Fear of pain, which is itself a form of pain, is a deterrent to violence. It is Starusch's fears about the painful consequences which his student will suffer that makes him urge Scherbaum to abandon his plan. Starusch's pain puts him in between Scherbaum and his proposed violence. In this sense, pain is a positive factor. It is an early warning system when seen in its strictly political context. Because pain is a constant, it alerts people against the dangerous belief that it can be banished. It guards against the notion that political utopias can abolish pain and are thus permissibly approached by means of violent revolution. In Bond's *Lear*, the two renegade daughters, Fontanelle and Bodice, share the same crude idea of a political heaven. Each plans to win over Warrington, the king's army commander, turn that army upon her sister, eliminate the king, have her husband murdered, and rule the whole land. Fontanelle or Bodice can then marry Warrington—Fontanelle later has the man's hands crushed and wants to "sit on his lungs"— and live happily ever after. Lear has no such illusions about the power of pain to conquer pain. Man has created the world in his own image, and suffering is therefore an eternal feature of that world. He has been blinded, de-throned and exiled by his daughters: man reproduces the source of his own pain. *Local Anaesthetic* treads on neighbouring territory. Starusch, Irmgard Seifert and General Krings, the three practitioners of the violence of National Socialism, reveal the absurdity of the idea that a Nazi millenium would have made pain redundant. Equally, the revolutionary dogmas of Scherbaum and Vero Lewand are no passports to the realm of the painless. Starusch and the dentist urge the acceptance of an enlightened resignation. It is better to live with a pain which can be controlled and minimised than to endorse a great pain—revolution—whose results are illusory.

Given the areas he wishes to explore, Grass could not have chosen two more apt professions than those of teacher and dentist. He persistently sets the two side by side—

(A dentist and a schoolteacher: maybe the parallel doesn't work. He gives painless treatment; I regard pain as an instrument of knowledge, even though I don't bear up very well under toothache and reach for Arantil at the slightest pang. He could manage without me; I am dependent on him. . . .)

(*Local Anaesthetic*, p. 158)

Dentist and teacher join forces to persuade Scherbaum that his plan to burn Max is pointless and ill-considered. Starusch begins to see the two professions as complementary—

Just imagine: a dentist and a schoolteacher rule the world. The age of prophylaxis has dawned. Preventive measures are taken against all evils. Since everyone teaches, everyone also learns. Since all are exposed to caries, all are united in the fight against caries. Care and prevention bring peace to the nations. . . . Just imagine.

(*Local Anaesthetic*, p. 170)

Starusch and the dentist represent the arguments for reformism in the novel, but they are polarities within the same camp. Starusch is highly subjective while the dentist is coolly objective. Starusch is a pessimist who has moments of Swiftian gloom while the dentist is an optimist with occasional tendencies towards a Panglossian vein. Starusch is a mediocre teacher who doubts the possibilities of his calling, while the dentist is a model of his profession who is confidant of the power and relevance of that profession. Starusch is troubled by guilt, the past, and by sexual failures with Irmgard Seifert. The dentist has no guilt, no past, and is happily married. Like some of the characters from the Danzig trilogy, Starusch is undergoing a severe identity crisis. He gropes around wildly in the past and in the present for a role which he can play consistently and to effect. The dentist, on the other hand, has an unshakable hold on his own identity and has no psychological worries. Starusch can be easily liked. The dentist can only be respected.

What begins as a professional relationship between patient and dentist soon takes on other dimensions. As Starusch's mind races around his past it is clear that he has not managed to build up any resistance against the attraction of violence. He constantly searches for new and savage forms of revenge to wreak upon Linde, his former fiancée. In this sense he falls within the pale of Seneca's judgement that 'Revenge is a confession of pain' (*De Ira*, Book III). He sympathises with Scherbaum's plan in his heart, but the liberal pedagogue in him has to argue against the burning of Max.

> As a teacher of German and history, I have a deep-seated horror of violence. And to my student Vero Lewand, who a year ago went in for picking so-called star-flowers, I said when she exhibited her collection of sawed-off Mercedes stars in the classroom: "To you vandalism is an end in itself."
>
> (*Local Anaesthetic*, p. 28)

The dentist starts by treating Starusch's dental decay but soon pays attention to what he considers to be the teacher's intellectual and moral decay. Eventually treatment turns into confrontation. The dentist remains nameless, faceless, even speechless but the words in the balloon convey his disapproval and reveal Starusch in his true colours. There is power and bite and momentum in the words. It is the kind of passage which shows that Grass's linguistic energy is still at his disposal, and that the general absence of free-flowing and mordant prose arises from choice rather than failure to produce it. The dentist shifts from the personal to the impersonal, thus giving the impression of being an omniscient narrator—

185

One look at your tartar tells the story. I suspected it the moment I saw your X-rays: here's somebody, another somebody, who wants the transvaluation of all values. Here's somebody who wants man to surpass himself. Who wants to take measurements with an absolute yardstick. I know, he pretends to be modern. He's not planning to dust off the moth-eaten Superman, he's foxy enough not to speak of a new socialist humanity, but everything: his way of sneering at small but useful improvements, his passion for cutting knots with swift but unaimed blows, his hankering after the most pompous possible doom, his outmoded hostility to civilisation, which for all its progressive trappings is nothing but nostalgia for the days of the silent film, his inability to work quietly and conscientiously for human welfare, his educational methods which oscillate between utopia and resounding nothingness, his restlessness, his capricious birdbrain, his malicious joy when something goes wrong, and his repeated incitements to violence—everything gives him away. Bulldozers! Bulldozers! Not another word. Off to the waiting room with him. I don't want to hear from you until the anaesthetic has fully taken effect. . . .

(*Local Anaesthetic*, p. 95)

Masochism and objective criticism coalesce here. Starusch is at once subjecting himself to a searing character-analysis and receiving the ruthless appraisal of his dentist. Stylistically, the passage shows the marriage of the literary and political which Grass sets out to solemnise joyfully in the novel. Linguistic verve marches down the aisle with political concept. The wedding photographs provide ready access to the novel. For the dentist is setting up all the antitheses which operate in the book: revolution and evolution, past and present, arts and science, energy and impotence, theory and practice, health and disease, action and inaction, pain and anaesthesia. In attacking Starusch's credo he is giving his own. As befits a man who is known only by his profession, his political views are rooted in dentistry. Because the dentist has made clear and positive progress over the centuries —Starusch later calls him a man whose profession "brings gaugeable results"—then society, too, should be able to make progress in the same way. Dentistry thus becomes a metaphor for social democracy, which must set about the task of preventing social decay with the same method, logic, and quiet conscientiousness that distinguishes the dentist.

186

Icily realistic when commenting on Starusch's political beliefs, the dentist becomes happily unrealistic when propounding his own idea of utopia. From the launching-pad of his narrow, scientific specialism he rises to the stars to view his concept of a "worldwide and socially integrated Sickcare". Starusch sums up the idea as "the world as hospital", but the dentist elaborates. The function of international Sickcare is to replace all existing systems, and yet, paradoxically, it is not itself a system. The dentist claims that Sickcare is free from any ideological associations. Its strength lies in the fact that it is "the base and superstructure of our human society". Sickness, as a version of pain, is an eternal feature of the human condition. It is as impractical to work for a system of medicine which aspires to a condition of perfect health as it is to work for a political system which aspires to a condition of perfect painlessness. To eliminate human failing is to eliminate humanity. Sickcare starts from a recognition of the permanence of sickness. The process of ageing is one of decay. What is needed therefore is not government but a policy of "all-embracing world Sickcare", which will care and help instead of trying to change. In this new order of things, health and the social obligation to be healthy will disappear. The world will become one gigantic, self-administered hospital.

Local anaesthetic, like all the other scientific advances, has its part to play. Pain, though an affirmative value, can distract and distort and cause unbearable suffering. It must therefore be limited by means of anaesthetic. But this anaesthetic must be local and temporary, so that sensitivity to all pain is not totally lost. To put it another way, pain is creative but only where pain is selective. Local anaesthetic can eliminate pain that is beyond our control and free the consciousness so that it can focus on the pains over which it does have some influence. Starusch's gums are numbed by the injection so that his mind can confront the pain of his past. Scherbaum's infatuation with global politics must be numbed so that he can concentrate on the more useful 'pain' of editing the school magazine. The forms which Scherbaum's local anaesthetic should take occupy much of the central part of the novel. Teacher and dentist compete in the search to find and inject the anaesthetic into the student.

The relationship between Starusch and the dentist, which

frames the novel, is intellectually stimulating. But it is the relationship between Starusch and Scherbaum, crucial to the argument of the book, which is more appealing on aesthetic and human levels. Philipp Scherbaum is an exceptional student. He is intelligent, industrious, rational, responsible, morally aware and kind to animals. Superior academic ability isolates him from all his classmates except Vero Lewand, and the 'middling muddlers' acknowledge this isolation by routinely laughing at his nickname of 'Flip'. To some extent, Scherbaum has already removed the distinction between student and teacher which Starusch sees as the essence of his educational pipe dream. In his relations with his teacher, Scherbaum is confident, outspoken, sceptical and prepared to trade quotations on equal terms. He obliges with the story of St. Apollonia when Starusch first mentions the dentist, at once promising to pray to the patron saint of those with tooth troubles and bringing home rather forcefully to his teacher the traditional association between dentistry and agony. Later, having refused to take over the school magazine ("You can't reform an absurdity"), he assures Starusch that the Apollonia story was properly researched. Scherbaum does his homework.

For obvious reasons, Scherbaum reminds Starusch of himself as an adolescent. He therefore absorbs his student into his personal fantasies and transports him back in time to a confrontation with General Krings. The scholastic and military worlds which plague Starusch converge in his febrile imagination to produce a quiz show devoted to "battles that helped to shape the destinies of Germany, Europe, in fact the whole world". In front of an audience which includes schoolchildren (heirs of the past) and members of the Parent-Teachers Association (a family professional link between past and present) Linde introduces the contestants with wit and control. Vero Lewand and Scherbaum are competing with General Krings. Students of history and war challenge a practitioner in the military arts. Those who search for the lessons of war struggle against someone for whom it is an end in itself. Whose picture of the reality of war is the more accurate— the younger generation's or the ex-Nazi's? The quiz battle is a parody of the sandbox battle which is in turn a parody of real battle. After successful sorties from both parties, General Krings is defeated and breaks the rules into the bargain. Subjective involvement gets the better of him when the question centres on the withdrawal in 1943 of German armies from positions on the eastern front. He leaps up and pours scorn on Zeitzler, former chief of the General Staff.

Starusch is delighted that Scherbaum has defeated the General, especially since his student, when asked why he studied history, replies that 'It's always been my hobby. But our history teacher, Herr Starusch. . . .' (p. 98). The teacher can feel instrumental in the humiliation of General Krings. It is significant that Linde is cast in the role of the quiz-master, the impartial, detached recorder of scores. This is the position Starusch would have liked her to occupy. In fact Linde threw herself wholeheartedly into a real-life struggle with her father and it was Starusch's attempt to intercede which jeopardised the engagement. In the quiz show, Linde—'in excellent form'—is a model of elegant restraint: in reality, she was so grimly determined to learn the truth about her father that she gives herself to Schlottau, Starusch's rival, in order to gain information. Starusch, too, is bribed to say all that he knows about the hapless General. Transposing all this into the terms of a quiz show enables Starusch to soften and adapt his memories. He takes an ironic pleasure in noting the prizes received by the contestants. Scherbaum and Vero share a steamer trip down the Rhine and a visit to Koblenz Military Archives. By way of consolation, Krings receives an edition of the *Letters of Lucilius* (a work later recommended to Scherbaum by the dentist) on Bible paper! It is worth recalling that Starusch's 'prize' for his part in the contest against Krings was the loss of his job as a pollution expert and a financial payment from Linde which helped him to become a teacher.

When Scherbaum decides to burn his dog, Max, he has thought out the decision very clearly. It is a case of 'enlightenment by demonstration'. The fact that he explains and justifies his decision to his teacher is indicative of the close relationship between them. Scherbaum is secure in his conviction that Starusch will not be able to dissuade him. His protest expresses genuine moral outrage against the Vietnam war. He loves Max. Burning the animal will be a great personal loss to him, but it is necessary because, in a city as dog-conscious as Berlin, it will have a stunning effect. Starusch is both excited and appalled by the notion. The bulldozer aspect of his thinking—revolutionary change via sensational action—responds to the notion; but the sober, circumspect, reformist is horrified. He must prevent Scherbaum at all costs. In David Caute's *The Demonstration*, Professor Bright tries to counsel a similar moderation to his student revolutionaries. They ignore him and carry out their plan to occupy the University and take over the theatre. Since argument has failed, Bright tries to make his point more theatrically. He puts the place at the disposal of hippies, drop-outs and other oddballs who, though strongly anti-University, have no coherent political views. Bright is mocking and hindering the demonstration by his action. Starusch never has to go to these lengths because Scherbaum's plan remains theoretical. But, like Bright, he does offer a stream of liberal arguments against extremist action. He taxes his student with historical analogies and illustrates his theme with colour slides. He tries to reduce the issue to metaphysical, then humanitarian, then philosophical, then literary terms. Scherbaum is proof against all this, rejecting out of hand the validity of any examples from literature. Starusch attempts compromise. Why not burn a dog other than Max, a spitz bought from the Lankwitz Kennels, say? Scherbaum remains steadfast. Like Starusch, he has a past which compels him on. His father was an air raid warden whose job it was to put out fires. He will start another fire to signal another war.

Starusch consults the dentist, whose suggestion that Starusch should offer to *buy* the alternative dog fails. The reformists are not trying to prevent the protest here only to re-direct it and remove much of its personal pain for Scherbaum. Starusch tries to get his student to sublimate his sense of moral outrage in protest poems or in songs which he can accompany with his guitar.[5] The dentist meanwhile urges him to keep Scherbaum talking—'Dialogue prevents action', but the student reaffirms his intentions. Starusch makes a futile threat of reporting him to the authorities, flirts with the idea of writing to the senator on the school commission, but the letter is never sent—"There are no statistics on unmailed letters. Cries for help that never get postmarked. There is toothache—and Arantil" (p. 149). In despair,

---

[5] c.f. Grass's poem "Powerless, with a Guitar".

Starusch asks the dentist to see the boy. The dentist first estab-
lishes a professional relationship with him. At length, the student
abandons his plan. This news is put into the mouth of the dentist
as he speaks over the telephone to Starusch, and he naturally
seems to be taking some credit for Scherbaum's change of mind.
It is a further proof of the dentist's superiority over the teacher.

The facts belie this assumption. The real turning-point in
Scherbaum's attitude takes place when he and Starusch visit the
scene of the projected burning outside Kempinski's. Theory and
practice collide and Scherbaum is a casualty of the collision. He
reacts in exactly the way that he hopes the cake-eaters would
have reacted to the burning of the dog—by being violently sick.
From this moment on, he has grave misgivings about his plan but
does not reveal them. Support for and against his proposal rises
in volume and intensity. Vero and Irmgard Seifert urge him on,
while dentist and teacher warn him to stop. Having built up the
crisis, Grass denies it a dramatic climax. Scherbaum's renunciation takes place offstage. Unwittingly, Starusch has helped to complete his student's conversion. If he sees Scherbaum as he once
was, the student suddenly sees his teacher as he might one day
become. It jolts him out of his plan because he does not want to be
"peddling the feats of a seventeen-year-old when he's forty".
Scherbaum's change of heart is more a reflection of his personality
than his political beliefs. He accepts the editorship of *Dots and
Dashes*. Local anaesthetic takes effect.

The female element in this novel is stronger than in any of
Grass's previous work, but none of the women emerges with any
real credit. Linde, Vero and Irmgard are all in the grip of an
obsession. Linde, as we have seen, is so enmeshed in her father's
past that she ruins her engagement and contracts an odd marriage
to electrician Schlottau. Vero has a wild revolutionary zeal, but
it is unsupported by any serious political thinking. She embraces
Mao because it is the current fashion and because it gives her a
spurious identity. Scherbaum's violent protest will give her a kind
of 'liberation'. It is something with which she can openly associate
and from which she will get the psychological satisfaction of
'belonging'. As a representative of the revolutionary arguments
in the novel. Vero is naïve, impulsive and ineffective. Her need to
identify is nowhere more clearly shown than in her seduction of

191

Starusch. She may believe she is helping Scherbaum but she is also aligning herself with progressiveness in sexual matters. That she is not the promiscuous creature she likes to think she is reveals itself in her reaction to the news of Starusch's engagement. An inscribed cake-spoon comes his way, hinting at betrayal. ('That's how you come by souvenirs'.) Ultimately, Vero's Maoist fervour evanesces into conventional romance. She fails to take her examinations and marries a Canadian linguist.

Irmgard Seifert is an altogether more sinister character. Her music students call her the 'archangel' because her manner of speaking "evokes the flaming sword". Yet no person in the book has less spiritual affiliation. Her sword is used viciously in the service of gratuitous and secular violence. While Vero is searching for her identity in the present, Irmgard is trying to shed her identity in the past. Letters found in the family attic—the fact that she has kept them speaks for itself—remind her of her days in the League of German Girls when she betrayed a peasant farmer to the Nazis. Although Starusch assures her that the farmer survived and that she has no call to blame herself, Irmgard insists on magnifying her guilt to dramatic proportions. Only a redemptive act of similar size can absolve her, and she finds that act in Scherbaum's plan to burn the dog. For her he is a redeemer who will bring her salvation. That the student sees the burning as an act of sin rather than redemption does not deter her. She instinctively adapts the protest to suit her own ends. Her socialist ideology is all the more dangerous because it is fired by these manic preoccupations with her own guilt. Like Matern her political stances are dictated by psychological traumas. Grass emphasizes the damage which such ex-Nazi expiators can do by putting them in influential positions. Matern's voice is one which the nation "wants to hear" on its radios: Irmgard's role as a teacher of history enables her to misguide the younger generation.

Her sexual encounters with Starusch amusingly underline his impotence and her frigidity. Scherbaum becomes the repository of her sexual as well as her political problems—"If I were younger and if as a teacher I didn't have to recognise this barrier . . . I'd love him, I'd love him passionately!—Oh, if I had his unperverted faith, how loudly and nakedly I should publish the truth" (*Local Anaesthetic*, p. 195). The 'new' Starusch, improved by dental treatment, eventually manages for the first time "to have inter-course with Irmgard Seifert in a manner that seemed relatively satisfactory to both of us" (p. 219). Compromise wins the day in the sexual as in the political context of the novel. Moderate pleasure rather than unexampled passion is suggested by Starusch's comment. His arch proposal to Irmgard and her ironic acceptance provide a genuine comic moment. Reformism becomes engaged to revolutionary expiation. The marriage will never take place, but at least the two recognise the uneasy bond between them. It is an open question which of the partners will influence the other most.

Davor omits the engagement between Starusch and Irmgard, losing both the comic and the symbolic possibilities. It also excludes the Linde episodes. A vital dimension of Starusch's insecurity is thus sacrificed and the notion of the simultaneity of time is weakened as a result. Where the novel ended on an ambiguous note of optimisim and resignation ("There will always be pain")[6], the play ends on a gesture of disillusion. Vero Lewand is disappointed by Scherbaum's failure to carry out his plan and tells Starusch that she will go back to Kempinski's to register her own protest by eating "all the most expensive things. Spoonful by spoonful". Scherbaum arrives on the scene, assuming that their political and personal friendship is unchanged—

SCHERBAUM: We're having an editorial conference. Aren't you
    coming?
VERO LEWAND: (After a pause) No.

(Davor, Scene 13)

Vero is taking her first step along the path of disenchantment here. At the end of that path—waiting in the wings—is a Canadian linguist who has visited a jeweller's.

Davor celebrates inaction. Its setting is the time-span between intention and realisation of that intention. In the first of the thirteen scenes that flow naturally into each other, Scherbaum outlines his plan; the remainder of the play is taken up with discusssion of that plan. In Heinrich Böll's hilarious novel, *The End of a Mission* (1966), a father and son stand accused of burning a jeep as a protest against militarism. The trial becomes a farcical

---

[6] "Immer neue Schmerzen". The literal translation is "Always new pain".

attempt to describe and interpret this event, and to allot responsibility for it. The culprits, Gruhl senior and Gruhl junior, com-
plicate matters by differentiating their roles. The father admits
to being a 'participant' while the son claims to be an 'artist',
creating an event, an authentic and unprecedented 'Happening'.
The artistic possibilities in the burning of Max are not ignored in
Davor, which follows Böll's novel in distorting the central event
(projected here, real in Böll) out of all recognition. Scherbaum's
scheme is praised, scorned, feared, defied, ridiculed, trivialised,
overloaded with significance and made the vehicle of other people's
psychological shortcomings. Its moral basis simply ceases to exist.
None of the five people in the debate speaks from a fixed, unequivocal point of view, and so the perspective on the burning
is shifting and kaleidoscopic. Since fluidity of this type exists,
there is no possibility of thought and action coinciding meaning-
fully. Nothing happens. Dialogue defeats drama.

In scope and approach, *Davor* differs somewhat from its prose
version. *Local Anaesthetic* predicated a new relationship between
author and reader. The works in the Danzig trilogy were warm,
sensuous, explosive; they welcomed, beguiled, shocked. While their
impetus was largely aesthetic, that of *Local Anaesthetic* is distinctly
political. To get its argument across Grass needed to induce a
different state of mind in his reader. He does this in a most
individual and daring way. Having put Starusch and, by extension,
society at large, into the dentist's chair, the author does precisely
the same to the reader. Whoever opens the novel will find himself surrounded by oppressive evidence of modern scientific and
technical advance—clipped phrases, hygienic metaphors, neat,
functional imagery, white-coated control, laundered situations,
and almost complete freedom from the element of chance. The
paragraphs are short, disconnected, unfinished. It is almost as if
Grass, like the dentist, is saying at regular intervals 'Rinse, please',
inserting the mouthwash prose in between those passages where
he is trying to remove the tartar from the readers' teeth. The
pain and irritation occasioned by discontinued themes and paragraphs is sometimes anaesthetised, but never totally absent. It
awakens the intelligence, incites to ratiocination. And the pain is
never long or intense enough to alienate the reader completely.
He is kept in his chair by the sight of Starusch's more painful

predicament and by the force of the relationship between teacher and student. Again, he feels—or is intended to feel—that, whatever its discomforts, the treatment he is undergoing is both essential and beneficial. The Novelist as Dentist. Literature as Prophylaxis. It is a bold concept but Grass brings it off by learning from his own dentist. The surgery of his novel has its own television set, which offers a continually changing series of programmes; and which, ultimately, present an entertaining allegory on its own nature. For as one astute critic has pointed out, the story of Möller's painting of the Last Judgement is "an ingenious summary of the thematic configurations" of the novel.[7]

Davor favours the poetic over the dental. Its strength lies in the quality of its evocation rather than in its technical expertise. As a non-naturalistic play, it relies on a wide range of poetic devices. Grass displays his usual assurance in juxtaposing a variety of speech levels with telling effect. Asides, soliloquies and blunt statements to the audience aid the departure of naturalism. Characters walk (or cycle) on and off the stage at will, so that all five of them are kept constantly in touch with the argument. Written for live performance in a theatre, *Davor* is closer to the condition of music. It appeals to the ear rather than to the eye. Its quintet combine harmoniously to produce infinite melodic variations on a theme called Max. The more extravagant pieces of improvisation come from Irmgard and Vero, while Starusch and Scherbaum are responsible for the poignant moments. Holding these four individualists together is the dentist who functions as musician and conductor.

If the novel gave its characters little environmental cover, the play sends them naked into the conference chamber. They are divested of their backgrounds and exposed to merciless analysis. Consequently, there is a much keener sense of interrelationships between them than there is in the novel. The women, in particular, gain in warmth and interest as a result of greater exposure. The literary associations are clarified as well. Goethe's *Tasso* is not just another example of Starusch's argument by quotation: it is a viable dramatic comparison. *Tasso*, too, presents its audience with five characters, two of whom are female, disputing the rightness of

[7] Erhard Friedrichsmeyer: 'The Dogmatism of Pain: *Local Anaesthetic*', from *A Günter Grass Symposium*, op. cit., p. 43.

a particular course of action. In Goethe, as in Grass, the argument remains unresolved. Scherbaum, like Tasso, might well cry 'Teach me to do whate'er is possible!' or even, under the strain of the opposition to his plan, 'Resign'd I yield myself and it is done'. The Senecan syndrome has an especial relevance to *Davor*, too. In novel and play, quotations from the Stoic are used as a kind of esperanto of debate. An element of parody is added in *Davor*. Seneca's own tragedies are famous for their lack of drama. Homily takes its toll. Time and again a dramatic moment is stillborn because the midwife uses precept and moralising. Grass apes this technique by using Seneca's own precepts to abort his dramatic situations in *Davor*. It is one of the ways in which he negates any real dramatic action in the play, and denies it the theatricality of *The Plebeians Rehearse the Uprising*.

Ultimately, this technique is counter-productive. *Davor* becomes static, detached, involuted. It lacks visual interest and dramatic momentum, and must be seen as an interesting experiment rather than as an assured artistic success. Starusch in *Davor* has nothing like the depth and variety of Starusch in the novel. He fails to engage the imagination in quite the same way. *Davor*, then, is the work of a poet *in* the theatre who is not yet a poet *of* the theatre. That the play has more value and resonance than many of its German critics thought was proved by a radio version of it broadcast in 1972 by the BBC.[8] Though entitled *Local Anaesthetic*, the radio version in fact followed the pattern of *Davor* fairly closely. It removed some of the more allusive passages, like the notable speech by Starusch at the end of Scene Five—"Ah, how is the gold become dim. I ought to get my junior class to write about these words from Lamentations, or perhaps just about the little words 'oh' and 'ah'." On the other hand, while following *Davor* in refusing admission to Linde, it gave the listener some insight into Starusch's past by lifting from the novel the long confession ("The boys called me Störtebeker. Yes, that was 1944") and placing it effectively near the opening of the play.

With its concentration on language, the radio medium transformed an unspectacular stage play into a brilliant listening ex-

[8] *Local Anaesthetic*, adapted and produced by Christopher Holme from Ralph Manheim's translation of the novel and from the German of *Davor*, was first broadcast on Radio 3 on Sunday, 29 October 1972.

perience. Mobility in time was achieved with ease and the musicality of the drama given point. Clever juxtaposing of characteristic sounds like the drill, the rinsing of the mouth, the bicycles, the class noise and laughter, and the ring of the telephone helped in the creation of a fascinating, multi-dimensional sound-picture. One scene which was especially successful in radio terms was the paralleling of the two lectures. Each armed with a clicking epidiascope, teacher and dentist alternated at speed on 'Death by Burning in History' and 'Caries. A Disease of Civilisation' respectively. This scene was a triumph of counterpointing. The whole production seemed to prove that *Davor* was handicapped rather than helped by its theatrical pretensions. In essence it is a superb radio play, whose auditorium is the individual human mind. It is too poetic and rarefied a creation to work at its best when fleshed out by actors on a stage. On radio its subtleties, its wit, its wordplay, its lucidity, its experimentalism and its more moving qualities were fully realised.

Whatever form it takes—novel, stage play, radio play—*Local Anaesthetic* is a repudiation of the claims made in the Princeton speech. Grass combines rather than separates the artistic with the political. This does not mean that it is a *"roman à thèse*, i.e. all artistic considerations have been subordinated to its message".[9] Nor does it mean that the work is an example of special pleading for the policies of the SPD. Scherbaum does not give way to political argument. In his change of heart, two personal relationships—with his dog, with his teacher—are decisive. Again, reformism is not presented as an infallible answer to the problems of government. The dentist's slow and systematic treatment of Starusch turns out to be a failure; the tooth has to be extracted, after all. And Starusch himself, the other representative of the case for evolution, is no model German citizen. He is a tormented figure, abnormally sensitive to pain of all kinds, self-doubting, rudderless, and vulnerable to absinthe green tights on white Berber rugs. He is human being as well as political animal, and his emotional problems are not all intellectualised. He is not simply out to influence the vote.

Local Anaesthetic is not a finer novel than *The Tin Drum* or

⁹ Irène Leonard, *Günter Grass*, 1974, p. 73.

Dog Years. They were immense undertakings carried through with an extraordinary measure of success. They sounded the depths and were, by their very nature, revaluations of the novel form. *Local Anaesthetic* is a revaluation of the role of its author. In the sense that he defines the limits of his intention and operates with complete success within those limits, it must be recognised as a technical masterpiece. Its severity of form is dictated by its artistic and political needs. Afterwards the fish was gone and the bones remained. But the bones remind us of the novel's firm structure, control of theme, and darting aesthetic movements in the cold waters of political debate.

7

From the Diary of a Snail

Doubt grows up with knowledge.

Goethe

Melancholie is an alienation of the mind troubling reason, and waxing foolish, so that one is almost beside himself. It commeth without a fever, and is chiefly engendered of melancholie occupying the mind, and changing the temperature of it.

Philip Barrough, *The Method of Phisick* (1583)

Wise emblem of our politic world
Sage snail, within thine own self curled
Instruct me softly to make haste
Whilst these my feet go slowly fast.

Richard Lovelace (1618–58), *The Snail*

From the Diary of a Snail is a celebration of the art of collecting. Stories, ideas, people, images, observations, definitions, fears, hopes, illusions, statistics, arguments, insights, memories and doubts are gathered together, arranged and re-arranged into intricate patterns. Three main collections dominate. First, there is the electioneering stamp album, which records the political and geographical movements of Grass during the 1969 Campaign. Then there is the photograph album of the Grass family. This contains a series of snapshots of his wife, Anna, and of his four children; it also contains a full-length portrait of Grass himself. Finally, there is the scrapbook history of the Danzig Jews, illustrated by cuttings from the life and times of Hermann Ott. Politics, autobiography and fiction are treated as related—often interchangeable—species. Election speeches, family conversations and cellared snails are collected with equal passion. The book is, in every sense, a collector's piece.

Appropriately, Grass's design for the book jacket collects the themes and moods of the work. A human face in close-up lies horizontal, eye dilated and mouth agape, as a large snail descends its nose. Four of the senses are alerted—sight, sound, touch, smell; the fifth, taste, is anticipated by the mouth as foretaste. There is helplessness and anxiety in the eye, the only coloured area in the vast white expanse of the face. The power of the snail is paramount. Slow, but vividly alive, it continues its progress over a human death's-head. Its patience and method outlive the more dramatic aspirations of man. Again, the snail is a symbol of the SPD ('Our campaign is going to be orange'), the party of evolutionary reformism in Germany. It is the emblem of Herman Ott, snail and collector of snails. It is a creeping threat to the undefended coastline of the face, in which the mouth of Danzig is particularly vulnerable. It is a creature of time, moving towards its own ghost on the horizon, a reminder of the simultaneity of past and present. It is a diarist who chronicles each stage of its advance with mucus. It is the unidentified slug which restores speech to the open but soundless mouth of Lisbeth Stomma.

Freudians will recognise the sexual symbolism of the snail, with its vaginal associations. The eye in the face observes and reacts to this symbolism, becoming itself an enlarged vagina from which the eye of the future generations looks out apprehensively. The mouth, too, has sexual affiliations, a foreshadowing of the relationship between Ott and Lisbeth. Other values of the book are captured in the design as well. There is the eye as moon, the target on which the man has set his sights and which he has attained, with dubious implications. There is the snail as teacher, communicating its sceptical melancholy. There is the familiar Grassian concept of beneathness—beneath water, beneath ground, beneath the snail. And there is the snail as book and as author, disturbing, yet reassuring, grotesque yet strangely human.

From the Diary of a Snail reveals an even greater politicisation of Grass's art than its predecessor did. Like the slug which Lisbeth Stomma finds in a cemetery, the book resists classification. It is not a political novel like *Local Anaesthetic*: it is a work which calls in question all the assumptions made about the dividing lines between literature and politics and autobiography. It is a re-examination of the purpose and of the possibilities of the novel. Where *Local Anaesthetic* dispensed with the artist in its title, its successor restores artist alongside political symbol; and, unlike Starusch, the diarist never allows the reader to forget that he is primarily an artist. The contents of the diary are directed at the author's children and, by extension, at the whole of the younger generation in Germany. With its opening sentences, the book states its terms of reference.

> Dear children: today they elected Gustav Heinemann president. I meant to start with Doubt, whose first name was Herman and last name Ott, but Gustav Gustav comes first. It took three ballots to elect him.
>
> *(From the Diary of a Snail, p. 3)*

The personal, the documentary and the fictional are to be the triple points of his compass, and Grass steers his course confidently by them. It is tempting to see the precedence which Heinemann is given over Doubt as a declaration of the supremacy of the political over the literary; but such a view would be foolhardy. Grass no longer accepts such distinctions. The ideal which he set out in his Princeton Speech, of compartmentalising political and creative activities, has been made redundant. *From the Diary of a Snail* eliminates all such lines of demarcation. Under the same snail shell, father, political activist, writer, voter and German live without scandal.

Though nominally autobiographical, the Danzig trilogy concealed as much about its author as it revealed. The childhood perspective enabled Grass to exploit a number of disguises, and to choose the moments to reveal himself in his own person. His voice was often heard in unison with that of Oskar Matzerath, most notably in the chapter, 'Faith, Hope, Love': but he remained well-hidden behind the guilty reminiscences of Heini Pilenz. In *Dog Years*, he made fleeting appearances as all three narrators and ran the risk of becoming his own fourth narrator when he related the parable of the rats. *Local Anaesthetic*, though forsaking the Danzig setting, gave him the opportunity to play occasional roles as teacher and dentist. Such authorial interventions tell us more about Grass's ideas and attitudes than about his background and personality. *From the Diary of a Snail* redresses the balance. It is an act of self-criticism, a portrait of the artist as a middle-aged snail. Like the tape recorder of the Boss, the book is at once a confessional and a mode of expression. Grass has something else in common with the Boss: he offers, in addition to his art, his character and his life as essential parts of his artefact. The decision to do this is a dangerous one. It is the contention of this chapter that in making this decision Grass is wholly vindicated.

The snail stands central. It is author, main character, writing method and political philosophy. It propels the story of Herman Ott and is crucial in his relationship with Anton and Lisbeth Stomma. In commending the virtues of the snail, Grass clearly has in mind the attributes of both snail and slug (the German word 'Schnecke' in the title means both). The snail suggests deliberation, self-sufficiency, protection; the slug denotes sensitivity, defenceless nakedness, the sluggish. In mythology both gasteropods were thought to possess curative powers. Both are resoundingly unspectacular in their life-styles. Grass makes the political identification early on.

> "What do you mean by the snail?"
> "The snail is progress."
> "What's progress?"
> "Being a little quicker than the snail. . . ."
>
> (*From the Diary of a Snail*, pp. 5–6)

As a political symbol, the snail is less dynamic and ostentatious than the rooster, the official emblem of the SPD. Grass urges that the snail is more realistic as a symbol because it is more ordinary, more honest. Like the tortoise of the Fabian Society, the snail stands for steady, undeviating, imperceptible progress. Unlike the tortoise, it has no pretensions to invulnerability.

The snail is Grass exuding a benevolent melancholy as it looks about for a place to rest and hide. To decide what species of snail he is, Grass goes snail-pace through alternatives open to him. Having ruled out pulmonate land snails, door snails, keeled slugs and so on, he arrives at a classification:

> I am the civilian snail, the snail made man. With my forward, inward drive, with my tendency to dwell, hesitate, and cling, with my restlessness and emotional haste, I am snail-like.

Still indeterminate, I am gradually evolving into the snail principle.

Even now I am a fit subject for speculation.

(From the Diary of a Snail, p. 63)

This passage reflects an aesthetic as well as a political judgement.
The tendency to "dwell, hesitate and cling" is a pronounced
feature of Grass's style. It gives rise to those many scenes in the
novels which are played out in slow motion, or which are deliberately delayed by the weight of copious detail. It also accounts
for the reiteration of a collection of favourite images to which
Grass has remained faithful for many snail years. In the present
work, it has a special relevance to the doubt story which, like
its creator, gradually evolves into the 'snail principle'. Artistic
means and political stance are thus mutually supportive.

Under pressure from his children to say something about himself which is not shrouded by metaphor ('What you're really like
when you're not making yourself up'), Grass provides a frank and
revealing profile of himself:

All right: about myself. It won't be much of a picture. Of all
flowers my favourite is the light-grey skepsis, which blooms all the
year round. I am not consistent. (No use trying to reduce me to
a common denominator.) My supplies: lentils tobacco paper. I own
a beautiful blank recipe pad.

In addition to telling stories and telling stories against telling
stories, I insert pauses between half-sentences, describe the gait
of various kinds of snails, do not ride a bicycle or play the piano
but hew stone (including granite), mould damp clay, work myself
into muddles (aid to developing countries, social policy), and cook
pretty well (even if you don't like my lentils). I can draw left-
or right-handed with charcoal, pen, pencil and brush. That's why
I'm capable of tenderness. . . .

But this much is certain: I used to be able to laugh a lot better.
I pass some things over in silence: my gaps. Sometimes I'm sick
of being alone and would like to crawl into something soft, warm
and damp, which it would be inadequate to characterise as feminine.
How I wear myself out looking for shelter.

(From the Diary of a Snail, p. 71)

Notwithstanding the conversational, shoulder-shrugging opening,
this passage gives a definite insight into Grass as writer and as

man. He begins by extolling scepticism, presenting it as a flower of gentle and unsensational colouring. It is a growing thing, a hardy perennial with a distinctive scent: sniff it and one smells Montaigne's dictum that "Philosophy is doubt". The emphasis on cooking, sculpture and drawing underlines the manual quality of Grass's art, that feeling he conveys of having put every word carefully in place by hand. That he reminds his children he is ambidextrous has its political implications. He shows a bias neither to the right nor to left. Extremism of both kinds is his enemy; he prefers the quieter paths of the middle way. Tenderness is conceivable in one who opts for peaceful evolution, who argues against violence. Among political extremists, aggression is the norm. Communism and fascism alike preclude the soft-hearted. The tenderness which Grass speaks of is in keeping with the snail image, which lies behind the whole passage. Flowers, lentils, stone and clay help to evoke the terrestrial and recall his earlier admission that in "thought, words and deeds I am categorically earthbound" (p. 9). He not only describes, but emulates, the gait of a snail—slow, lymphatic, close to the ground. A bicycle holds no attraction for him because it is a symbol of self-propelled progress. But slowness is not lethargy, and change does occur. In himself, Grass perceives a decreasing aptitude for laughter and a developing seriousness. The snail is often fatigued and searches for shelter and comfort. It learns that sex is a palliative and not a permanent solution. A solution does not in fact exist but it is the purpose of the snail to seek it nevertheless.

The passage under discussion is a fine example of the union of autobiography, politics and fiction into a single mode. Father, campaigner and fictional hero cannot be separated. Grass has heeded the advice which he makes Volumnia give to the Boss: he has dovetailed his sentences and left no openings for scissors. With the same words, he describes himself, his political views and Hermann Ott. There are many occasions in the book when Doubt can claim that his first name is Günter and last name Grass. Indeed, the function of the nickname, Doubt, apart from reducing the burden of the argument to one word, is to provide accommodation for the author at any given moment. Grass's doubt frequently informs that of Hermann Ott. In the case of the self-portrait, it is Ott who becomes Grass. He, too, cultivates the flower of scepticism and is inconsistent. He, too, tells stories and counter-stories, observes the locomotion of snails and is capable of tenderness. Like Grass he seeks refuge in the snail's mirror-image, the vagina, and finds its comfort transient. Like Grass he succumbs to a kind of enlightened melancholy. Like Grass he spurns the bicycle which he had hitherto loved, descends to a cellar beneath the bicycle shop (stasis beneath progress), and behaves like a snail hibernating below ground till milder political weather comes.

The fluctuating relationship between Grass and Doubt is handled adroitly, unpredictably and persuasively, and controls the narrative approach. When recalling political meetings or personalities, Grass often indulges in special pleading for the SPD. At such times Doubt is used to challenge, re-define or distance these lapses into partisanship. The fictional character with the factual basis (Doubt has his real counterpart in the critic, Marcel Reich-Ranicki) ensures that the factual character is subject to fictional checks and balances. That Grass sometimes doubles as Doubt deepens and broadens the perspective even more. The relationship allows a whole gallery of confrontations, insinuations, juxtapositions, parallelisms, and contradictions. It links the past with the present, the fate of the Jews under Hitler with the fate of the Germans under Heinemann. By softening political assertion with doubt, it helps to join propaganda with art and to dissolve the dividing line between them.

As a teacher, Doubt differs considerably from Starusch. Where the latter was confused, guilt-ridden and mediocre, Doubt is clear-headed, free from remorse and an example to his profession. He teaches at a Jewish School in pre-war Danzig, though he is not Jewish himself. Ironically, his subjects are German and Biology; his pupils later become the victims of Nazi theories of genetics. If Starusch is a teacher by default, then Doubt is one by choice. He applies for the job at the Rosenbaum School, conscious of the dangers of associating with Jews. Though he announces that "all religious usages are intensely alien to me", his very position at the school has made him intensely alien to the German authorities. He loses his post as assistant secretary of the Schopenhauer Society because, a letter informs him, "immediate contact with the Jews is incompatible with the values of pure-bred German philosophy"

(p. 37). Beatings, injustices and the flight of many of his pupils do not force him to resign. He remains, true to his vocation, in front of a dwindling class. Doubt is an unlikely candidate for the teaching staff at the Rosenbaum School and it is this very unsuitability which compels Grass to appoint him, introduce him to the school, and justify his presence there. To convince the reader of Doubt's fitness for his teaching post, Grass has to answer many questions about his character, has to still the doubt in his audience. As a result, Doubt "turns out to be more versatile than I had originally planned". Aesthetic needs promote the first signs of independent growth in the character. Since Doubt is only of value to the Danzig story if he teaches in a Jewish School, then he must be allowed to act and develop in a way that makes such a situation credible. This is only one of many examples of Grass's equivocal relationship with his protagonist.

To explain is to equip with a history. Doubt is shown as a youthful collector of snails in his native Müggenhahl, cycling off enthusiastically in search of specimens. Instinctively siding with the underdog, he has a sympathy for slugs and snails because they face periodic persecutions at the hands of Müggenhahl schoolchildren. The same instinct leads him later on to side with the Jews. When he becomes a student in Berlin, he stops collecting snails. He takes up the hobby when he is teaching at the Rosenbaum School, when in fact, he is once more in the presence of those who face "destruction like common field slugs". At university it is philosophy which absorbs him.

> The little word "why" became for Herman Ott the specimen box in which he collected everything that set itself up to be a datum or valid hypothesis or, once proved, had gone into retirement, preparatory to mounting each item on a pin and subjecting it to the acid test of doubt. *(From the Diary of a Snail, p. 45)*

Grass doubles as Doubt here, encapsulating, in a sentence characteristic of Hermann Ott, the essence of his book. Observation before knowledge. Questions before answers. The snail before the horse. Schopenhauer before Hegel. The younger generation calls for elucidation:

> "Who's Hegel?"
> "Somebody who sentenced mankind to history."

"Did he know a lot? Did he know everything"?
"Thanks to his subtlety, every abuse of state power has to this day been explained as historically necessary."

(From the Diary of a Snail, p. 46)

The enemy has been identified, and the problem with which all Grass's prose work has wrestled is taken on again: how does one tell the truth about history? If Hegelians urge that change is a natural part of the cycle of history, and that all must bow to the necessity of that change, how can one focus attention on an attempt at genocide? In a court which believes that such crimes were the inevitable concomitant of the laws of change, how can one even gain a fair hearing?

The Danzig trilogy grappled with this problem by employing protest, parable and satire. *Local Anaesthetic* tried dispassionate analysis and made its narrator a teacher of history. *From the Diary of a Snail* modifies these approaches. It fuses past and present. It binds the descent of Doubt into the cellar with the ascent of Heinemann to the presidency of the Federal Republic. It combines two kinds of political change—a pogrom and an election—into a single unit. The exemplary story of Hermann Ott becomes an allegory which is at once fictional and real, a tiny segment of a nation's history and a continuing event with daily relevance. The symbiosis between Grass and Doubt is one means to this end. The other is the additional and authentic perspective given on the Danzig Jews by Ruth Rosenbaum, whom Grass met —"Today, in Haifa, she gives private lessons (English and French) and would prefer not to be mentioned". Doubt, on the other hand, insists on being mentioned. While Grass calls on him in his cellar, he returns the visits by interrupting his author's election campaign. They discuss all kinds of issues. ("We avoided the present, and it punished us with ignorance of the past".) This ability to summon up Doubt at will as his *alter ego* strengthens the role of Ott. Inside and apart from his author, he helps to prevent the snail being trampled beneath the hooves of the horse.

The story of Hermann Ott signals the rebirth of Grass the story-teller. He controls, paces and unfolds the tale with admirable skill. He makes it a part of his recommendation of the snail principle, teasing his readers with snippets and ancedotes, then warning them to be patient ('I mean to speak to you by (round-about) by-paths'). Patience brings its reward by the middle of the second chapter:

> Only now, children, can Doubt come to the surface, predominate, take on body, cloud the atmosphere, pour vinegar on hope, behave bravely and amusingly, be outlawed—only now, in short, is it finally permissible to speak of Hermann Ott.
>
> *(From the Diary of a Snail, pp. 18–19)*

Grass is committing himself to the Doubt story here, and discussing and illustrating the mechanics of narration. When he has sketched in Doubt's background, and explained the origin of his nickname in the Jewish transit camp on Troyl, he makes a brief but significant reference to *The Tin Drum* and *Dog Years*. He mentions Doubt's grandmother who had four husbands to match the four skirts of Anna Bronski. At the very moment when an eccentric and individual character is about to grow, Grass halts the process—"I've already written too much about active grandmothers". There is no room in the Doubt story for rich and varied characterisation of his first two novels: cellars are confined areas. Nor is Doubt himself described in any detail. He is a "man who inflicts pain only in shaking hands", but he lacks precise shape and temperament and bearing. Grass warns his readers not to try to conjure up a mental picture of Doubt. He should be imagined in terms of his qualities rather than his appearance. For Doubt is an attribute as well as a person. To resist the temptation to flesh him out is to enable Doubt to become what he often becomes for Grass—a state of mind.

Understatement disposes of Doubt's sex life. Engaged to the daughter of a crane operator at the Schichau shipyard, Doubt comes up against the fact that his prospective father-in-law is an organiser for the National Socialist German Labour Front; and "this engagement went out of existence when Doubt started teaching at the Rosenbaum School". His subsequent engagement to Erna Dobslaff, librarian, is another casualty of his compassion for the Jews. As the boycott of the Danzig Jews intensifies and becomes "increasingly official", Doubt has corresponding difficulties to face. He makes no complaint, and would endorse his author's euphemistic description—"Doubt seems to have had his troubles at this time". On 9 November 1938, Danzig suffers its version of 'Kristallnacht'. Doubt immortalises the event in his waste book with typical brevity and pungency—"The Reich Kristallnacht is a specious metaphor". The exodus begins. Doubt goes to see off some friends and pupils who are departing by bus, then sealed train, then ship. Doubt's own application for emigration has already been rejected without explanation. The Danzig 500 set out for an uncertain destination. The horrors and privations suffered on their journey are later retailed to Doubt in a letter from one of his former pupils, Simon Kurzmann. Emigration is not escape.

Doubt has no illusions about the ferocity of anti-Semitism or the direction which it is to take. It was brought home to him at a bus stop, when a "lovable little grandma" pulls out a hatpin and stabs the lettuce which Doubt has bought from Isaak Laban, friend and vegetable dealer.

> "Shame!" she shouted, and wiped her hatpin on her sleeve. When he got home, Doubt didn't mention the incident to his snails.
>
> (*From the Diary of a Snail*, p. 84)

Police interrogation, warnings and beatings convince Doubt that he must seek refuge. He first repatriates his snails, choosing the most ideal habitat. This act is an ironic comment on the German "repatriation" of the emigrant Jews. Doubt's emigration is like that of Oskar and Bebra and Eddi Amsel. It is an inner exile and moves him to the cellar below the home of Anton and Lisbeth Stomma. In his wake Doubt leaves grim statistics of the murder, persecution and flight of the Danzig Jews. When the turning-point comes and Doubt himself needs shelter, Grass deliberately freezes the moment of crisis and introduces details of current political personalities—"Before Doubt goes down the cellar and starts to get used to it, I catch up on my entries" (p. 127). The private tragedy is of a piece with the public event.

Anton Stomma is a wise choice for someone who wishes to hide. He has neither friends nor visitors, radio nor dog. He is a solitary man who "cursed himself in an undertone". He speaks bluntly but to the point: "There's nobody else here but Lisbeth; that's my daughter. She's not quite right in the head. I'll tell her to keep her mouth shut." A cellar at the north-east edge of Karthaus.

Doubt, Anton Stomma, Lisbeth Stomma. Setting and characters have been established. It is through the behaviour of this trio that the rise and fall of National Socialist military ambitions is viewed. It provides a deliberately unflattering perspective on what many saw as the great achievements of National Socialism. The snail in Grass and in Doubt alike dictates the place of refuge. Carnage and injustice are best watched from below ground. The death of six million Jews can be effectively described through the inter-relationships of three non-Jews.

At the beginning Doubt's stay with the Stomma family is put on a financial basis. He is a paying guest rather than a desperate refugee. He gives Stomma three marks a day "until November 1942, shortly before Stalingrad, when he ran out of money" p. 132). Grass here resorts to his familiar device of dismissing a major happening of the war in a casual aside. The first serious resistance to German advance on the Eastern Front is no more than a convenient marker of the time when Doubt entered a period of poverty. Goodwill keeps him in his cellar. He has already taught Stomma to write in order to fill in an application form for Germanisation. And he is fully aware of the paradox involved in his helping a man to become an ethnic German, at one with the very people who are persecuting him. The patience of a snail is required to help the brutish and uneducated Stomma form his letters. The teacher–pupil relationship fosters goodwill, and Doubt appreciates this. His teaching is selective. Stomma does not learn to read. Doubt reserves for himself the task of reading out the *Danziger Vorposten* to his host. It gives him a function in the household, buys him more time. There is, however, no danger of Stomma evicting his guest. Boasting about his freedom of action ('I do what I want'), Stomma walks into a demonstration of Doubt's fondness for philosophical disputation. Doubt confronts his host with the alternatives from which he can choose, pointing out that he will be the prisoner of the action that is not performed, of the decision which is not taken. The bewildered Stomma is lost in the vacuum between thought and action. He satisfies himself with ignoring Doubt's claims to being a non-Jew. If he is to harbour a refugee, that person must conform—"he wanted a Jew in his cellar".

The relationship with Stomma affords Doubt some intellectual amusement, but it is the relationship with Lisbeth Stomma which strikes deeper chords in him. She is the product of her past, another victim of history. At nineteen she had an affair with an employee of the Polish Railways, and a child resulted. The father paid towards its upkeep regularly but rarely saw the child and made no mention of marriage. On the fourth day of the war, the father was killed in battle. On the first day, his son, aged three, was run over by a military vehicle whose horses had bolted. Lisbeth Stomma loses son and lover to the antediluvian Polish army. The experience makes her dull-witted, taciturn, introspective. She is oppressed by melancholy and finds comfort only in visiting cemeteries. Like Leo Schugger in *The Tin Drum*, the cemetery is her natural element; unlike Leo, Lisbeth is no symbol of death, no scatterer of condolences. Cemeteries relieve the burden of her melancholy and send her home, cheerful. Asked to describe cemeteries, she supplies the word 'pleasant', and later, 'cosy'. Doubt intercedes on her behalf with Stomma who tries to stop his daughter's visits with a stick. Doubt argues in practical terms:

> "Where else can the poor thing go? You and I are too this-worldly to take the place of graves and ivy in her mind."
>
> Stomma respected Doubt's advice, because he looked on Doubt as a Jew and the Jews are shrewd.

(*From the Diary of a Snail*, p. 135)

Having taught his host to write, Doubt starts to read him Aesop's Fables. He later experiments with his own fables. He talks about the "snail, the weasel, the lark that towered over the snail, and the swift horse, who, whenever he won a race, wished he were a snail" (p. 150). Lisbeth listens to these fables but it is impossible to know how much of them she heard. Doubt's inventions are a microcosm of Grass's book, which is a superbly convoluted essay in the tradition of the animal fable. Doubt's snail, weasel, lark and horse are as easy to identify as Aristophanes' Frogs or Čapek's Insects or George Orwell's Farm Animals. Stomma copies out the fables laboriously into a school exercise book but he is unable to read them. He can write down but he cannot understand. He hears but without comprehension.

When Doubt reads the newspapers to Stomma and his daughter, he subtly edits them, moderating any German successes and highlighting any advances made by the Allies. The political situation is reflected in his own. When, after Stalingrad, the tide of the war seems to turn against the Germans, Doubt's own position improves. Before Stalingrad, he was at his lowest point. Now his food improves, his host's manner towards him improves, and the comforts which he is offered take on a new and unexpected dimension—"and from February on, he regularly sent his daughter Lisbeth to the cellar to lie down on Doubt's mattress and to take him in" (p. 186). For Lisbeth the love-making is a duty ('Father wants me to'): for Doubt it is, at first, a pleasurable habit. He soon learns that Lisbeth's visits frustrate as much as they satisfy.

Liszeth Stomma submits to his passion but is unable to respond to it. Torpid, unaroused, disengaged, she lies beneath her lover with her mind in the cemetery. Her body becomes a grave in which Doubt buries his urges, his tenderness, his love. Nothing he can do brings about the shared happiness he longs for: like Herbert Truczinski he struggles to awaken love and sensuality in a wooden Niobe and is injured by the power of silence. Grass heightens the prose to accentuate Lisbeth's problem. He incorporates a reference to Dürer's *Melencolia I*, the engraving which was partly an inspiration for his book.

A petrified carp's mouth
Word balloons from the past and blocks of basalt are piled high
Hieroglyphics hewn in lava
Words begotten in Capricorn.
With clammy fingers she holds the compass and cannot
Close the circle.
No cry consents to rise, to be long and sustained.

(*From the Diary of a Snail*, p. 188)

Lisbeth is not the prototype of the frigid woman. She is representative of the feminine response to war. It has deprived her of the little love she has known and left her stunned and insensible. "The widespread case of Lisbeth Stomma" is a judgement on the past. She is the symbol of the wastage of war, a wasted woman, a creature, who will go through the motions of family life and of the intimacies of the bed, but who will do so joylessly, pointlessly.

Doubt cannot come to terms with his failure to arouse Lisbeth. He feels impotent at the very moment when he is publishing his potency. His failure is mental rather than sexual, however. Love-making is the one aspect of his life where his sceptical philosophy deserts him. He wants to give himself too completely, too un-critically. There is an element of total abandon in his passion— "he had more to get rid of than juice". Hermann Ott, the master of Doubt, becomes its slave in sexual matters. It leads to dejection and sluggishness. It prompts a search for a 'cure' for Lisbeth. Diagnosing her condition as melancholy, seated in black bile, Doubt prescribes a potion which engenders diarrhoea in the girl. The blackness of her faeces confirms Doubt in the belief that he has driven melancholy out of her by medical means. Stomma, a sufferer from gout, is so impressed that he insists on a purgative, too. Doubt joins father and daughter in "hellebore parties", which are very cheerful occasions, notwithstanding the "strenuous violence of their evacuations" as they take turns in the outhouse. Grass combines the comic with the tragic here. Misguided science, brute simplicity and unprotesting womanhood are joined in the persons of Doubt, Stomma and Lisbeth. They suffer pain and humiliation in pursuit of a spurious remedy. The laxative pro-duces more than the obvious results. Lisbeth is provoked into prattling and Doubt into theatrical presentation. As a result of one of the hellebore sessions, he inaugurates his cellar theatre.

Oskar's art was at its height in the Onion Cellar and Eddi Amsel's talents flourished best underground. Doubt tries to emulate them as subterranean creators, attempting to reach Lisbeth's emotions by aesthetic means, if not by sexual and medical. The cold which the German soldiers are suffering at Stalingrad is duplicated by the cold of the cellar, where another theatre of war is in operation. Doubt performs simplified versions of the great classics. He parodies the German war effort by his rendering of Kleist's *The Prince of Homburg*, the great Romantic tragedy in which the agony of decision over his own life is placed in the hands of the Prince. Having isolated key moments of the plot and explained Doubt's treatment of them, Grass punctures the high-flown sentiment with the observation that the old hats used by Doubt belonged to Stomma and his late wife. The choice of the drama presented is always considered. Hauptmann's *Rose Bernd* follows, a working-class drama which shows a poor girl seduced, then abandoned, by a rich villain. Its moving portrayal of the fate of unwed motherhood connects with Lisbeth's own experience. She groans in dismay when Rose strangles her child at the end of the play. The last line of Hauptmann's work—"This girl . . . what she must have suffered"—is an appropriate epitaph on Lisbeth Stomma, too.

Art not only awakens Lisbeth, it brings out the best in Doubt and inspires noble responses in Stomma. Doubt inserts political jokes ('A committed theatre') and Stomma rises to the sight of the freedom-fighter in Goethe's *Egmont*. Stomma's cry of "Freedom to all Kashubians" comes oddly from the lips of one who took such pains to become an ethnic German. Again, his excitement is ironic in view of the fact that Doubt has given the heroine of the piece, Klärchen, features which he has borrowed from Lisbeth Stomma. Alarmed by the noise and vigour of Stomma's revolutionary fervour, and fearing that it might attract attention, Doubt tries to calm his host down. He tries to discredit the fictional Egmont by pointing out that he is very different from the factual Egmont. In indicating that Egmont was, in reality, a debtor with eleven children, Doubt is using the same argument against the play which was contained in Schiller's critique of it; namely, that it departs too completely from historical truth (Schiller's own *Mary Stuart* is also part of the repertoire of the theatre in the cellar.) Doubt succeeds in deflating the heroism of Egmont, but has to suffer the consequences. Deprived of his inspiration and his chance to liberate Kashubia, Stomma beats Doubt with his leather belt. Such is the fate of the artist whose work does not excite the wilder political dreams of his audience: the corrective of fact is not welcome when it complicates a surging emotional response.

Art reaches but does not resurrect, Lisbeth Stomma. She remains "cryless, alien and dry". It is only when Doubt begins to collect snails again that the 'cure' becomes possible. Stomma and Lisbeth assist the collector in various ways, and then the latter brings home one day a slug which she has found in the cemetery. Doubt does not know its name and certainly does not guess at its powers. For him the new slug is a challenge to his scientific method— it stimulates his doubt. For Stomma it is just another potential competitor in the snail races which are held, and into which he enters with spirit. But for Lisbeth the slug represents a new life.

214

When Doubt puts it on her forearm, and hand and knee, the effect is instantaneous. She begins to stammer, then grunt, then form intelligible words. The miracle slug has restored her speech. It enables her to speak of her son, to confront her past and face up the source of her anguish. The slug sucks the melancholy out of her, darkening itself in the process but leaving Lisbeth increasingly more 'normal'. Having spent her time collecting cemeteries, she now switches to "collecting proofs of being alive". She is transformed into a sexual dynamo, demanding, inventive, insatiable. In love-making it is she who is the initiator, the comforter, the 'man'. Doubt is able to forsake all doubt as they lie together on his mattress. But there is a problem. The more normal Lisbeth becomes, the more she is revolted by snails. Doubt notes in his copybook: "The beauty of snails cannot overtake disgust with snails. Normalcy wins out and remains stupid."

In acquiring tenderness and love, Lisbeth also acquires callousness and hate. With her new laughter comes a new perversity. On the first Sunday of Advent, Lisbeth, whose growth to full normality is marked by the latest hairstyle, can stand the slug no more. She tramples on the miracle slug:

> It burst from the breathing aperture to the end of the keel. It burst with a full-bodied report. On the inside, too, it was black. Inky-black and odourless it drained.

> (*From the Diary of a Snail*, p. 264)

Grass points up the religious parallels—"Nail the slug to the cross". Lisbeth has killed her Redeemer. The snail as Messiah. Once again the fictional overlaps with the political and autobiographical. Lisbeth's private act becomes a nation's public act and, in turn, relates to Grass's own situation. For the slug is writer too, signing its own death warrant in black ink. The artist who tries to suck the black bile out of society in order that society may live more wholly, tempts the fate of the slug. To purge evil and darkness, he must imbibe them. It is easy to mistake him as a devil rather than a saviour. That Grass intends a personal reference here is made clear by the fact that the subsequent paragraphs, which switch back to the election campaign, focus on threats of violence to him and his family—"The bullet's ready".

215

The war ends, Doubt and Lisbeth marry, she becomes more and more cantankerous. Doubt now haunts cemeteries in search of the miracle slug but is himself overcome by melancholy. At length he is committed to an asylum. This does not represent the failure of Doubt: it reflects the weakness of Hermann Ott in abandoning his doubt in the crucial area of love. He believed that a cure was possible for Lisbeth, that a snail existed which could provide the panacea. The message of the book is that no such panacea is possible. Nothing can transform Lisbeth Stomma from *Melencolia I* into a version of her sister-figure, Utopia. The snail can alleviate but not remove melancholy. The two must be seen as mutually helpful things, not as diametrical opposites. Snail and melancholy form a positive alliance. Doubt tried to make the one drive out the other, and takes in reverse, the path which Lisbeth Stomma follows. At a surface level, she has made a gain, having replaced both son and lover. For Doubt, there is only loss. And the greatest loss of all is his surrender of his doubt.

Grass and Hermann Ott duplicate each other in a variety of roles—as collectors, tabulators, educators, diarists, snails, artists, political commentators, storytellers, supporters of the underdog, melancholiacs. Where Ott cannot follow his creator is in the matter of reputation. Grass is handicapped by Fame. The burden of Fame is as central a theme in the book as it is in *The Plebeians Rehearse the Uprising*. In that play, the Boss is destroyed by his fame: workers and state alike need the rubber stamp of his name. Grass faces similar difficulties. Like the Boss, he is an artist whose critical reputation has gained him an audience for his political views. Where the Boss prevaricates, Grass is perfectly ready to state his position in unequivocal terms. But it is the artist's fame rather than the political activist's reason which communicates itself to the bulk of his listeners. Throughout *From the Diary of a Snail*, Grass signs copies of his novels during political meetings. An artist's autograph has some value: political figures only sign letters of protest. Grass speaks movingly and revealingly about the fame which has dogged him since the publication of *The Tin Drum*:

> Since then, Fame has been with us as a roomer. He's always standing around, he's a nuisance, hard to get away from. Especially Anna hates him, because he runs after her, making obscene propositions.

Inflated and deflated by turns. Visitors who think they've come to see me look around for him. It's only because he's so lazy and so useless when he besieges my writing desk, that I've taken him with me into politics and put him to work as a receptionist: he's good at that. Everybody takes him seriously, even my opponents and enemies.

(*From the Diary of a Snail*, p. 75)

Coming as it does after Grass's fairly explicit and realistic self-appraisal, this passage emphasises that he has no illusions about his fame. Since he can never separate man from legend, he makes the legend earn its keep, winning for his political speeches the kind of attention which he would not otherwise get. Again, this extract touches on the allied theme of the relation between reality and imagination, between the thing as it really is and the way in which others perceive it.

In the Plebeians Rehearse the Uprising, Volumnia tries to close this gap between action and interpretation of that action when she urges the Boss to speak out. She wants man and legend to cohere, event and reading of that event to bear a marked resemblance to each other. Grass, too, strives to reconcile his private with his public self, reality with fame. This is why he maintains such a direct link between the familial and the political, presenting the story of his election tour in terms of a lecture with lantern slides for his children. Although he offers eulogies of certain political personalities (Willy Brandt, Wehner, Ehmke, Leo Bauer), he does not glamourise the context in which they operate. The faults and follies of parliamentary democracy are clearly spelled out, and Grass makes no attempt to hide the boredom and repetition and futility of much of his campaigning. Another way in which he modifies the image of himself as a famous artist is in his discussion of the case of Manfred Augst. That Grass chooses to relate the Augst story in real terms rather than fictional ones is itself an indication of his desire that the story should speak directly about himself and his own shortcomings.

Augst was a pharmacist who attended one of Grass's meetings, interrupted it with a protest, and then committed suicide by swallowing poison. The incident preys on Grass's mind. After a "protracted attempt to dispose of him in a footnote", he writes to Augst's widow. She agrees to see him to talk about her hus-

217

band. The storyteller becomes listener. Like Grass, Augst had three sons and lived in a family house. Each of the sons has a different view of the father, supplementing or contradicting the view taken by Frau Augst. Grass is impressed by their candour:

> None tried to whitewash or embellish. No game of father construction, no family court of justice at the living room table. Each son let the next keep his (admittedly) distorted picture. All were agreed that they hadn't known him, that he had been a (strange) stranger in their midst. . . .
> *(From the Diary of a Snail, p. 212)*

With painful slowness, Grass pieces together his own picture of Augst, hoping to understand him as husband, father and political idealist by sifting each detail of his personal history. Augst emerges as a grim, haunted, embittered creature. Produced by the war generation, Augst was brought up by a grandmother who wanted to make him take piano lessons. But Augst's vision is political rather than musical. In his relentlessness, single-mindedness and inability to compromise he is oddly reminiscent of Walter Matern. Like Matern, he seems to have had a love-hate fixation on the figure of Hitler. Like Matern, he is a "seeker, driven by hunger". Like Matern, he resorts to poison from political motives. So obsessed is Augst with the urge to speak out in public, that he takes elocution lessons and joins five or six organisations—"Every discussion gave Augst a small advance towards the community he was looking for . . . To stand shoulder to shoulder, to belong, to have the right to pledge allegiance" (p. 214). Though given to violent gestures and speech, Augst's only act of aggression was against himself, at the last.

Grass underlines the affiliations between Doubt and Augst in Chapter 24, alternating snippets of discussion at the Augst home with details of the snail races in the Doubt cellar. Doubt and Augst are victims of melancholy, men who do not learn to season it with doubt. Doubt's belief in a cure for melancholy and Augst's belief in a political utopia are one and the same thing: quests which are doomed to increase the very condition which the questors hope to shed. Grass is restating the argument of *Local Anaesthetic* in new terms. Pain cannot be abolished by one great act of violence: melancholy cannot be conquered by a vision of utopia. Pain and melancholy are permanent conditions which can be turned into positive values with the aid of local anaesthetic. For the pain of melancholy, doubt is the local anaesthetic. Together they produce a state of mind which is critical, realistic, but in no way depressed. Melancholy can become an affirmative condition. To prove his point, Grass closes the lecture with a portrait of Leo Bauer, the sad but inspiring character who was Brandt's chief speechwriter in the SPD.

> He, too, is not isolated case. A biography among thousands. Abjuring faith, Leo Bauer has become a Social Democrat. The distrust of his new colleagues, the hatred of those he has lost, and the baseness of his political enemies have put their mark on him. You would expect him to give up, to drop out. But a will such as only men who have many times been broken and given up for dead, men whose consciousness of guilt springs from their own inner resources, enables him, if not to go on living in the fullest sense of the word, at least to be active. . . .
>
> (*From the Diary of a Snail*, p. 309)

Leo Bauer is offered here as a model snail, a prototype of the positive melancholiac. Grass sees him as a man in whom darkness and disenchantment have taken up permanent lodging, but who has written a safety clause of scepticism into the terms of the lease. Bauer, who died in 1973, belonged to the brotherhood which included Willy Brandt, Hermann Ott and Günter Grass among its numbers. He was another "man of the tribe of Doubt". Life and death sat upon him with equal weight: he was by turns flesh and stone, eager involvement and total disengagement. Intense personal suffering and a lifetime on the treadmill of political disillusion had acted as the preconditions of his melancholy. Most men in his position would have given up and succumbed to depression and recrimination. He remained active and useful to the end, striving to take that small and tentative step forward, questioning it when it was taken, feeding on doubt. Such was the completeness of his melancholy that success had no power to delude him and disappointment had no strength to hurt him. Affliction had placed him at once beyond further affliction, yet hopelessly susceptible to it. Leo Bauer was the perfect example of the man to whom Grass refers in the concluding paragraph of his book:

Only those who know and respect stasis in progress, who have once and more than once given up, who have sat on an empty snail shell and experienced the dark side of utopia, can evaluate progress.

(From the Diary of a Snail, p. 310)

The resignation of Willy Brandt from the Chancellorship in 1974 added a strange poignancy to Grass's portrait of his friend. The death of Leo Bauer in 1973 made the author's tribute to him almost unbearably moving. There could be no more fitting epilogue to the book.

Like *The Plebeians Rehearse the Uprising*, Grass's fourth major prose work has its origins in a lecture. He was invited in, 1969, to contribute a lecture as part of the celebrations marking the Dürer year 1971. He chose as his subject the engraving *Melencolia I*, "done in 1514". As he campaigned around Germany, he kept looking for material for the lecture. Entitled "On Stasis is Progress", the lecture became the final chapter of *From the Diary of a Snail*. It clarifies the book, extends its scope, reinforces its message. In its discussion of Dürer's engraving the work provides itself with a visual correlative in much the same way that *Local Anaesthetic* employs Möller's painting, 'Last Judgement'. Both novels benefit from his relationship with an established artistic masterpiece. Dürer's engraving anticipates Grass's book in the subtlety of its collecting. The female figure of Melancholy, plump, Teutonic, grave, sits and broods in the company of the very things which symbolise human endeavour and hope. The mood of deep spiritual unease, of angst, of inertia is captured memorably. *Melencolia I* is a classic version of stasis in progress, of the angel whose feet are on the territory of the snail. The emblems of art, science, craft and the new learning lie about her unused and therefore useless. The plane, the hammer and nails, the inkwell, the knife, the geometrical compass and so on are mere objects without the exercise of human will and spirit. The illumined hands which hold the compass are inactive: the head, which could initiate decisions, is in shadow. The ladder stays unascended. The scales remain balanced by neglect. Time passes endlessly in the enlarged hour-glass. The beckoning sun arouses no response.

The mood of helplessness, of the creative spirit choked by its own inner agony, is the more effective for being expressed in such harmonious form. Symmetry frames anguish. Technical perfection connives at its own malaise. Dürer has supplied Grass with many of the elements for *From the Diary of a Snail*. Stylistically, he gives the author the same technical dexterity which his engraving possesses, the same passion for precision, the same love of detail, the same sureness in factual definition. Where Grass's art becomes more sophisticated is in its use of image and metaphor, in its counterpointing of the factual with the imagined or suggested. Like the figure of Melancholy, Grass and his real or fictional characters belong on the ground. They have no wings of faith or mistaken idealism to help them soar into utopia. When, like Augst and Ott, they believe that heaven lies at the top of the ladder if only they will climb it, their fall is sudden and tragic. The positive melancholiac must be like the dog in the engraving, bred for speed but favouring stillness. The emblems of human achievement must be seen for what they are in the true perspective of their enforced idleness. A book that is shut with a clasp can communicate no learning unless Melancholy opens it. Literature is futile when there is no will to read.

Grass follows Dürer, too, in the prominence he gives to time. His treatment of time has been one of his most distinctive idiosyncrasies in all his prose works. Here, too, time is a central preoccupation. Its more sinister attributes are taken up in a passage which goes to the very core of his argument:

> It's time that makes terror habitual: time is what we must write against.
>
> An old trick. Before their crime, criminals figure out how long it will take for their crime to be forgotten, to be overlaid by the crimes of other criminals, reduced to marginal history . . . time, the passage of time, benefits the criminals; for the victims time does not pass,
>
> (*From the Diary of a Snail*, p. 139)

In ten meagre months, time faded the memories of tyranny and thwarted hope which were contained in the names 'Svoboda' and 'Dubček', and which Grass saw being eroded away on walls in Czechoslovakia. Time bestows its blessing on the criminal: in 1966, an ex-Nazi, Kurt Georg Kiesinger, became Chancellor of the Federal Republic. Time turns its back on the victim: Ruth Rosenbaum still lives in Haifa with her painful recollections of the inhuman treatment of the Danzig Jews. *From the Diary of a Snail* sweeps the sands of time energetically away from the crimes it is drifting over and covering. Grass freshens up the slogans, increases the volume of the accusations, points the finger with more embarrassing directness.

Like Dürer, then, Grass is challenging the myth of human perfectibility. For the Nuremberg artist, the Renaissance held no sure guarantee of a limitless progress. For the Danzig writer, modern man is equally unimpressive as an infallible guide to utopia. Grass pours scorn on the Utopianism of America, where happiness has become a consumer product, as much a mass-produced artifice as the guilt and atonement on sale in the Onion Cellar. He berates the Communist countries for including utopia as the aim of their political programmes. He criticises West Germany where the equally pernicious myths of "youth and productivity" spur on a nation towards a heaven where doubt, compassion, self-appraisal and, above all, melancholy, are unknown. For, as Grass points out, melancholy is the reverse side of the coin of utopia. To trust in the latter presumes the former. One cannot legislate melancholy out of existence without sabotaging utopia as well. And since melancholy precludes utopia, it is best to approach it in an affirmative way. Informed scepticism is the only realistic attitude to take. It is with the snails that the possibility of progress—dishearteningly slow progress at that—really lies. Grass has spoken out for melancholy.

In view of his subject-matter and his avowed aims, Grass might be expected to attract the same adjectives which greeted Dürer when his engraving was circulated. People talked of the sick artist, the diseased, depressed and depressing Dürer. *Melencolia I* illustrated a malady which all recognised but which all strove to avoid. Grass's illustration is animated. For a companion of the snail, it has tremendous power and zest and effectiveness. His Anatomy of Melancholy has lifted rather than dampened Grass's spirits. The book is full of anxiety and self-doubt and even humility; but it is always red-blooded and alive, always deliberate and totally realised. The style is the man and the man is commending melancholy. It is no philosophy of despair. It is a firmly-based, logically-argued, intelligent attitude of mind. That it can give rise to a book as trenchant, energetic, and aesthetically satisfying as *From the Diary of a Snail* is dramatic proof of its worth. Melancholy, as evinced by Grass, is its own best propaganda. Lamartine once described utopias as "often only premature truth". Grass exposes them as always only premature delusions. In doing so he plays the roles of father, political activist and famous writer without incongruity. Far from confirming that Grass the artist has become more politicised because he lacks faith in 'pure' art, *From the Diary of a Snail* is his greatest act of faith in the writer. It enlarges his responsibilities, assumes a wider hearing. Grass goes beyond the irresponsible satire of a dwarf, beyond the venomous parody contained in his scarecrows, beyond the political solutions expressed in dental metaphors. He takes it upon himself to endorse a state of mind. He instructs his countrymen in a view of time which they must take. He elects himself as the vital link between the different generations. To trumpet his belief in the increased responsibilities of the artist, he puts himself at the heart of his book as both factual and fictional protagonist. The resulting work is quite unique, an amalgam of opposites which might seem to vitiate each other but which Grass synthesises with unerring skill and assurance.

The tin drummer has come a long way. He began by revelling in his freedom and individuality and artistic power. The absurd presumption that he was the father of Maria's child prompted the firstlings of parental duty in him. Now, dog and snail years later, he has become an exemplary father. To convert his children to the religion of doubt, he has told them the story of the Jews, and justified the nature of the telling in the process. His art has matured with his outlook. *From the Diary of a Snail* extends the conventional boundaries of the novel. It disposes of the complaint that politics and literature do not blend by making the author, in whom the didactic and the artistic self-evidently unite, central. It goes a stage beyond *Local Anaesthetic* in this respect, and is a testimony to the health and versatility of Grass's talent. It moves, it debates, it excites, it teases, it is artful in its artistry. Like Dürer, it communicates mood and message with graphic suddenness. The reader is left as the Boss is left at the end of the play about the Berlin Uprising—'with fewer and fewer certitudes'. One can ask no more of a book.

8

Conclusion

There was once a moustache that grew in the dark without applause.

There was once a bird, which lacked a moustache, but which grew a thick fable. This fable with a long bird threw a party to begin all parties. Time was invited but was not able to stop.

There was once a party attended by flowers, respectable flowers like lilies and asters. On wicked petals they danced their stems red. Gardeners implemented. Tenors sang of school. Zebras played mazurkas on black and white teeth. In a knife and fork tango, murder was observed. Yet this party, held in a windless cellar at the top of a house, this party, crouching in the hollow of a trumpet by gaslight, this party, open to wardrobes and moustaches alike, timeless because time was busy elsewhere, this party lived in an attic which never got off the ground.

There was once a rocking-horse called time. It raced towards a party but marked itself painfully. A clown with six legs missed the festivities. An artist on horseback never climbed those stairs.

There was once a railway track which led nowhere and everywhere. Three of its three destinations were called despair. The other was known as hope. On this track was an engine, rusted by time. In fact, it was these same rusting duties which kept time away from attic celebrations with a blood-red carnation. This engine, this metal eternal, was only ten rusty minutes away from home. To the beat of a hot stork's wings, it strained to move forward but transported no-one, not even the nun.

There was once a flood which gate-crashed a party, suggesting bedrooms as dry places to be moist. Beds given freedom kicked their legs in the air. Liberated pillows put their heads down to rest. Rats read philosophy on the university roof. Water rose and water fell. Chamber pots collected evidence. Time collected chamber pots. Grandfather clocks collected time. Children collected grandfather clocks.

There was once a murderer who was never party to murder. The trigger of circumstance refused to be pulled. In a bed, in a bath, in a pit, in a quandary, he let thought kill the killer in him and gun down his trade. The children who found him, coffined on roller skates, saw something in his notebook and took it away.

There was once a recipe, stolen from a dead man, and if he was alive then he had to be shot. This deadly concoction was ideal for parties. Spoons held its mystery with hollow politeness. Cats spoke of eating from inside the egg. The soup, which was never made, tasted of whiteness. And whiteness means Christmas and Christmas is the time for giving some time.

There was once a tin drum which had no name but whose playing was too beautiful for words. The drum was not a Christmas party but went to bear witness of a Christmas party, and wore its best party moustache. It lay in ambush behind a Christmas tree then held up the guests by pointing its middle drumstick. Party members lifted their hands, in some cases, one arm. Noisily, the drum deprived them of their deafness. Innocently, it emptied their pockets of innocence. Deftly, it extracted old photographs from their wallets and acquainted them with themselves. This robust robber, this drum with a flame-red grin, this uninvited intruder made the party famous. In all three corners of the world, they heard about its games.

There was once a parish hall secretary who befriended an Adam's apple and taught it to swim. Time crept up like a cat on the Adam's apple, which dropped in fear into the mouth of the sea. The teeth of a virgin sank into the apple. Holiness below water is the Eve of disaster.

There was once a scarecrow which had the party spirit and which joined as a member. It knew a tin drum and a mouse that gathered moustraps. This scarecrow was scared of dogs unless it met them below ground. It held subterranean parties and intoxicated rock. These parties were hell-bent and made guests sweat. Fame wrote out invitations to each guilty party.

There was once an artist with a view of the cemetery and a

friend in Rome. When he sat at his desk, it was covered in demonstrators. They lifted his pen by way of protest, and donated their blood to his inkwell. But his words remained blue. For his part, he did not know. He did not know, for example, why a desk could not be built out of freedom but had to wear a red paper hat. He did not know why those who want your autograph will tear up your opinions. He did not know who it was who first tried to blot out pain with the pressure of his fist, or what revolution can be achieved by the power of quotation, or how history came by its historic hump.

There was once a snail which cared for its teeth. Consumed by food and nursed by nurses, this snail was fond of children. Its cellar was a skyscraper, an address to the world. With a melancholy grin, the snail told stories and did tricks with beer mats. It, too, had its desk but made use of those demonstrators, political paperweights. Slowed down by fame, the snail crawled across its desk, left behind by uprisings and by guitars and by suicide. It has time on its side and time on its back.

There was once a moustache which looked strange on nuns. Beneath this moustache was a row of teeth and teeth are for eating, that's why they're like gold. Above this moustache is an army of barbers with razors and scissors. Yet whatever they do, the moustache looks the same.

Which is something. Which, in an age of impermanence, is very definitely something. A collection of hairs keeps the snail on course. Since the flood. Because the bird. Despite the drum. As a result of the slapping. Until the kennel. Whereas the tape recorder. If the dentist. Hot dogs. Cold snails. Damp cellars. White hopes. Black facts. How the child.

Beneath begins above. Parties lead to parties. Time is the bad fairy who always turns up. Aftertaste. Afterbirth. Aftermath. When the party is over, the snail clears up the mess.

There was once a moustache which grew in the light with too much applause.

There was once a snail who was exemplary in its choice of examples.

There was once a party and if it isn't stopped soon it will continue with its games and its partisan fun.

There was once and there still is. Yet he does not know.

226

He does not know, in his quieter moments, if the past has got a future. Or if he travels in a circle of pain.

There was once a drummer.

There was once a drum. This object abolished faith, hope, love in a way that was too final for words.

There was once a conclusion which concluded with love, hope, faith.

And doubt.

Select Bibliography

For more detailed information about Grass's own writings and the secondary literature concerning him see the following:

Görtz, Franz-Josef. 'Kommentierte Auswahl Bibliographie' in *Text und Kritik* I/Ia, ed. H. L. Arnold, Munich, 1971.
Schwarz, W. J. *Der Erzähler Günter Grass*, Bern and Munich, 1971.

Works by Günter Grass

Die Vorzüge der Windhühner. Neuwied: Luchterhand, 1956.
Beritten hin und zurück. Ein Vorspiel auf dem Theater, in *Akzente*, 1958.
Die Blechtrommel, Neuwied and Berlin, 1959.
Noch zehn Minuten bis Buffalo, in *Akzente*, 1959.
Fünf Köche. Ballett. First performed, 1959, Aix-les-Bains and Bonn.
Gleisdreieck. Neuwied: Luchterhand, 1960.
Hochwasser (first version), in *Akzente* 2, 1960.
Katz und Maus. Neuwied: Luchterhand, 1961.
Die Bösen Köche, in *Modernes Deutsches Theater* I, ed. Paul Portner, Neuwied and Berlin, 1961.
Hundejahre. Neuwied: Luchterhand, 1963.
Die Ballerina. Berlin: Friedenauer Press, 1963 (limited edition).
POUM oder die Vergangenheit fliegt mit, in *Der Monat*, June, 1965.
Onkel, Onkel. Berlin, 1965.
Was ist des Deutschen Vaterland? Neuwied: Luchterhand, 1965.
Loblied auf Willy. Neuwied: Luchterhand, 1965.
Es steht zur Wahl. Neuwied: Luchterhand, 1965.
Ich klage an. Neuwied: Luchterhand, 1965.
Des Kaisers neue Kleider. Neuwied: Luchterhand, 1965.
Die Plebejer proben den Aufstand. Neuwied: Luchterhand, 1966.
Ausgefragt. Neuwied: Luchterhand, 1967.
Über das Selbstverstandliche. Neuwied: Luchterhand, 1968.
Über Mein Lehrer Döblin und andere Vörtrage. Berlin, 1968.

Örtlich Betäubt. Neuwied: Luchterhand, 1969.

Davor, in *Theater Heute*, April 1969.

Theaterspiele (containing *Hochwasser*; *Onkel, Onkel*; *Noch zehn Minuten bis Buffalo*; *Die bösen Köche*; *Die Plebejer proben den Aufstand; Davor*. Neuwied and Berlin, 1970.

Gesammelte Gedichte. Neuwied and Berlin, 1971.

Aus dem Tagebuch einer Schnecke. Neuwied and Berlin, 1972.

Works by Grass in English Translation

Unless otherwise stated all the works have been translated by Ralph Manheim.

The Tin Drum. London, Secker and Warburg, 1962.

The Tin Drum. New York, Pantheon Books, 1962.

Cat and Mouse. London, Secker and Warburg, 1963.

Cat and Mouse. New York, Harcourt, Brace and World, 1963.

Dog Years. London, Secker and Warburg, 1965.

Dog Years. New York, Harcourt, Brace and World, 1965.

The Tin Drum. Harmondsworth, Penguin Books, 1965.

Cat and Mouse. Harmondsworth, Penguin Books, 1966.

Selected Poems. trans. Michael Hamburger and Christopher Middleton, London, Secker and Warburg, 1966.

Selected Poems. trans. Michael Hamburger and Christopher Middleton, New York, Harcourt, Brace and World, 1966.

The Plebeians Rehearse the Uprising, London, Secker and Warburg, 1967.

The Plebeians Rehearse the Uprising, New York, Harcourt, Brace and World, 1967.

Four Plays (*Flood; Mister, Mister*; *Only Ten Minutes to Buffalo;* trans. Ralph Manheim; *The Wicked Cooks*. trans. A. Leslie Willson) New York, Harcourt, Brace and World, 1967.

Four Plays (as above), London, Secker and Warburg, 1968.

Rocking Back and Forth, trans. Michael Benedikt and Joseph Goradza, in *Post-war German Theatre*, ed. Michael Benedikt and George Wellwarth, Macmillan, 1967.

Speak Out! Speeches, Open Letters, Commentaries. With an introduction by Michael Harrington, New York, Harcourt, Brace and World, 1968.

Local Anaesthetic. London, Secker and Warburg, 1968.

Local Anaesthetic. New York, Harcourt, Brace and World, 1968.

Dog Years, Harmondsworth, Penguin Books, 1969.

Speak Out! London, Secker and Warburg, 1969.

Poems of Günter Grass, trans. Michael Hamburger and Christopher Middleton, with an introduction by Michael Hamburger, Harmondsworth, Penguin Books, 1969.

Four Plays (as above). With an introduction by Martin Esslin. Harmondsworth, Penguin Books, 1972.

The Plebeians Rehearse the Uprising. Harmondsworth, Penguin Books, 1972.

Local Anaesthetic. Harmondsworth, Penguin Books, 1973.

From the Diary of a Snail. New York, Harcourt, Brace, Jovanovich, 1973.

From the Diary of a Snail. London, Secker and Warburg, 1974.

Note: Most of the references in the text of this book are to the hardback editions published by Secker and Warburg, London. The only exceptions are *Local Anaesthetic* and *Poems of Günter Grass*, where the Penguin editions have been used.

Secondary Reading

Anon. 'Drum of Neutrality', in *Times Literary Supplement*, 5 October 1962, p. 776.

Anon. '*Katz und Maus*', in *Times Literary Supplement*, 5 October 1962.

Anon. 'Dogs and the Deflation of Demons', in *Times Literary Supplement*, 27 September 1963.

Anon. 'Leaves of Grass', in *Time*, 1 April 1966.

Anon. 'The Plebeians Rehearse the Uprising', in *Nation*, 204, 13 February 1967.

Anon. 'Rome in Berlin', in *Times Literary Supplement,* 28 December 1967.

Anon. on *Örtlich betäubt*, in *Times Literary Supplement*, 25 September 1969, p. 1077.

Anon. 'The Dentist's Chair as an Allegory of Life', in *Time*, 13 April 1970, p. 52.

Anon. 'Germany's Günter Grass', in *Time*, 13 April 1970.

Anon. 'Forward with the Gasteropods', in *Times Literary Supplement*, 22 December 1972.

Anon. 'Dingsbums und Espede', in *Der Spiegel*, No. 35, 1972, pp. 101 ff.

Ackroyd, Peter. 'Growing up with Grass', in *The Spectator*, 18 May 1974.

Andrews, R. C. '*The Tin Drum*', in *Modern Languages*, 45, No. 1. 1964, pp. 28–31.

Arnold, Heinz Ludwig. 'Die unpädagogische Provinz des Günter Grass', in *Text und Kritik*, I, 1963, pp. 13–15.

Arnold, Heinz Ludwig. 'Zorn Arger Wut: Anmerkungen zu zen politischen Gedichten in *Ausgefragt*', in *Text und Kritik*, I–Ia, 1971, pp. 71–3.

Ascherson, Neil. Review of *The Tin Drum*, in *New Statesman*, 28 September 1962.

Ascherson, Neil. Review of *Dog Years*, in *New Statesman*, 26 November 1965.

Ascherson, Neil. 'The Lonely German', in *The Observer*, 26 July 1970.

Augstein, Rudolf. 'William Shakespeare, Bertolt Brecht, Günter Grass', in *Der Spiegel*, January 24 1966.

Baring, Arnulf. 'Kipphardt, Grass und die SPD', in *Die Zeit*, 25 June 1971.

Batt, Kurt. 'Groteske und Parabel', in *Neue Deutsche Literatur* 12, No. 7, 1964, pp. 57–66.

Baumgart, Reinhard. 'Günter Grass: *Katz und Maus*', in *Neue Deutsche Heft*, Berlin, January 1962.

Baumgart, Reinhard. 'Plebejer-Spätlese', in *Neue Rundschau*, May 1966.

Becker, Rolf. 'Mässig mit Malzbonbons', in *Der Spiegel*, No. 33, 1969.

Blöcker, Günter. 'Rückkehr zur Nabelschur', in *Frankfurter Allgemeine Zeitung*, 28 November 1959.

Blomster, W. V. 'The Documentation of a Novel: Otto Weininger and *Hundejahre* by Günter Grass', in *Monatshefte*, No. 61, pp. 122–38.

Boa, Elizabeth and Reid, J. H. *Critical Strategies: German Fiction in the Twentieth Century*, London, 1972.

Brooks, H. F. and Fraenkel, C. E. (eds.) Background and introduction to *Katz and Maus*, London, 1971.

Brooks, H. F. and Fraenkel, C. E. (eds.) Background and introduction to *Die Plebejer proben den Aufstand*, London, 1971.

Bruce, James C. 'The Equivocating Narrator in Günter Grass's *Katz und Maus*', *Monatschefte* VIII, 2, pp. 139–149.

Carlsson, Anni. 'Der Roman als Anschauungsform der Epoche', in *Neue Zürcher Zeitung*, 21 November 1964.

Cunliffe, W. G. *Günter Grass* (World Authors Series No. 65), New York, 1969.

Durzak, Manfred. 'Abschied von Kleinburgerwelt. Du neue Roman von Günter Grass', in *Basis*, No. 1, 1970, pp. 224–37.

Domandi, Agnes Körner. (ed. and compiler) *Library of Literary Criticism of Modern German Literature*, 2 vols., New York, 1972.

Emmel, Hildegard. 'Das Sebstgericht. Thomas Mann-Walter Jens und Edzard Schaper-Günter Grass', in *Das Gericht in der Deutschen*

Literatur des 20. Jahrhunderts, Berlin and Munich, 1963, pp. 92–120.

Enright, D. J. '*Dog Years*: Günter Grass's Third Novel', in *Conspirators and Poets*, London, 1966.

Enright, D. J. Review of *The Plebeians Rehearse the Uprising* in *New York Review of Books*, 29 December 1966.

Enzensberger, Hans Magnus. 'Trommelt weiter', in *Frankfurter Hefte*, December 1961, pp. 491 ff.

Enzensberger, Hans Magnus. 'Wilhelm Meister auf Blech getrommelt' in *Einzelheiten*, Frankfurt am Main, 1962, pp. 221–33.

Enzensberger, Hans Magnus. 'Günter Grass: *Hundejahre*' in *Der Spiegel*, 4 September 1963.

Esslin, Martin. *The Theatre of the Absurd*, London, 1962.

Esslin, Martin (introduction to) *Günter Grass: Four Plays*, London, 1968.

Esslin, Martin. Review of *The Plebeians Rehearse the Uprising*, in *Plays and Players*, September 1970, pp. 38–9.

Fischer, Heinz. 'Sprachliche Tendenzen bei Böll und Grass', in *German Quarterly*, 40, No. 3, 1967, pp. 372 ff.

Forster, Leonard. 'Günter Grass', in *University of Toronto Quarterly*, October 1969.

Fried, Erich. '1st *Ausgefragt* fragwürdig?', in *Konkret*, July 1967.

Friedrichsmeyer, E. M. 'Aspects of Myth, Parody and Obscenity in Grass's *Die Blechtrommel* and *Katz und Maus*', in *The Germanic Review*, 40, No. 3, 1965, pp. 240–50.

Frisch, Max. 'Grass als Redner', in *Die Zeit*, 24 September 1965.

Frisch, Max. *Tagebuch 1966–71*, Frankfurt am Main, 1972, pp. 325–55.

Garrett, Thomas J. 'Oskars Empfang in England', in *Die Zeit*, 26 October 1962.

Gaus, Günter. *Zur Person: Porträts in Frage un Autwort*, vol. 2, Munich, 1966.

Gelley, A. 'Art and Reality in *Die Blechtrommel*', in *Forum for Modern Language Studies*, No. 2, 1967, pp. 115–25.

Gilman, Richard. 'Spoiling the Broth', in *Newsweek*, 6 February 1966.

Grathoff, Dirk. 'Dichtung versus Politik: Brechts *Coriolan* aus Günter Grassens sicht', in *Brecht Heute*, Vol. I, Frankfurt am Main, 1971.

Hamburger, Michael. *From Prophecy to Exorcism*, London, 1965.

Hartung, Rudolf. 'Günter Grass: *Hundejahre*', in *Neue Rundschau*, November 1963.

Hatfield, Henry. 'The Artist as Satirist', in *The Contemporary Novel in Germany*, Austin: University of Texas Press, 1967.

Holthusen, Hans Egon. 'Günter Grass als politischen Autor', in *Der Monat*, No. 216, September 1966.

Holthusen, Hans Egon. 'Der neue Günter Grass. Deutschland, deine Schnecke', in *Welt des Buches*, No. 196, 24 August 1972.

Horst, Karl A. 'Die Vogelscheuchen des Günter Grass', in *Merkur*, 8, No. 10, 1963.

Janhke, Jürgen. 'Günter Grass als Stückeschreiber', in *Text und Kritik*, I, 1964, pp. 25–7.

Jenny, Urs. 'Grass probt den Aufstand', in *Süddeutscher Zeitung*, 17 January 1966.

Jens, Walter. 'Das Pandämonium des Günter Grass', in *Die Zeit*, XVIII, 36, 1963.

Kahler, Erich. 'Form und Entformung', in *Merkur*, 19, 1965, pp. 318–35, 413–28.

Kaiser, Joachim. 'Die Theaterstücke des Günter Grass', in *Text und Kritik* I–Ia, 1971, pp. 52–66.

Kesting, Mariann. 'Günter Grass' in *Panorama des Zeitgenössischen Theaters*, Munich, 1969, pp. 300–4.

Kielinger, Thomas. 'Günter Grass's *Örtlich betäubt*', in Neue Deutsch *Hefte* 16, No. 124, 1969, pp. 144–9.

Kielinger, Thomas. 'Günter Grass's *Aus dem Tagebuch der Schnecke*', in *Neue Deutsch Hefte*, No. 139, 1972, pp. 155–60.

Kohn, Hans. *The Mind of Germany*, London, 1965.

Kruger, Horst. 'Das Wappentier der Republik', in *Die Zeit*, 25 April 1969.

Lebeau, Jean. 'Individu et société, ou le métamorphose de Günter Grass', in *Revue Germanique*, No. 2, 1972, pp. 68–93.

Leonard, Irène. 'The Problem of Commitment in the Work of Günter Grass' (M.Phil. Thesis, London), 1973.

Leonard, Irène. *Günter Grass*, Edinburgh, 1974.

Löschutz, Gert. ed. *Von Buch zu Buch: Günter Grass in der Kritik*, Neuwied: Luchterhand, 1968.

Magill, C. P. *German Literature*, O.U.P., 1974.

Mander, John. Review of *Speak Out!*—'Germany's Voice of Democracy' in *The Guardian*, 20 September 1969.

Mander, John. Review of *From the Diary of a Snail* in *The New Review*, vol. I, No. 2, May 1974.

Mayer, Hans. 'Felix Krull und Oskar Matzerath', in *Süddeutscher Zeitung* 14 October 1967.

Migner, Karl. 'Der getrommelte Protest gegen unsere Welt', in *Welt und Wort* 15, 1960, pp. 205–7.

Moore, Harry T. *Twentieth Century German Literature*, London, 1967.

Morton, Frederic. Review of *The Tin Drum* in *New York Review of Books*, 7 April 1963.

Neuveux, J. B. 'Günter Grass le Vistulien', in *Études Germaniques*, 21, No. 4, pp. 527–50.

Parry, Idris. 'The Special Quality of Hell', in *The Listener*, 3 February, 1966.

Parry, Idris. 'Aspects of Günter Grass's Narrative Technique' in *Forum for Modern Language Studies*, 8, No. 2, 1967, pp. 99–114.

Ratcliffe, Michael. 'Lessons from a Grounded Angel' in *The Times*, 16 May 1974.

Reddick, John. 'The Eccentric Narrative World of Günter Grass (D.Phil. Thesis, Oxford), 1970.

Reddick, John. 'Action and Impotence in Günter Grass's *Örtlich betäubt*', in *Modern Language Review*, No. 3, July 1972, pp. 563–78.

Reddick, John. *The 'Danzig Trilogy' of Günter Grass*, London, 1975.

Reich-Ranicki, Marcel. 'Günter Grass: unser grimmiger Idylliker' in *Deutsche Literatur in Ost und West*, Munich, 1963, pp. 216–30.

Reich-Ranicki, Marcel. 'Günter Grass's *Hundejahre*', in *Literatur der Kleinen Schritte*, Munich, 1967, pp. 22 ff.

Reich-Ranicki, Marcel. 'Eine Müdeheldensosse', in *Die Ziet*, 29 August 1969

Ruhleder, Karl H. 'A Pattern of Messianic Thought in Günter Grass's *Katz und Maus*', in *German Quarterly*, 39, No. 4, 1966, pp. 599–612.

Schwarz, Wilhelm Johannes. *Der Erzähler Günter Grass*, Bern and Munich, 1971.

Spender, Stephen. 'Günter Grass', in *The Sunday Telegraph*, 30 September 1962.

Spender, Stephen. 'Scarecrows and Swastikas', in *New York Times Book Review*, 23 May 1965.

Steiner, George. 'A Note on Günter Grass', in *Language and Silence*, London, 1969, pp. 133.

Subiotto, Arrigo V. 'Günter Grass' in *Essays on Contemporary German Literature* (*German Men of Letters* IV), London, 1966.

Sutton, Ellen. 'Grass and Bobrowski', in *Times Literary Supplement*, 17 February 1966.

Tank, Kurt Lothar. *Günter Grass*, Berlin, 1965. (English translation by John Conway, New York, 1969).

Thomas, R. Hinton and Van Der Will, W. *The German Novel and the Affluent Society*, Manchester, 1968.

Thomas, R. Hinton and Bullivant, Keith. *Literature in Upheaval*: *West German Writers and the Challenge of the 1960's*, Manchester, 1974.

Toynbee, Philip. 'A Torch for Brandt', in *The Observer Review*, 7 September 1969.

Wagenbach, Klaus. 'Günter Grass', in *Schriftsteller der Gegenwart*, ed. Klaus Nonnenmann, Olten and Freiburg, 1963.

Waidson, H. M. 'Günter Grass' in *Twentieth Century German Literature*, ed. August Closs, London, 1969.

Wiegenstein, R. H. 'Noch ein Vorschlag Günter Grass zu verstehen', in *Frankfurter Hefte*, December 1963, pp. 370–3.

Wiese, Theodor. 'Fabulier und Moralist', in *Merkur*, 13, 1959, pp. 1188–91.

Wiese, Theodor. *Günter Grass: Porträts und Poesie*, Neuwied and Berlin, 1968.

Wiggin, Maurice. 'Casting out Doubt', in *Sunday Times Review*, 12 May 1974.

Van Der Will, Wilfried. *Picaro heute. Metamorphosen des Schelms bei Thomas Mann, Döblin, Brecht, Grass*, Stuttgart, 1967.

Willson, A. Leslie. 'The Grotesque Everyman in Günter Grass's *Die Blechtrommel*', in *Monatschefte*, 18: 2, Summer 1966, pp. 131–8.

Willson, A. Leslie. ed. *A Günter Grass Symposium*, University of Texas Press, 1971.

Wilson, Angus. 'Blood Brothers and Scarecrows', in *The Observer*, 7 November 1965.

Woods, Ann. 'A Study of *Die Blechtrommel* by Günter Grass' (M.A. Thesis, Liverpool), 1966.

Yates, Norris W., *Günter Grass: a Critical Essay*, Grand Rapids, Michegan, 1967.

Zimmer, Dieter. 'Kriechspur des Günter Grass', in *Die Zeit*, 29 September 1972.

Zwerenz, Gerhard. 'Brecht, Grass und der 17. Juni, II Anmerkungen', in *Theater Heute*, July 1966.

Index

237